Environmental Issues

Population, Pollution, and Economics

The Author

Lawrence G. Hines is professor of economics at Dartmouth College. He holds a Ph.D. from the University of Minnesota, and has taught there and at the George Washington University, American University, and the University of Michigan. He has served as a consultant to the Water Pollution Control Division of the Department of Health, Education, and Welfare, the Federal Reserve Bank of Boston, the Department of Transportation, and the Department of the Interior. He is co-author (with B. W. Knight) of *Economics*.

Environmental Issues
Population, Pollution, and Economics

LAWRENCE G. HINES

DARTMOUTH COLLEGE

W · W · NORTON & COMPANY · INC ·
NEW YORK

Contents

Preface   vii

Chapter 1   How the Environment Became a
              Problem   1

PART I   The Resource Background   13

Chapter 2   Population, I: The Pressure of People   15
Chapter 3   Population, II: The Impact Upon
              Resources   37
Chapter 4   Economic Growth—Friend or Foe of the
              Environment?   61

PART II   Economic Decision-Making   83

Chapter 5   The Market Economy and Its Operation   85
Chapter 6   The Public Sector: Benefit-Cost Analysis   109
Chapter 7   Benefit-Cost Analysis in Action—The
              Middle Snake River Hydroelectric
              Project   132

PART III   Environmental Problem Areas   163

Chapter 8   Energy—A Contest Between Demand
              and Supply   165

Chapter 9   Water Pollution, I: The Sources and
                    Magnitude of the Problem   195
Chapter 10 Water Pollution, II: The Options of
                    Control   225
Chapter 11 Air Pollution—Its Extent and Control   253
Chapter 12 Solid Waste—Disposal and Resource
                    Recovery   290

PART IV   Conclusion   315

Chapter 13 Environmental Protection—Tomorrow
                    the World?   317

Index   333

Preface

This book has three main objectives: to appraise environmental pressures in the United States, to determine the role of the government and of the market economy in environmental deterioration and its abatement, and to examine the range of corrective actions that are available to check environmental abuse.

Given these objectives, it is not possible to adhere strictly to the jurisdiction of a single discipline. No matter how much the specialists may wince or the angels fear, excursions into the territories of both the social sciences and the natural sciences are necessary to present the complex nature of environmental issues. This does not mean that this work is "interdisciplinary," however—that most dubious of compliments—but that in its pragmatic approach, information is drawn from a variety of sources.

The book is problem-oriented. In the analysis of particular environmental issues, such as air and water pollution, the emphasis is upon the technical arrangements and policy options that are available to correct these conditions. Ways of coping with specific environmental abuses are examined against the background of existing programs and regulatory controls. More generalized approaches to environmental deterioration that have but slight chance of adoption, such as the freezing of economic growth or increased reliance upon the pricing system, are considered largely in terms of the validity of the proposals rather than as likely alternatives or supplements to existing programs.

In the main, this study focuses on the nature of environmental deterioration in the United States and the question of how it can best be checked. Understanding how we got into this situation, however, and what needs to be done to get out, requires acquaintance with the way decisions affecting the use of natural resources are made in the private and public sectors of the economy. This involves determining not only where the market economy has fallen short in protecting the environment, but also how this deficiency has been carried over to the public sector through the use of market-oriented benefit-cost criteria. A section on decision-making in the private and public sectors of the economy covers these areas. The way in which benefit-cost analysis is employed by federal agencies, such as the Army Corps of Engineers, the Federal Power Commission, and the Bureau of Reclamation, is illustrated by a chapter-length case study of a series of proposed hydroelectric dams in the Hells Canyon reach of the Snake River. This complex Middle Snake case raises a multitude of issues: legal, administrative, and economic questions; the determination of whether the project should be financed by private or public investment; and—finally—the matter of whether it should be undertaken at all.

In an attempt to compensate for my considerable inadequacies in the many areas covered in a book of this kind, I have drawn heavily upon the talents of a variety of specialists. At Dartmouth, I have benefited greatly from the advice and assistance of Edward S. Brown, Thayer School of Engineering; Meredith O. Clement and Martin L. Lindahl, Department of Economics; William A. Reiners, Department of Biological Sciences; and Franklin Smallwood, Department of Government. Robert B. Dishman, Department of Political Science, University of New Hampshire, and Lawrence Goss, Department of Geography, New York State University College at Oswego, have reviewed with a critical eye material in their areas of specialty; and David V. Ragone, College of Engineering, University of Michigan, has given much time and effort to improving my understanding of air pollution. James J. Flannery of the Department of the Interior, Washington, D.C., has read critically much of the book in draft form and has provided information, wisdom, wry humor,

PREFACE ix

and an endless stream of good conversation. Although he is mentioned last, my indebtedness to him is greatest.

The National Science Foundation, through a curriculum-development grant to Dartmouth's Environmental Studies Program, provided support in the preparation of the Middle Snake case study and the air-pollution material. My students at Dartmouth in Environmental Studies 3 and Economics 12 have served as generally willing and helpful captive audiences in testing earlier drafts of this book. May they all graduate *summa cum laude* for valorous combat with the disjointed sentence.

Environmental Issues

Population, Pollution, and Economics

Chapter One

How The Environment Became a Problem

Mankind has a long past and an uncertain future.—Abba Eban [1]

Speaking of a turbulent era almost exactly two centuries ago, Charles Dickens said in the opening of *A Tale of Two Cities*, "It was the best of times, it was the worst of times. . . ."

So it is today.

Economic growth is mounting in a large part of the world, but pollution of the environment is more than keeping pace; employment is high and leisure is increasing, but great numbers of people clog our cities and overrun the few remaining wild areas; science and technology have brought man within reach of the stars, but the accomplishments of science, in unexpected misdirection, have also produced the horror of the near extinction of species through poisoning by pesticides and chemical wastes; an abundance and variety of output hitherto unknown has come from industry, but it has been distributed among the world's population with a cruel unevenness, causing some have-not nations to cry out

[1] Israeli delegate to the United Nations Conference on the Human Environment, Stockholm, June 1972.

1

against efforts to reach international accords for environmental
protection as the pastime of the wealthy nations.

The Heritage of Land Abuse

Abuse of the environment is not new. Earlier cultures have
mined the soil and deforested the land with little thought for the
future. Some find in the opening of the American West to farming, mining, and logging, an era of unparalleled disregard for the
environment, but this country has no monopoly on abuse of the
resource base. China, though it decries the need for population
control and the curtailment of resource exploitation, has a land
scarred from the mining of the soil and the deforestation of the
countryside. The Yellow River, which flows through an area of
great population, rides high on silt from the surrounding lands
and periodically floods the region through which it travels.
Through the ages, overcutting of forests and exploitative farming
practices have reduced China's cultivable land so severely that
today the despoiled areas, together with those climatically and
physically unsuited to agriculture, constitute 80 percent of its
total land—all now useless for farming.

The Mediterranean region, with a civilization younger by far
than China's but still respectably mature by Western standards,
has suffered the twin scourges of deforestation and overgrazing.
Greece retains little more than 5 percent of its land area in
productive forest, although originally this constituted 65 percent
of the nation's land. Removal of the forest has not simply meant
the extension of cultivation; more often, heavy grazing has been
followed by land-destroying erosion. On the other side of the
Mediterranean, North Africa long ago suffered accelerated deforestation and destructive farming-grazing practices that converted the fertile continental rim into a desert that now supports
only nomadic herdsmen. The interior of Africa has fared better,
but it has not escaped the marks of man—marks that are likely to
be deepened in the years ahead. Tropical soils are fragile; when
the forest cover is removed, even without cultivation, destruction
may be quite rapid. And when Western cultivation practices are

introduced to grow successive cash crops, such as tobacco, cotton, or coffee, soil depletion and erosion may reach heroic proportions.

Europe used the environment better than many other areas of the world, at least up to the Middle Ages. European agronomy evolved gradually, and cultivation techniques were well adapted to the soil and climate. Although there is ample evidence of large-scale deforestation—England was heavily forested until the Norman Conquest, for example—generally land abuse in the early period was limited, as a result of sparse population and primitive methods of cultivation. Later, abuse of the land accompanied the changes in agricultural technology. The spread of the metal plow throughout Europe and other areas of the world caused a break with past farming practices and sometimes left havoc in its wake. Reaching deep to turn the heavier soils, the iron-moldboard plow was introduced in America and in other parts of the world in the late 1830's; it raised crop output substantially, but often at the cost of accelerated depletion of the soil.

If by world standards European agriculture has been protective of the land, that of the Western Hemisphere—especially South and Central America—appears largely indifferent to the destruction of the soil in its early history. The vast areas of virgin land in the Americas, fertile but unprotected by land-use traditions such as those of Europe, provided a necessary precondition for highly exploitative agriculture. Whether in fact the Maya Empire, an early Central American civilization that disappeared by the tenth century, suffered the backlash of exploitative slash-and-burn agriculture is an intriguing question that probably will never be answered with certainty. But clearing land by burning and planting in the ashes was a common practice in the Americas when virgin land was brought under cultivation. Unfortunately, the rich yields of the early plantings quickly gave way to lowered output once leaching and erosion of the tropical soil occurred in the absence of protective vegetation.

In the early extension of farming westward, the slash-and-burn method of clearing the land was also used in North America, but fortunately the soils were generally less fragile. However, the combination of a limited population and an abundance of land encouraged depletion of the soil. Land was virtually a free good to be had by preemption—if not close at hand, then on the way west. The austerity of frontier life and the seemingly unlimited expanse of land and profusion of wildlife made depletion of resources by the early settlers inevitable. Land, timber, minerals, and wildlife were abundant to the point of encumbrance, and the emergence of a "land ethic" not only had to await a later age, but it had to come from those who did not struggle in the shadow of the forest or with a backdrop of grasslands reaching to the horizon.

The buffalo, the passenger pigeon, the heath hen, and the plains antelope were early victims of the frontier men's indifference—either totally exterminated or so severely reduced in numbers that they survive now only as protected remnants. The list of endangered species continues to grow. Today, encroachment upon habitats and the indiscriminate use of pesticides have brought new candidates to the point of extinction, but the early extermination of species was more direct. It was brought about by hunting—unthinking at times, callous at others, and frequently undertaken in disbelief that the largess would ever run low.

The Passing of the Frontier Philosophy

The frontier reached the Pacific well in advance of a change in the American attitude toward exploitation of natural resources. Indeed, holdovers of the early attitude still show up in some commercial developments. However, by the turn of the twentieth century there was growing evidence of a break with the past. The establishment of Yellowstone National Park in 1872, although possibly reflecting a greater interest in the bizarre than in the preservation of nature, represented an innovative approach that later spread to other segments of wild America. In the early 1900's, President Theodore Roosevelt and his chief forester, Gifford Pinchot, worked effectively for the adoption of the sustained-yield approach in forest management and for recognition of the danger of natural-resource depletion, although the Roosevelt-Pinchot conception of conservation was narrowly commercial by today's standards.

It was the early 1930's, however, the years of drought and dust storms, that shocked the nation into taking stock of its depleting resource base. With faith in the market system already suffering severely from the collapse of the economy, evidence of its further failure to protect natural resources led to the establishment of the Soil Conservation Service, the Civilian Conservation Corps, and other federal agencies to cope with resource damage. This was a period in which natural-resource policy was extensively examined, but the issues raised were largely confined to questions of depletion and scarcity.

In the meantime, the shock of the development of a dust bowl in the Midwest and the south-central United States and of severe erosion of the land in other parts of the country lessened as the drought lifted and the shifting soil was brought under control. Actually, the ravaging of a large area of the Midwest had not so much resulted from a failure of the market economy, as from its excessively short-run, private orientation. In the high-price era of the 1920's, the farmers in the Plains states who had done so well in cattle raising during World War I turned to the dry farming of wheat. The return was satisfactory, if not impressive; the yield per acre was less than farther east, but so was the investment per acre. The stress upon the land from dry farming was entirely different from grazing, however, in the western areas of short buffalo grass. With a cover of undisturbed grass, the prairies could wait out the drought phase of the irregular rainfall cycle. When it rained, the prairie bloomed, and without rain, the thick-matted buffalo grass held the soil together until the cycle turned again to moisture. But wheat farming broke the hold of the buffalo grass on the soil, and the collapse of wheat prices in the late 1920's left the submarginal lands uncultivated, vulnerable to the winds that swept across the prairie.

The dust that darkened the skies of the nation's capital in the early days of the Great Depression was the result of 150 years of soil abuse in the Midwest. The productivity of more than 280 million acres of farmland had been seriously impaired and much of the topsoil of another 775 million acres had been lost by the time the Franklin Roosevelt administration took stock in the early 1930's. Destructive sheet erosion, which leaches away the soil's minerals, and gully erosion, which carries away the soil itself, had greatly reduced agricultural productivity, and reforestation had gone forward at too leisurely a pace. But these were abuses that could be corrected, and gradually the miscues of the market system were brought under control. During World War II, however, the preoccupation with maximum industrial and agricultural output for national survival pushed aside questions of resource abuse, and if the air over Pittsburgh and Gary was polluted from the steel mills' round-the-clock operation, so much the worse for the enemy.

After the war, fear of a return to the mass unemployment of the Great Depression period from economic dislocation in converting to peace reduced the concern with natural-resource policy to occasional congressional hearings and department memoranda. And although World War II had drawn voraciously upon raw materials, the resource base appeared to survive in remarkably good shape. Innovations such as high-nitrogen fertilizers, long-lived pesticides, and disposable containers were viewed benignly as improvements in the lot of mankind; their harmful environmental side effects were to show only over time, with increased use. As late as 1952, an exhaustive study by President Truman's Materials Policy Commission examined natural-resource policy mainly in terms of the adequacy of domestic resources. The Commission found the United States reasonably well off.

The Emergence of Broad Environmental Deterioration

Side effects of industrial output and overall environmental deterioration were still largely unnoticed in the 1950's, but changes were at work that would surface later. Population growth in the postwar period had turned sharply upward, and much of this increase was concentrated in the already congested metropolitan areas. Technology had poured forth a welter of new materials and processes, and with increased output, affluence and leisure had grown. By the late 1960's, what had previously been random cases of localized environmental damage, such as the air pollution from smelters in Donora, Pennsylvania, that caused twenty deaths in October, 1948, and the heavy industrial use of some segments of the Ohio River, became a matter of more widespread complaint.

Seemingly overnight the air had become befouled and the rivers contaminated. Actually, of course, environmental deterioration had not taken place so rapidly, nor was it so universal as it sometimes appeared, but once the recuperative power of our rivers and streams had been exceeded and the air above our cities overburdened, the change in air and water quality from acceptable to intolerable was rapid. The pollution buildup in a stream can go largely unnoticed until its capacity to degrade wastes is overrun, at this point the stream's debasement is likely to be quite apparent to all. The case of air pollution is similar. By dilution, large amounts of airborne waste can be dissipated under favorable atmospheric conditions, but a continued increase in emissions, or an atmospheric change such as a temperature inversion, may trap the pollutants, producing near-lethal conditions overnight. Moreover, the threshold point at which pollution of air and water endangers man is not the same for plants and other animal species; some are less resistant to environmental deterioration and others more. In short, man is an unsatisfactory indicator of environmental stress.

The Habitat Issue

In earlier times, environmental blight, such as erosion of the land by wind and water, could generally be traced to a specific set of causes—the clear-cutting of timber, the overgrazing of livestock, or inappropriate farming practices. By contrast, the environmental abuses that seemed to emerge so suddenly in the early 1970's were largely the product of broader common causes —advances in technology, growth in population, and increased output—that represented a new and potentially greater threat to mankind. At stake was the basic question of whether the earth as a habitat for plants and animals—including man—could be effectively insulated against the destructive by-products of a rapidly expanding industrial system and a growing population. The traditional conservation problem—how to minimize natural-resource depletion and provide for the future—still occupied men's minds, but was now subordinated to the broader habitat consideration.

The Controversy Over Causes

In the early 1970's, there was almost universal agreement on the need for environmental protection. But there was less than general accord on what the basic causes of environmental abuse were—too many people, rising industrial output, new products and processes, or industrial and metropolitan concentration. Some found our habitat threatened primarily by rapid population growth and emphasized the need to bring the birthrate under control. Others considered economic growth and high living standards to be the basic cause of environmental damage and urged a no-growth "stationary state." Still others pointed out the sharp increase in new products and production techniques that had taken place in the late 1960's and recommended that technological innovation be somehow channeled away from environmentally harmful avenues.

Because environmental damage can be traced to a number of contributing causes, sharp disagreement has developed among those examining this problem. Two leaders of the environmental movement, Barry Commoner and Paul Ehrlich, have emphasized different factors—the former, technology, and the latter, population growth—in explaining the deterioration in our environment.[2] In itself, the difference of opinion between these two

[2] See the review of Barry Commoner's *The Closing Circle* (New York: Alfred A. Knopf, 1971) by Paul R. Ehrlich and John P. Holdren in *Environment*, XIV (April 1972), p. 24; and the rejoinder by Barry Commoner, *ibid.*, p. 25.

biological scientists who manage to demonstrate such a considerable disregard for each other's views might well go unremarked, but it illustrates an important aspect of the environmental problem—its complex and multi-causal nature.

Enter the Economist

The Commoner-Ehrlich controversy has by no means exhausted the opportunity for dispute over the identity of the most important sources of environmental damage. Undoubtedly the greatest disagreement surrounds the issue of economic growth and its contribution to the decline in environmental well-being. The discussion of this question has been greatly stimulated by the unusual publicity given the release of an MIT computer simulation study [3] of the role of economic growth as an environmental influence. Economists, most of whom view growth as a boon to mankind, have been quick to align themselves on the pro-growth side of the argument. But more important, the growth controversy has focused attention upon the underlying economic nature of the environmental problem. Although the actual damage to the environment is primarily physical and biological, the main reason that it persists is economic: The burden of foul air, contaminated water, and other abuses of the habitat is frequently shifted to the public by producers who do not wish to bear abatement costs. Protecting the environment involves using resources that could otherwise be put to work producing products—and profit.

The Need to Choose

If resources were available without limit, we could have products and abatement, with no need to choose between them. But almost all resources are scarce to some degree, as shown by the fact that they are available only at a price. The range of prices established in the market indicates the considerable difference in the availability—or scarcity—of different resources. Futhermore,

[3] Donella H. Meadows *et al.*, *The Limits to Growth* (A Potomac Associates/Club of Rome Book; New York: Universe Books, 1972).

the spread of environmental damage has been accompanied by a reversal in the established patterns of scarcity and abundance. Both the ambient air and the waters of the sea, previously thought beyond the power of man to diminish or permanently degrade, have felt increasing pressures from population growth and waste disposal, while the supply of material products has been vastly increased.

The technologists who have raised the growth issue see this reversal, and the pressures upon the environment, as the inevitable consequences of rising industrial output, and they have postulated a future in which we will be overwhelmed by wastes or decimated by the wholesale depletion of resources unless output is checked. Economists are less inclined to subscribe to such immutable projections and find in the market economy the mechanism for corrective adjustments rather than entrapment in rigid relationships. That these corrective adjustments frequently fall short of the social ideal—as they clearly do in the case of environmental damage—is in large part the result of the system's preoccupation with the goal of private gain from resource use. This need not be the only goal. Through price and cost inducements—different kinds of subsidy and tax programs—and prescriptive rules of industrial behavior, the market system can be made to function so that the choices of consumers and producers protect the environment rather than endanger it.

Choice, the necessary response to the scarcity that underlies all economic activity, is not confined to our private affairs of getting and spending. It is also at the heart of government decisions, in which highway development, military procurement, pollution abatement, and the many other resource-using options must be ranked in order of priority. Moreover, the choice decisions in government and private resource use are not mutually exclusive; what is done in one sector affects what can be done in the other. Controlling pollution and protecting the environment may not usually be viewed as components of such a broad and interacting system, but in spite of the attention to the details of programs and problems in the chapters that follow, much of this book concerns the choices imposed upon our society by the scarcity of resources.

References and Readings

Benarde, Melvin A., *Our Precarious Habitat,* rev. ed. New York: W. W. Norton & Company, 1973.
> This work surveys the medical effects of the deterioration in the human habitat resulting from air and water pollution, the addition of chemicals to food, the increased use of pesticides, noise, and other features of modern life.

Commoner, Barry, *The Closing Circle.* New York: Alfred A. Knopf, 1971.
> Commoner in this book argues for natural control—"closing the circle" by limiting wastes from our industrial society to by-products that can be recycled or degraded. He elaborates his position concerning technology as a cause of environmental deterioration and covers a wide range of ecological topics.

Darling, F. Fraser, and Milton, John P., eds., *Future Environments of North America.* Garden City, N. Y.: The Natural History Press, 1966.
> A collection of papers presented at a 1965 conference supported by the Conservation Foundation, in which the broader aspects of the environmental problem are sometimes recognized.

Graham, Frank, Jr., *Man's Domain: The Story of Conservation in America.* New York: M. Evans & Company, 1971.
> A readable and comprehensive account of the conservation movement in the United States, covering the period from the middle of the nineteenth century to the passage of the Wilderness Act in 1964. A final brief chapter notes the broader environmental problem, but does not really examine it.

Hays, Samuel P., *Conservation and the Gospel of Efficiency: The Progressive Conservation Movement, 1890–1920.* Cambridge: Harvard University Press, 1959.
> A scholarly study of the emergence of the conservation movement in the United States, especially illuminating of the Roosevelt-Pinchot era. Hays finds the role of the federal government during this early period to be that of supporting professional control of resource decisions as opposed to direction by the private market. Maximization of economic output was the primary goal of the so-called "wise use" of resources, but this was to be achieved through public management.

Leopold, Aldo, *A Sand County Almanac.* New York: Oxford University Press, 1949. Reprinted (together with essays from a posthumous work, *Round River*) by Ballantine Books, New York, in 1970.
> The Ballantine Books volume presents a wide range of Leopold's

work, including his essays on nature as well as those setting forth his conception of the land ethic and the worth of wilderness. Leopold's writings are classical statements of the conservation issues of the years before 1970.

Nash, Roderick, ed., *The American Environment: Readings in the History of Conservation*. Reading, Mass.: Addison-Wesley, 1968.

An excellent collection of materials on the development of conservation in the United States from the early 1800's to the mid-1960's. The introductory essays and the explanatory passages preceding each selection greatly enhance the worth of this book.

PART I

The Resource Background

Chapter Two

Population, I: The Pressure
of People

*It is quite reasonable to assume that the world population
crisis is a phenomenon of the 20th century, and will be
largely if not entirely a matter of history when humanity
moves into the 21st century.—Donald J. Bogue* [1]

*Over a billion births will have to be prevented during the
next 30 years to bring down the world's population growth
rate from the present 2 percent per year to an annual rate of
1 percent by the year 2000. The task may well be the most
difficult mankind has ever faced, for it involves the most
fundamental characteristic of all life—the need to reproduce
itself. An unprecedented effort is demanded, yet success
will depend on the private actions of hundreds of millions
of individual couples.—National Academy of Sciences* [2]

The Dutch geographer Hendrik Willem van Loon calculated in 1932 that the whole human race could be loosely packed
in a box measuring half a mile in each direction. This somewhat
macabre speculation assumed that the average displacement of

[1] "The End of the Population Explosion," *The Public Interest*, VII
(Spring, 1967), p. 11.

[2] *Rapid Population Growth: Consequences and Policy Implications* (Baltimore: Johns Hopkins Press, 1971), p. 4.

15

each individual was 1 foot by 1½ feet by 6 feet and that there were 2 billion people in the world. Van Loon would undoubtedly be distressed to learn, if he were to extend his speculation to the turn of the century, that his box would have to be three times as long by the year 2000 in order to hold the earth's growing population.

The Explosion of World Population

Some demographers may object to calling the recent increase in world population an "explosion," but Figure 2.1 seems to demonstrate graphically that the pace of growth over the past fifty

Figure 2.1.   The Growth in World Population *

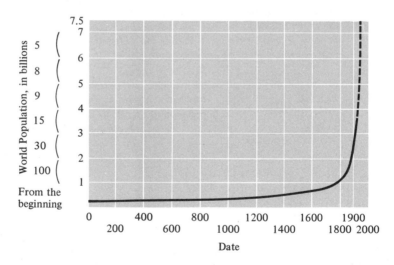

Date

* UNA-USA National Policy Panel on World Population, *World Population: A Challenge to the United Nations and Its System of Agencies* (New York, United Nations Association of the USA, 1969), p. 12. Population estimates frequently differ—as the reader of this chapter will note. In part such differences may be the result of varying assumptions concerning birth and death rates, but the basic data of world population are subject to con-

years has indeed been explosive and that the future portends even greater growth. From some 250 million at 1 A.D., it took the world roughly 1,800 years to reach the billion-people mark, but another billion were added within the next hundred years—and the time interval required for doubling the population continues to shrink. Barring a spectacular reversal of the rate of growth, by the end of the twentieth century, world population will have risen to at least 6 billion people, and in only two centuries beyond—by 2200—an undiminished growth rate would bring to the earth the unthinkable total of 500 billion people. Fortunately, there is no real likelihood that the earth will be flooded with such an overabundance of people. Long before any such massive increase takes place, a reduction in the growth rate will occur either by design or by calamity. In the immediate future, however, the course of world population will continue upward.

Where Are All the People Coming From?

The answer is not simple. Numerous factors interact to account for the recent rapid growth in population: the birthrate, the death rate, and the age composition of the population. At times, these factors may change, accelerating or slowing the population rate of growth, and in some cases working against each other. In the developed countries of the world, such as those of western Europe and North America, changes in the birthrate in recent decades have been most important in determining the rate of population growth, but in the low-income, underdeveloped countries, such as India, Egypt, and various Latin American states, a lower death rate has been primarily responsible for the surge in population. Moreover, a lowering of the death rate in the underdeveloped countries adds more to world population than a similar reduction in the death rate of developed countries because there are more people in the underdeveloped nations and their birthrate is higher. Figure 2.2 shows the inverse relationship

---

siderable question. Data from some of the world's most populous areas are little more than guesses, and even in countries where systematic measurement is undertaken, errors may be substantial.

between population and gross national product in the developed
and underdeveloped nations.*

In Europe and the United States, life expectancy at birth has

Figure 2.2. The Distribution of Population and Income
between the Developed and Underdeveloped Countries †

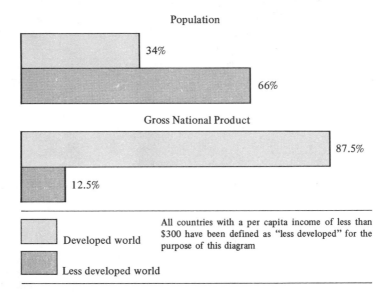

Population

34%

66%

Gross National Product

87.5%

12.5%

Developed world

Less developed world

All countries with a per capita income of less than
$300 have been defined as "less developed" for the
purpose of this diagram

† UNA-USA National Policy Panel on World Population, *World Population: A Challenge to the United Nations and Its System of Agencies* (New
York, United Nations Association of the USA, 1969), p. 27.

* A less developed country is defined in Figure 2.2 as one in which the
annual per-capita income is less than $300. This definition is in accordance
with the economist's sometimes confusing practice of expressing a country's
stage of economic development by the use of either "product" or "income" statistics. The two measures actually come down to the same thing.
"Product" is the money value of goods and services produced in a given
area, such as a nation, whereas income is the return from the sale of these
items when distributed as wages, profits, rents, and other shares; they are
essentially equivalent. "Gross national product," the statistical version employed in Figure 2.2, is the most frequently cited measure of a nation's
economic output; it is the aggregate dollar value of goods and services produced without deductions for depreciation or replacement of the machinery
and equipment used in production.

made great long-term gains, doubling from thirty-three years in 1700 to more than sixty-six by the middle of the twentieth century. The advances in medicine, nutrition, and sanitation that have been primarily responsible for lowering the death rate in Europe and North America have gradually spread throughout the world. Foreign-assistance programs financed by the more affluent nations have introduced these life-extending practices to many backward areas, and over the past forty years the death rate in the low-income countries has fallen sharply, from 40 to 50 deaths per thousand to 10 to 20 deaths per thousand. This is a great change, and since the reduction in the death rate has taken place mainly in infancy and early childhood, its net effect is to reduce the average age of the population and eventually to increase numbers in the childbearing age group.

Professor Jean Mayer, of Harvard's Center for Population Studies, describes the demographic effects of increasing life expectancy in the nations with high birthrates as follows:

> In the United States, 97 out of every 100 newborn white females reach the age of 20; 91 reach the age of 50. In Guatemala, only 70 reach the age of 20; 49 that of 50. If the death rate in Guatemala fell within the next decade to somewhere near the 1950 United States level, a not unlikely development, this alone would increase the number of women reaching the beginning of the childbearing period by 85 percent. Because of the high proportion of young people in underdeveloped countries generally—a country like Costa Rica has twice the proportion of people under 15 that Sweden has—this drop in the death rate in the pre-childbearing period has now and will have in the next few years a gigantic effect on the birth rate. Brazil had 52 million people in 1950, 71 million in 1960, and 83 million in 1966. If present rates prevail, it should have 240 million by the year 2000, or 14 times the 1900 population. With a drop in mortality in the young age groups, the increase could be even more spectacular.[3]

The typical underdeveloped country is plagued by its high fertility. Most such areas have birthrates in the neighborhood of 40 per thousand population, with at least 5 births per childbear-

[3] Jean Mayer, "Toward a Non-Malthusian Population Policy," *Columbia Forum*, XII (Summer 1969), p. 7.

ing couple by the age of fifty. The developed countries, including most countries of Europe, the Soviet Union, and North America, have birthrates of about 20 per thousand and a total fertility of 2 to 3½ children per family by the end of the childbearing period. Recently the United States birthrate has taken a downward tack, but prior to this dip the United States was on the upper end of the fertility scale among the industrialized nations, while Japan, as a result of a concerted effort to depress its birthrate, in part to check the congestion from increasing numbers, had virtually stabilized its population.

Although most nations—developed as well as underdeveloped —have much to gain from limiting population growth, an actual decline in an ethnic group's or a nation's relative population position is likely to cause anxiety among some. For example, Poland, which had a population rate of 8.5 per thousand in the early 1970's, has undertaken a public campaign to encourage larger families because its projected rate indicates a further decline. The campaign for more births in Poland includes increased government subsidies to large families and decreased availability of various population-control practices, such as abortion. Within the Soviet Union, those groups that have fallen behind, such as the Russians and Slavs, have been exhorted by their spokesmen to marry earlier and produce more children. Some Central Asian minorities in the Soviet Union, by contrast with the Russians and Slavs, have increased by as much as 52 percent. The fear of eclipse by faster-growing peoples is also found in some of the racial and ethnic groups in the United States. Jews, for example, who have been active in the Zero Population Growth movement have been criticized by some Jewish leaders, who argue that by reducing their numbers they lessen their influence in society. At the same time, some militant blacks view public programs to control births as an ill-concealed form of genocide, a means of checking the growing proportion of blacks in American society.

Control of Birth in the Developing Nations

The major upward thrust of the world's population comes from those countries that can least support it and are least able to control their birthrates—the underdeveloped nations, as a brief inspection of Figure 2.3 indicates. Ironically, the more advanced nations have contributed to this population pressure by their

Figure 2.3 Distribution of World Population *

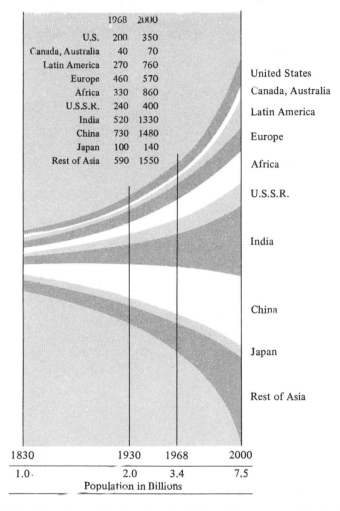

	1968	2000
U.S.	200	350
Canada, Australia	40	70
Latin America	270	760
Europe	460	570
Africa	330	860
U.S.S.R.	240	400
India	520	1330
China	730	1480
Japan	100	140
Rest of Asia	590	1550

United States

Canada, Australia

Latin America

Europe

Africa

U.S.S.R.

India

China

Japan

Rest of Asia

1830	1930	1968	2000
1.0	2.0	3.4	7.5

Population in Billions

* UNA-USA National Policy Panel on World Population, *World Population: A Challenge to the United Nations and Its System of Agencies* (New York, United Nations Association of the USA, 1969), p. 14.

humanitarian efforts in making available to the developing nations the more recent advances in disease control, since they have not at the same time provided effective means of checking the birthrate. The inevitable consequence for the low-income countries is more rapid population growth, an increased need for additional food, and intensified pressure for economic growth and development. But the simple fact is that the eradication of disease in these countries is considerably easier than checking births or raising economic output.

The public-health measures that are most frequently responsible for cutting back the death rate in the developing nations—such as control of malaria-carrying mosquitoes, improvement in water quality, and immunization programs—are not dependent, as are birth-control programs, upon the virtually complete participation and approval of the total population. Nor do the measures that reduce the death rate raise the cultural and religious issues that at times limit the acceptance of some birth-control techniques. Successful population limitation in an underdeveloped country requires not only an inexpensive birth-control method but a literate population and widespread public acceptance.

Economic Growth and Population Growth

Although it is easier to prevent death than it is to control births in the emerging nations, a foreign-assistance program that concentrates upon extending life expectancy and simply raising economic output without regard to population growth is almost certainly on a self-defeating course. The economic-growth goal, the pursuit of greater output, is now a tarnished symbol of achievement in the industrial nations, but it has lost little of its attraction in the low-income countries; indeed, higher per-capita output has an obvious appeal to the developing nations, as was indicated by the controversy surrounding the growth issue at the United Nations Stockholm conference on the environment in the summer of 1972. But a country's standard of living can also be raised by spreading its output among a smaller number of claimants. In short, its rate of population growth can be slowed.

Population growth in the low-income nations is a prime enemy of rising living standards. It restrains them in two ways: through numbers and through the population composition. Obviously, the more people there are to share a given output, the smaller will be each share, but this is only part of the problem. The age composition of a population is a critical determinant of its productive capacity. A population that is growing adds more mouths to feed than workers to the labor force, necessarily decreasing the per-capita standard of living. A population growth rate of 2 or 3 percent per annum, typical of many underdeveloped nations, largely nullifies the income assistance from foreign-aid programs. Not only does rapid population growth increase need by raising the number of nonproducing younger members of the population, but it also reduces the developing nation's output potential by confining large numbers of females to child rearing. For the most part, children under fifteen are unproductive—both in developing nations and in more advanced societies—and during the period of infant dependency and for a varying number of years thereafter, the mother is at least partially removed from the labor market. The net effect is to hold back output while need increases. By contrast, a declining population growth rate not only permits the economy's output to be shared by fewer people, thus increasing per-capita income, but it provides the opportunity for the emerging nation to convert some of this output to productive machinery and equipment, establishing a base for further economic growth.

Investment in Decreased Population

Within limits, a population decrease can be thought of as an investment opportunity for an underdeveloped country, one that provides a more immediate return than the construction of hydroelectric-power projects or the operation of international airlines. Unfortunately, the desire to emulate the established industrial nations is strong, and steel mills, hydroelectric plants, and airlines have become the status symbols of growth for the developing nations. The donor agencies and states do exercise some direction over the projects they support, but to require birth control as a condition of aid is likely to outrage many in the developing nations and to raise disturbing ethical questions. The object of foreign aid—improving the underdeveloped country's standard of living—can be achieved in more than one way, although the conventional approach has emphasized added machinery and equipment and more advanced techniques of production. The effects of introducing modern machinery and equipment to increase output have frequently fallen short of expectations, because of the difficulty of changing a backward agricultural economy to more advanced industrial production. And even when a modern industrial enterprise, such as a steel plant, is successfully grafted onto the developing economy, the increase in output may be dissipated by rapid growth in population.

By contrast, a foreign-aid investment to reduce population growth, if successful, promises a more immediate improvement in the standard of living. Furthermore, a substantially smaller investment is required to prevent the birth of an additional child than to provide that child with goods and services once it is born.

Population Control—The High-Yield Investment

Stephen Enke, an economist who has investigated the effects of population control upon the living standards of developing countries, declares, "If economic resources of given value were devoted to retarding population growth rather than accelerating production growth, the former resources could be 100 or so times more effective in raising per capita incomes in many less developed countries." [4] Obviously, the actual cost of reducing population growth depends upon the techniques of birth control involved—some, such as the pill, are substantially more expensive than others. For all control techniques, however, the benefit of increasing income exceeds the cost of birth suppression. This is not to imply that the only tenable policy objective of the developing nation is an ever-increasing gross national product. But if a

[4] Stephen Enke, "The Economic Aspects of Slowing Population Growth," *Economic Journal*, LXXVI (March 1966), p. 56.

country's per-capita income is falling, especially when it is near the borderline of subsistence, malnutrition and starvation may be the stark consequence. For this reason, the goal of higher output per capita is most urgent for the underdeveloped country.

The more severe the economic privation in the developing country, the greater will be the benefit from limiting births. The affluent countries need not greatly change their life style in order to support an increasing population, as the United States did in the early 1960's when its birthrate was higher than that of India, but the poorer countries do not have an output large enough to support noncontributing additions to the population without reducing the share of necessities for all.

As a means of raising the living standards of developing nations, investment in birth control not only has a more immediate impact than attempts to increase productivity, but can be funded for a trivial amount—about 1 percent of postwar foreign-aid expenditures. Unfortunately, however, investment in the control of population growth involves a wide range of administrative complexities, personal and religious values, and sometimes conflicting nationalistic objectives. Achieving widespread participation in a program for birth control is more difficult than reaching a decision on the desirability and location of a steel mill or hydro-electric plant. Indeed, any program that requires large-scale participation of the population in a country where literacy and means of communication are limited will encounter difficulty from the start. As a result, the investment cost is probably the least important of the factors influencing the introduction of birth control in developing nations. But since the desirability of reducing the pressure upon a poor nation's slowly increasing productive capacity is self-evident, a comprehensive birth-control program is a low-cost way of pursuing this objective.

Population Composition and the Standard of Living

With rapid growth, increasing births reduce the average age of a population. As the growth of the population slows, its composition changes. The average age rises and eventually the productive age groups enlarge; the number of unproductive dependents decreases at the same time that the proportion of the population in the labor market rises, expanding per-capita output. But what if population growth continues to decline until members of the older unproductive age groups outnumber young entrants into the labor market? Then a new class of dependents or semidependents is created, those who have contributed to output in the past but must now be supported by the output of others.

Population growth can seriously dilute even a rapidly rising national output. If output increases 5 percent annually with a stable population, it takes only 12 years to double per-capita income. But with a 2.4-percent annual population increase, the projected trend of the low-income nations of the world, more than twice as long—27 years—will be required to double per-capita income. And if the rate of economic growth is 4 percent instead of 5 percent, the 2.4-percent population increase will extend the time required for doubling per-capita income to 43 years.

An increase in population that is not matched by an equivalent increase in output does more than simply spread the resources of a country thinner, however. It sharply accentuates some needs. Where the population doubles every twenty-five years or less, as in an underdeveloped country, the youth component in the population may exceed 40 percent and seriously overburden the country's educational system. In spite of heroic efforts, illiteracy is likely to increase at the same time that more resources are devoted to education.

Population growth depends not only on what happens today but also on what happened yesterday. How many children are born now is, in large part, the result of how many were born earlier and have reached childbearing age. Even though the number of children per family decreases, population growth may continue more or less unabated until the lower birthrate compensates for the increase in the number of childbearing couples in the population. A high past birthrate, increasing the number of childbearing couples, will raise the rate of population growth even though the average number of children per family remains the same. Ten million families averaging two children per family add more to the population than 7 million families averaging the same number of children.* The importance of the past in determining present population growth is shown graphically in Figure 2.4.

Population Growth in the United States

In the United States, the problem of too many people is a recent one. In the formative years of our nation, increasing population was consciously sought, for the more abundant labor supply and the military manpower it provided. As late as the 1930's, the sagging birthrate was a cause for serious concern. The Great Depression delayed marriages and reduced the average number of children per family. The resulting decline in the rate of population growth was considered by some to portend continued economic distress and adjustment problems for the American economy. Professor Alvin Hansen, of Harvard, one of the more prominent economists of this period, noted the contribution of the decreasing rate of population growth in the 1930's to what he called "secular stagnation," a condition of long-run depressed investment and employment. A downturn in population growth, it was reasoned, reduced the amount of expansion that would be necessary to satisfy future needs, thus eliminating an important stimulant of economic growth. Against the background of the mass unemployment and malnutrition of the 1930's, only the most dedicated Malthusian could find benefits in declining population growth.

* The casting of this illustration in terms of "families" does not represent a kind of Victorian refusal to acknowledge the importance of illegitimate births. Indeed, in the United States these have become an increasing source of population growth, countered somewhat by the spreading acceptance of abortion. Eight percent of the births in the United States—one in twelve—are illegitimate. Moreover, this estimate probably seriously understates the extent of illegitimacy because of the difficulty of collecting information on this aspect of population growth. But since illegitimate births, like legitimate births, occur only among people of childbearing age, no different principle is involved.

Figure 2.4   Why Two Births per Family Will Not Halt United States Population Growth by 2000 *

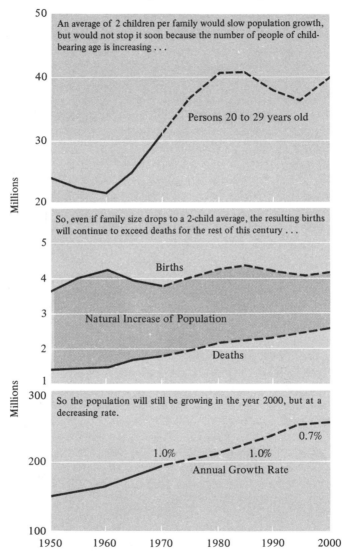

An average of 2 children per family would slow population growth, but would not stop it soon because the number of people of child-bearing age is increasing . . .

Persons 20 to 29 years old

So, even if family size drops to a 2-child average, the resulting births will continue to exceed deaths for the rest of this century . . .

Births

Natural Increase of Population

Deaths

So the population will still be growing in the year 2000, but at a decreasing rate.

0.7%

1.0%   1.0%

Annual Growth Rate

Millions

* Reproduced from *Population and the American Future: Report of the Commission on Population Growth and the American Future* (Washington, D.C., Government Printing Office, 1972), pp. 20–21.

Population Size and Economic Efficiency

Small nations may not be able to take advantage of some kinds of large-scale production opportunities because of their limited market and restricted technical and other skills. But the American economy has not been seriously constrained by insufficient population since well before the turn of the twentieth century. By 1915, our population had reached 100 million; it is now over 200 million, and whether we like it or not, it will eventually reach 300 million. Economic advantages from adding more people to our industrial system are hard to find. By the early twentieth century, large-scale production was well established in many American industries, and by the middle of the century, most production facilities had attained their optimum size, with little cost advantage to be gained from further expansion. Indeed, at times the opposite can occur: Lower productivity and higher costs may result from the lower efficiency of the large, bureaucratic firm and from the higher relative prices for materials whose supply cannot keep up with the pressure of expanding industrial output.

At the time when the American economy began to duplicate the size of assembly lines and plant facilities instead of enlarging them, the productivity-increasing effect of a growing population was starting to run its course. Innovations in technology and improvements in labor skills can still raise output above previous levels in the American economy, but they are no longer dependent upon increases in the size of the production unit. The business firm has continued to grow, and massive conglomerates have been formed, but the object now is control and diversification of holdings rather than more efficient operation.

The Difficulty of Demographic Forecasting

Demographic forecasting has established an unenviable record over the past half century in the United States. Birthrates have seldom followed the expected projections in the recent past, and the period extending from the Great Depression well into the postwar years has eluded the demographers' forecasts. So the demographers have responded with a larger offering of projections based on different assumptions.* Following this procedure, the Census Bureau—emphasizing that it is not "forecasting"—points out that if there were no change in immigration and if American families were to average three children, which is clearly unlikely, the United States would pass the 300-million population mark before the year 2000. But if the average number of children per family is reduced to two, a more realistic prospect and the goal of the Zero Population Growth movement, the United States will not reach 300 million people until near the second decade of the twenty-first century. As indicated in Figure 2.5, the population replacement rate is actually 2.11 children per couple to compensate for population reduction through death.

How long before or after the year 2000 the United States actually reaches the 300-million mark depends upon the decisions of those in the childbearing age groups. Modern contraceptive techniques, such as the pill, and more widespread acceptance of abortion have greatly increased the control over birth in the developed countries. And where birth-control techniques have improved,† making the size of the family largely a matter of

* There are still some uninhibited generalizers, however. For example, Professor Donald J. Bogue, a University of Chicago demographer-sociologist, predicts the end of the population explosion by the turn of the century. He contends that "it is probable that by the year 2000 each of the major world regions will have a population growth rate that either is zero or is easily within the capacity of its expanding economy to support." ("The End of the Population Explosion," The Public Interest, VII, Spring, 1967, p. 11.)

† The use of the pill has increased significantly the efficiency of birth prevention. Moreover, its use will continue to rise for some time, since it has been more extensively adopted by the younger childbearing couples than by the older. As those using the pill become older, a higher proportion of fertile women will rely upon this form of contraception. But the pill appears to be just the first step in more effective contraception. It is likely to be superseded by methods that are equally effective and more acceptable—such as a single tablet for the full oestrus cycle, medication that will not prevent ovulation (one of the basic Catholic objections to the use of the pill), oral contraceptives for males, and other hormonal control devices. The medication covering the whole oestrus cycle with one oral

Figure 2.5.   The Projections of the Census Bureau

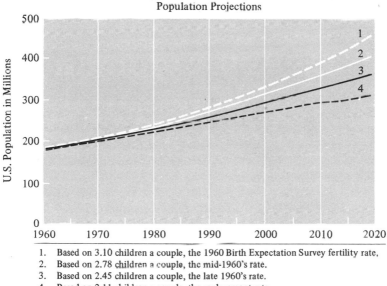

Population Projections

U.S. Population in Millions

1. Based on 3.10 children a couple, the 1960 Birth Expectation Survey fertility rate,
2. Based on 2.78 children a couple, the mid-1960's rate.
3. Based on 2.45 children a couple, the late 1960's rate.
4. Based on 2.11 children a couple, the replacement rate.

choice, population forecasting has become more uncertain. When birth can be prevented by conscious choice, human decisions can be anticipated only imperfectly. By contrast, where birth-control practices are limited or ineffectual, population forecasts can be tied more closely to the fertility of the childbearing age groups. In the more advanced nations, however, abrupt changes in the birthrate may take place in response to altered economic conditions, social unrest, or shifting personal views of the ideal number of children per family. Moreover, the demographer cannot be sure whether a lower birthrate represents a decision to reduce family size or simply a postponement in reaching the usual goal. Only time will answer this question; meanwhile, demographers are to be found on both sides of the

dose may combine the simplicity and the economy necessary for success in the underdeveloped nations.

issue. Even if the reduction in early births by younger couples does not reflect the goal of a smaller family, however, some decrease in family size is inevitable because to delay birth means to decrease births somewhat.

Population Growth in the Late 1970's

So what is going to happen to population growth in the United States in the rest of this decade? Nothing close to a precise answer can be given, but some of the basic determining factors can be identified. Well before the widespread use of the pill and before the Zero Population Growth movement had attracted attention in the United States, population growth had started to fall off. The population is still growing, but the rate of growth has decreased since 1957. Two factors may contribute further to this downward trend: concern for the environment, which is likely to reinforce decisions for smaller families, and the use of the pill by an increasing proportion of childbearing couples.

On the other side of the population equation, however, is the coming of age of those born during the "baby boom," a consequence of the postdepression surge in the birthrate that reached its peak in 1957. As these individuals attain sixteen years and over, the proportion of the population within the childbearing age range becomes larger. As a result, even if by 1975 each new family limits itself to two children, it will take seventy-five years, until 2050, for the United States population to stabilize. And even with the two-child family, the population will have increased to three people in 2060 for every two in the early 1970's. On the other hand, if the larger family of the early 1970's continues until 2060, there will be seven people for every two in 1970—clearly a massive population increase.

The Costs of a High Birthrate

Raising children involves costs in addition to the familiar outlays for food, shelter, and education. There is an "opportunity" cost of having children, which represents the productive activity—such as gainful employment—that would have been undertaken in the absence of child-rearing responsibilities. The

Commission on Population Growth and the American Future, appointed by President Nixon, estimates this opportunity cost to be in the neighborhood of $70,000 for the average American mother who stays home until the younger of two children reaches fourteen years of age. In addition, direct outlays—for food, shelter, and the like—are set by the Commission's economists at $40,000 per child in terms of 1971 prices. These direct costs of child-raising are of course not the same for all parts of the country, and the opportunity costs depend upon how much of the parents' earning capacity remains unused during the period of child-raising.

The Commission reports that direct costs are somewhat higher in the West, and that on the whole, child-raising is less costly on the farm. The variations in opportunity costs due to dissimilar earning capacities can probably be reliably compressed in an average figure, but the Commission's opportunity-cost estimate seems to overlook the usual alternative to waiting for the youngest child to reach fourteen years: nursery-school or day care for the children until they reach school age. The figure $70,000 greatly overstates the available alternatives to parental care in the child-raising years.

Zero Population Growth and the Quality of Life

Even though the impact of an increasing population upon such things as schools, housing, and medical services is reasonably predictable, at times the adjustments to society's changing needs may leave much to be desired, involving temporary classroom arrangements, insufficient medical facilities, and inappropriate housing. Needs may be quite apparent, but the mechanisms for private and public decision-making may produce sluggish or unsatisfactory responses. With zero growth, however, the task of adjustment is greatly reduced. Some aspects of life in the United States would improve with a stable population: Such difficulties as air pollution, noise, water pollution, and traffic congestion would be reduced; and some functions—such as education and job training—can generally be more efficiently undertaken with small numbers of people.

The "Law of Large Numbers"

Large populations have both advantages and disadvantages. Although the number of geniuses, or concert pianists, or great chemists, in similar cultures may be much the same *per million people,* the larger population will normally have more of such individuals, and this fact is sometimes cited as an advantage of large populations. This does not mean, however, that small nations are denied the benefits of the talents that are sometimes found in more populated areas. The contributions of Nobel chemists, concert artists, and great writers are seldom confined to the country of their origin. Moreover, the law of large numbers is not a one-way proposition. It yields unwanted events as well as benefits—psychopaths as well as geniuses are produced in greater abundance, and since the former are considerably more difficult to detect and control in a large population, individual responsibility tends to be eroded, and the by-products of the concentration of urban population—conflict, lawlessness, congestion—outrun the attempts at remedy.

The Threshold Effect

Some resources are impaired if used by too many people: space in and around cities, national parks, wilderness areas, wildlife populations, and commuter routes, to mention a few. Increasingly, the large metropolitan area has been beset with problems —economic decay, racial conflict, paralyzing traffic, bankrupt public transportation—but through it all the thrust of growing population piles more and more people into the congested areas. So inexorable has been the expansion of most large cities that some find in metropolitan growth a kind of irreversible "iron law."

The Period Ahead

At the start of the 1970's, the Census Bureau finds the birthrate in the United States to be lowering significantly. But a decline in the birthrate is no guarantee that the population will eventually stabilize. Birthrates in the past have shown a marked capacity to oscillate in disregard of demographers' projections, and a low reproduction rate may trigger national and ethnic anxieties that increase the population once again. Nevertheless, the recent decline in the birthrate to approximately two children per family is a basis for hope of a break with the past.

On a broader scale, the promise of population restraint in the low-income nations, where it is most needed, is less bright. Continuing illiteracy, poor systems of communication, and inadequate medical facilities frustrate attempts to carry out comprehensive population-control programs. Moreover, some emerging nations have shown little enthusiasm for population control. Instead, they have opted for population expansion. In following such a course, the low-income nation pays the price of a lower standard of living at the same time that it adds to an already excessive world population.

References and Readings

Bogue, Donald J., "The End of the Population Explosion," *The Public Interest*, VII (Spring 1967), pp. 11–20.
> An extravagantly optimistic view of mankind's ability to control future population growth, by a University of Chicago demographer-sociologist.

Bureau of the Census, *Population Estimates*. Washington, D.C.: Department of Commerce, various dates.
> These population reports, such as the P–25 Series, contain both the official estimates of the Bureau of the Census and various analyses of population projections.

Chamberlain, Neil W., *Beyond Malthus: Population and Power*. New York: Basic Books, 1970.
> A rather wide-ranging examination of the variety of effects of increasing population other than its impact upon the food supply.

Commission on Population Growth and the American Future, *An Interim Report to the President and Congress*. Washington, D.C.: Government Printing Office, 1971.
> A short informative discussion of United States population trends.

—— *Population and the American Future*. Washington, D.C.: Government Printing Office, 1972.

> A comprehensive study of the population problem in the United States, with recommendations for remedial action. The report is the work of a full-scale professional staff, and the policy proposals are endorsed by a commission of prominent citizens appointed by President Nixon. The Commission strongly favors population control in the United States.

Ehrlich, Paul R., and Ehrlich, Anne H., *Population, Resources, Environment: Issues in Human Ecology*. San Francisco: W. H. Freeman and Co., 1970.

> A vigorous statement of the need for world population control, and an examination of a wide variety of environmental problems, many of which stem from excessive population. Some of the same ground is covered by one of the authors, Paul Ehrlich, in an earlier book, *The Population Bomb*. The approach is exhortatory, sometimes based on highly selected evidence, rather than analytically objective.

Enke, Stephen, *Zero U. S. Population Growth—When, How, and Why*. Santa Barbara: Tempo Center for Advanced Studies, General Electric Company, 1970.

Mayer, Jean, "Toward a Non-Malthusian Population Policy," *Columbia Forum*, XII (Summer 1969), pp. 5–13.

> Mainly discounts the Malthusian doctrine and describes other features of the population problem.

National Academy of Sciences, *Rapid Population Growth: Consequences and Policy Implications*. Baltimore: Johns Hopkins Press, 1971.

> Volume I includes an examination of the demographic setting, a discussion of the consequences of rapid population growth, and policy recommendations. Volume II consists of seventeen research papers on a variety of topics related to population problems, such as resource adequacy, abortion, family size, and the like.

Thompson, Warren S., and Lewis, D. T., *Population Problems*, fifth ed. New York: McGraw-Hill, 1965.

> A comprehensive examination of population composition, factors affecting fertility and mortality, changing population-growth patterns, and the problems that arise from population changes.

UNA-USA National Policy Panel on World Population. *World Population: A Challenge to the United Nations and Its System of Agencies*. New York, United Nations Association of the USA, 1969.

> A brief account of the nature of world population growth and the involvement and obligations of the United Nations organizations.

Chapter Three

Population, II: The Impact Upon Resources

The battle to feed humanity is already lost, in the sense that we will not be able to prevent large-scale famines in the next decade or so.—Paul Ehrlich [1]

. . . Widespread famine that could reasonably be attributed to economic incapability has not been observed in any of the less developed regions for decades. Fear of famine reached a peak in the mid-1960's, largely as a result of crop failure in parts of Asia coupled with dwindling international food reserves. These fears have been allayed by the elimination of recent shortages and the prospects for a long-run sharp upward trend in output of food grains.—National Academy of Sciences [2]

In early 1972, a group of distinguished British scientists produced a document, called "Blueprint for Survival," that would have brought cheers from the early-nineteenth-century English clergyman and economist Thomas Malthus, who is most frequently associated with the view that population is likely to

---

[1] From *The Population Bomb* by Dr. Paul R. Ehrlich. Copyright © 1968, 1971 by Paul R. Ehrlich. Reprinted by permission of Ballantine Books, Inc., p. 36.

[2] *Rapid Population Growth* (Baltimore: Johns Hopkins Press, 1971), p. 23.

outrun the food supply. The British scientists raised this specter—and more. They likened modern man to a bull in the "environmental china shop," with the unreasonable expectation that the environment should adapt to his destructive behavior. To survive, according to these British scientists, man must not only change his ways but also reduce his numbers. The twenty-two-page document questions many aspects of modern industrial society, especially the preoccupation with economic growth, but its most arresting recommendation is that the British population be gradually reduced to about half its present size.

Once the British population had been shrunk from 55 million people to 30 million, a "steady" or "stationary" state would be established. The "Blueprint for Survival" suggests that the population be brought to this figure over a period of 150 years; this would undoubtedly be the longest period of population aging ever experienced by a major nation, and would cause England to take on many of the features of an old-age nursing home. No state has ever accomplished such a long-term reversal in its population growth, no matter how great the pressure of numbers or how poor the country. And where the upward movement in the birthrate has been deliberately checked, as in postwar Japan, agitation to break away from the zero or near-zero growth rate generally develops. For all its daring, the "Blueprint for Survival" is reminiscent of an earlier time in England when other famous British intellectuals warned of the dangers of increasing population.

Restraint of Population Growth—
A Long-Standing Issue

Malthus and Mill, Early Advocates of Population Control

Although no major nation has ever held its birthrate much below its death rate for long, the goal of stabilizing population is in the best British intellectual tradition. John Stuart Mill, a giant among English philosophers and economists in the mid-nineteenth century, advocated that the more economically advanced nations keep their population steady; otherwise, he foresaw a continued worsening of the advanced nations' living standards. Mill believed that a decline in both innovation and capital accumulation is inevitable for the developed nations and that to maintain output per capita, the natural rate of population growth has to be checked. In Mill's view, the inevitability of zero *economic* growth requires a zero *population* growth rate. This is the total opposite of the present-day view of the critics of the economic-growth goal, who believe we are endangered by runaway economic growth. On the broader goals of life, however, Mill would have found himself in substantial agreement with those who emphasize the quality of life. He said:

> I cannot . . . regard the stationary state of capital and wealth with the unaffected aversion so generally manifested toward it by political economists of the old school. I am inclined to believe that it would be, on the whole, a very considerable improvement on our present condition. I confess I am not charmed with the ideal of life held out by those who think that the normal state of human beings is that of struggling to get on; that the trampling, crushing, elbowing, and treading on each other's heels, which form the existing type of social life, are the most desirable lot of human kind, or anything but the disagreeable symptoms of one of the phases of industrial progress. . . . It is only in the backward countries of the world that increased production is still an important object: in those most advanced, what is economically needed is a better distribution, of which one indispensable means is a stricter restraint on population.[3]

Where Mill's concern was with the slowing down of the capitalist system, Thomas Malthus directed his attention to the social consequences of the reproductive capacity of mankind. His *Essay on the Principle of Population* was a best seller in the years following its publication in 1798, and his basic proposition—that population has the potential to overwhelm the food supply—has had a number of highly successful reruns since its original introduction.

[3] John Stuart Mill, *Principles of Political Economy*, ed. by Sir W. J. Ashley (London: Longmans, Green, 1940), pp. 748–749.

Others before Malthus had warned of the dangers of an increasing population, among them Aristotle, who observed in *Politics* that "neglect of an effective birth control policy is a never-failing source of poverty which, in turn, is the parent of revolution and crime." But Malthus not only raised the specter of misery and starvation from overpopulation; he detailed how the catastrophe would arrive. If unchecked, population would expand geometrically—2, 4, 8, 16—whereas the food supply would fall behind because it could increase only arithmetically—2, 4, 6, 8. One might dispute this relationship, but it was hard to ignore its message.

From the first, the doctrine took a strong hold on men's minds, although it is open to question whether this influence has served society well. Malthus' views spread quickly throughout intellectual circles and found their way into the British political arena. In the world of politics, Malthus is frequently given credit (or blame) for the decreased support of poorhouses and work-relief programs in nineteenth-century England, justified on the basis that "the constant tendency of all animate life to increase beyond the nourishment prepared for it" causes such assistance to be self-defeating. Sooner or later, according to the Malthusians, the improved living standard afforded by poor-relief payments would be wiped out by the larger numbers of poor that survived because of these programs. To Malthus, poor relief was an explosively expanding system: More relief begot more births, increasing the need for more relief—hardly a state of affairs likely to appeal to the propertied, tax-paying classes, then any more than now.

The Malthusian doctrine provided the justification for breaking this expanding cycle. But Malthus' opposition to the English poor laws was not confined to the population effect; he also believed that they generated idleness and dissipation, impairing resource use, as well as creating "the poor which they maintain." On a broader scale, the Malthusian interpretation of the role of population growth as a social force provided the intellectual justification for a *laissez-faire* approach in public affairs. It encouraged the policy of noninterference with "natural developments" that may have reached a high point in the Irish famine during the late 1840's when the British refused to divert Irish grain from sale abroad.

The pessimism generated by the spread of Malthus' doctrine and its message of the futility of social reform led Thomas Carlyle to label economics the "dismal science," even though economists then as now were not to be found among the more enthusiastic of Malthus' followers. Others—particularly the biological scientists—were more attracted to the doctrine and to this day they are numbered among his stronger supporters. Charles Darwin, for example, even found a parallel between the Malthusian pressure of the human population upon a lagging food supply and the experience of other organisms, that led him to his theory of biological evolution, where natural selection arises from the struggle of a species to survive.

The Survival of the Controversy Over Malthus

But why does the controversy over Malthus' principle of population continue? Isn't more than 150 years enough to prove or disprove a proposition as straightforward as his seems to be? The answer is that since 1798 the evidence has been conflicting, varying with time and country and sometimes with the preconceptions of the investigator. Moreover, even though the Malthusian doctrine is old, it is cast in terms of future expectations—and the future extends forever: if not this year, then maybe later population pressure will reach the crisis level. What in fact are the chances that population pressure and the by-products of unchecked growth will jeopardize mankind's future? All too great, according to recent commentators.

Here Comes Doomsday—Computer Style

If we are to believe Donella Meadows and a group of her colleagues at the Massachusetts Institute of Technology who have undertaken a look into the future with the aid of a computer, the consequences of continuing economic growth and rising population may bring the world to the verge of collapse as early as the year 2000—unless society's present course is drastically altered. Although the MIT study, *The Limits to Growth*, makes the traditional disclaimer that its computer models are not to be considered predictions of what actually will happen, there is no concealing that the message of the book is impending disaster. The Meadows projections cover a variety of different resource-using and population-growth conditions and therefore specify a number of different times for the arrival of disaster, along with the possibility of indefinitely forestalling collapse by imposing zero population and zero economic growth. Some are impressed with this message, but others find the study unconvincing.

Compared with the simple Malthusian proposition, in which the scourges of pestilence and starvation ultimately check growing population, the MIT projections are more complex and the consequences more devastating. The Meadows models examine population growth and the food supply, but they also trace the interactions of economic growth, capital creation, pollution, and resource use. Assuming that society blithely ignores or is unable to check increasing population, that the resource base suffers irreversible impairment, and that burgeoning pollution cannot be stemmed, the computer print-out sets the date of society's collapse at around the turn of the century. This early doomsday is shown in Figure 3.1, in which industrial output and per-capita food production reach peaks around 2000, but pollution and population continue to grow for some years before turning down. Throughout the period of increasing population, the supply of resources declines sharply, finally flattening out after the system has collapsed; population falls because the death rate (indicated by the D's on the chart) passes the birthrate (indicated by the B's).

The Steps to Disaster

The key to the collapse shown in Figure 3.1 is the interaction between economic growth and resource depletion, which takes the following pattern:

Expanding industrial output imposes increasing strain upon resources, depleting the resource base.

Figure 3.1. The Meadows World With Uncontrolled
Pollution, Population, and Economic Growth *

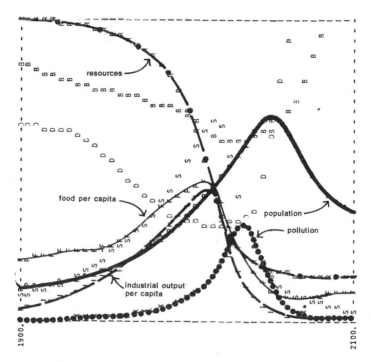

* Donella H. Meadows *et al., The Limits to Growth* (A Potomac Asso-
ciates/Club of Rome Book; New York: Universe Books, 1972), p. 124.
The horizontal axis of the Meadows diagram represents the linear passage
of time, but the vertical axis obviously does not provide a common de-
nominator for the variables depicted—units of food, people, and pollution,
for example, are hardly the same. The plotted but unconnected notations
B, D, and S refer respectively to crude birthrate, crude death rate, and
services per capita.

As the resource base is depleted, resource prices rise dis-
proportionately and a greater share of industrial expenditures goes for raw materials.

This increase in expenditures for raw materials reduces the

funds available for general capital creation, causing new investment to fall below depreciation.*

As capital depreciates more rapidly than new investment is added, the industrial sector collapses.

In collapsing, the industrial sector carries with it the agricultural and service sectors, decreasing food production and disrupting medical services; a sharp rise in the death rate results.

The postcollapse period is marked by continuing decline in the population, but a leveling off of the per-capita industrial output and food production. Pollution also reaches a relatively stable lower level, due to the sharp decline in industrial output. But the apparent stability in pollution, food production, and industrial output should not be interpreted as the onset of the happy equilibrium of the stationary state. The overburden of population continues to press upon resources and the food supply in the postcollapse period, resulting in a living standard near or below subsistence. Only when population has been reduced to a level that does not strain the economy's output capacity will there be a rise in the standard of living. This improvement in the standard of living does not occur during the time span presented in Figure 3.1, however, as is shown by the low, flat per-capita food curve and the relatively high population curve. Somewhere off the graph, beyond 2100, if there is a sufficient resource base left, the economy may right itself after undergoing the ordeal of depopulation.

Figure 3.1 depicts the Meadows Uncontrolled World; Figure 3.2 shows the Meadows Stable World, Model I. Between the "uncontrolled" world and the "stable" world, a variety of resource–growth–population relationships are explored by the MIT group. Invariably the conclusion is that unless mankind controls population and industrial growth, both industrial output and population will be brought to a halt within the next century by internal self-destruction. According to the group's reasoning, if

---

* Depreciation in the Meadows models is the outlay necessary to keep the capital sector productive by replenishing worn-out machinery and equipment.

resource depletion doesn't destroy the operation of the present world economic order, something else—such as skyrocketing pollution—will. If instead pollution is held in check and unlimited resources are plugged into the model, collapse is moved farther into the twenty-first century, but the irresistible effect of mounting population and decreasing food output brings disaster before the year 2100.

If resources are deemed adequate, breakdown may come from excessive pollution; if pollution is controlled, the food supply may lag behind population growth. So what does the MIT group propose—submissive acceptance of inevitable disaster? Not at all. To avert disaster, both population growth and industrial output must be brought under rigid control by the turn of the century. *Both* zero population growth and zero economic growth are required to save the world, and according to Meadows and her associates, the sooner the better.

The MIT Stable World

Stable World, Model 1, halts population growth at approximately the year 2000 and industrial output shortly thereafter. Because of the restraint upon population and economic output, pollution does not constitute a threat to the system. Resources are slowly depleted, but at so gradual a rate, as a result of zero economic growth, that technological innovation is presumably able to compensate for the resources used up. New investment just equals depreciation in Stable World I and no increase in output is permitted after 2000, but the average living standard of the world is significantly higher than the 1970 level because of economic growth in the years before 2000. World per-capita income at the turn-of-the-century stabilizing point is set by the Meadows group at $1,800, which is less than half of the 1970 United States average but more than three times that of the world as a whole.

What of the Postfreeze World?

After the freeze on growth, the Meadows world as a whole will have a higher standard of living than during the 1970's, but the

Figure 3.2.   The Meadows Stable World, Model I *

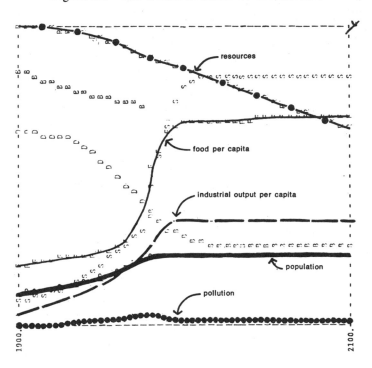

* Donella H. Meadows *et al.*, *The Limits to Growth* (A Potomac Associates/Club of Rome Book; New York: Universe Books, 1972), p. 165. See Figure 3.1 for an explanation of the axes.

lower-income nations may be locked into their lower-income status, and the question of how they will react to this situation is discreetly left aside. Even if the wealthier nations are cut down to the world average by the spreading of their greater output among the poorer nations, conflicts arising out of economic self-interest may destabilize the Meadows world. If the nations of the world—especially the have-not nations—accept a ceiling on their economic growth, it is likely to be only after they have attained more of the comfortable life they see others enjoying. At best, such a reaction provides a tentative equilibrium, rather than the stable world of no-growth.* So far, however, the validity of the Meadows projections have not been questioned. But will the world economies actually collapse so easily? Are there in fact no options for mankind except zero economic growth and zero population growth?

The Steps to Disaster Revisited

In the uncontrolled world, the first step dooms the world. After this step—the depleting of resources—there is no real hope; the only question is when doomsday will arrive. And so it is with the other Meadows models based upon different but exponential rates † of resource depletion and pollution build-up, and less-than-exponential rates of food production, without controls on population growth and industrial output. Different data inputs yield different time patterns of collapse, but the inevitability of disaster is assured by the rate relationships that are fed into the computer. Not only are the results of this study predetermined by the data inputs, but the models created are both oversimplifications and distortions of the real world.

When we look behind the computer plots of the various Meadows models, we see our old familiar Malthusian friend, dressed up in flashy new clothes and contemplating the twentieth-century problems of economic growth and the environment as well as the prospect that population may outrun the food supply. Although the terminology is different—"exponential" is used in place of Malthus' "geometric" to point up the potential of population increase and the threat of pollution—the critical relationship is still the high increasing rate of need that overwhelms a

* Those advocating zero economic growth generally ignore the problem of the important consequences that follow from the method adopted to stifle growth, quite aside from the effects of preventing an increase in economic output. A brief consideration of these effects occurs in Chapter 4.

† For discussion of the population question, exponential and geometric growth rates may be considered essentially the same, although the geometric rate is a special case of exponential growth. An exponential increase occurs when a growth rate is a constant percentage of the whole, which is true of the geometric rate—2, 4, 8—but some exponential rates diverge from this pattern.

lower rate of increasing capacity to meet this need, sealing mankind's fate. Once again, as in Malthus, starvation and pestilence
are the destructive forces that bring population back into line.

The Meadows worlds plunge headlong into catastrophe because the pressure upon resources is unabated, the food supply
lags behind need, population growth resists control, or pollution
reaches devastating levels. Neither the government nor the economy can respond in a manner that prevents the eventual collapse. Nothing—abatement programs, market readjustments, or the
development of resource substitutes—forestalls disaster. Innovation goes forward in the resource-using industries, but somehow
stops short of adding to the resource base through substitutes or
more efficient resource use. As a result, in the Meadows Uncontrolled World, for example, the rising resource prices drain funds
from other uses, such as investment in machinery and equipment,
and do nothing to encourage the development of substitutes for
the shrinking supply of industrial raw materials. Indeed, the quality of resources deteriorates so much that a larger and larger
share of investment funds is taken for such activities as processing
low-grade ores and mining deeper deposits. Collapse comes when
the heavy financial demands of the resource sector prevent the
economy from meeting the depreciation and maintenance outlays required to keep its industrial plant in operation.

Resource Scarcity and Depletion

It is true that resource depletion is a possible consequence of a
rapidly growing industrial world, especially if the underdeveloped nations swiftly change status from producers to users of
raw materials. World industrial output at a rate equivalent to that
of the United States, especially if achieved in a short time, would
find the world resource base spectacularly inadequate. But the
underdeveloped nations are hardly on the threshold of becoming
important resource users and this threat to the resource base is at
least not immediate.

Do market prices of resources provide any insight as indicators
of scarcity or the depletion of the resource base? They show

what is happening in the present and how the system has adjusted in the past. This is useful information. Far from taking an increasing share of the cost of producing industrial products, raw materials have taken a progressively smaller share; their prices have risen much less since the mid-1930's than have consumer prices or wages. Indeed, lagging raw-material prices have been a matter of distress to the low-income developing nations, which rely on resource sales for much of their income. As a result, the income of the resource-producing nations has not kept pace with that of the rest of the world, and it has become harder for them to close the income gap with the developed nations.

The Market Effect

Not only is there no evidence of a trend toward relatively higher prices for most natural resources, but in those few instances where higher resource prices do occur, the substitution of lower-priced materials is encouraged—plastics for metal, particle board for plywood, synthetics for wool, and the like. The market economy carries on the production and distribution of goods and services with little overall direction and control, but price movements are very effective in signaling scarcity. The high-price signal brings a redirection in resource use that economizes on scarce materials and stimulates innovative effort to create new materials.

Both the market's corrective adjustments and its stimulus to innovation are lost sight of when resources are regarded as a depleting fund. Some innovations, such as larger and more complicated automobiles, can deplete resources by using more materials than their predecessors did, but there are also resource-saving innovations. Many innovative techniques of production, such as the sulfate papermaking process, reduce resource waste; and labor and materials requirements are frequently decreased by innovative products, such as coaxial cable, which is capable of the simultaneous transmission of messages, and computers, which perform routine recording tasks as well as more esoteric problem-solving. Indeed the whole idea of fixed funds of resources,

such as petroleum, iron ore, and coal, that have specific exhaustion dates is misleading. Changes in techniques of extraction,
economy in the use of the scarce resources, and the development of substitutes make some exhaustible resources quite flexible in supply over the years. In addition, shifts in resource use
from exhaustible to renewable materials that can be produced
from the soil or in the laboratory will extend the life of the more
scarce exhaustible resources.

Before the seemingly unlimited abundance of natural resources
began to show signs of diminishing, raw materials in the United
States were generally used with little regard for conservation
because of their cheapness. The market economy does not encourage conservation of a resource until the supply decreases
enough so that the price rises, making it worthwhile to econo-
mize by limiting its use. In spite of an almost profligate rate of
consumption, some resources have such a broad base of lower-
quality reserves that final exhaustion stretches far into the future.
A number of the early landmarks in the extraction of minerals
are still producing: Israel's King Solomon copper mines, England's Cornish tin deposits, and the Mesabi iron range in northern
Minnesota. To be sure, not all mineral resources are indefinitely
available, awaiting only a favorable price and appropriate technology to bring them to market. There are wide differences
among various minerals in overall availability and in the responsiveness of the supply to changes in price, ranging from the great
abundance of iron ore and bauxite to the scarcity and economic
intractability of mercury and tungsten. Copper, zinc, and lead
occupy a middle ground. Broad generalizations concerning
either resource abundance or scarcity are risky, but such risks
have never discouraged such speculation.

The Different Views of Depletion

One of the causes for disagreement about resource depletion
stems from the use of different measures of the resource supply.
On the whole, the applied and natural scientists—the engineers,
geologists, biologists—view resources in terms of their physical

characteristics and are most likely to express resource adequacy in rates of physical use. Economists, less familiar with the physical aspects of resources, are likely to concentrate on prices, finding evidence of scarcity when resource prices rise more rapidly than other prices. Both approaches leave something to be desired: The natural science approach may seriously underestimate the responsiveness of materials supply and technology to rising prices, whereas the economics approach may sometimes overstate the influence of price and ignore the side effects that frequently accompany higher resource prices and increased reliance upon technology in resource exploitation. The perspective from which the question of scarcity is approached influences the answer to the question of whether we are running out of resources.

The different views are illustrated by Richard H. Jahns, a geologist who is dean of Stanford University's School of Earth Sciences, and Hans Landsberg, an economist with Resources for the Future, a Ford Foundation organization devoted to the study of resource-related issues. Jahns, in a paper presented before the United States National Commission for UNESCO in November, 1969, warned, "Such nonrenewable resources as mineral fuels, metals, and industrial minerals and rocks must be of grave concern to all of us . . . some of them already are in serious short supply, and known reserves of others will be exhausted within two or three decades." [4]

"Serious short supply" can only be interpreted as a cause for concern, but exhaustion of "known reserves" is not an unambiguous indicator of future resource availability because we have no way of knowing the extent to which the amount of known reserves is a measure of total supplies.

The view of Hans Landsberg, by contrast with Jahn's position, is one of unruffled confidence. Landsberg says:

> Neither a long view of the past, nor current trends, nor our most careful estimates of future possibilities, suggest any general running out of resources in this country during the remainder of

[4] Jahns, "Mineral Resources and Human Ecology," from, *No Deposit-No Return*, edited by H. D. Johnson, 1970, Addison-Wesley, Reading, Mass., p. 152.

this century. The possibilities of using lower grades of raw material, of substituting plentiful materials for scarce ones, of getting more use out of given amounts, of importing some things from other countries, and of making multiple use of land and water resources seem to be sufficient guarantee against across-the-board shortage.[5]

This benign overview of resource sufficiency is in part the result of an abiding faith in the operation of the market economy and its pricing system: A moderate increase in resource prices will encourage use of abundant lower-grade raw materials. Scarcity and resource depletion are unthinkable to an economist without some signal of rising relative prices. Although even moderate resource depletion within the present century appears to be unlikely, in dismissing the prospect of depletion it is important not to endow the market system and prices with a kind of mystic infallibility. How well price reflects the full impact upon the economy of the use of a particular resource depends upon whether the price of the resource covers all the costs that are generated in bringing it to the consumer. Increasingly, as population and economic output rise, the prices of raw materials and finished products fail to cover the full costs of production, and therefore afford an incomplete accounting of the full burden of producing various products and services: The market prices understate what is given up—in the way of clean air and water, quiet and tranquility, uncluttered scenic and natural areas, and the like—in order to attain some output.

The Social Costs of Resource Production

"Cost," although generally thought of in money terms, has a broader application in economics that includes any loss, injury, or damage, such as the destruction of a scenic area, the pollution of a stream, or the congestion of a freeway. When the full cost, including damage to the environment as well as monetary out-

[5] Hans H. Landsberg, *Natural Resources for U. S. Growth—A Look Ahead to the Year 2000* (Baltimore: Johns Hopkins Press, 1964), p. 13. Published for Resources for the Future, Inc. by The Johns Hopkins Press.

lays, is incompletely covered by the price of a raw material or finished product, the portion shifted elsewhere is sometimes called the spillover cost.* The rise in spillover costs, unrecorded in market prices, is well illustrated by the extractive industries.

Strip-Mining: Environmental Devastation

The use of strip-mining and auger-mining in the coalfields has reduced mining costs well below those of underground operations —if the widespread environmental degradation and property loss in areas where these practices are employed is disregarded. Although underground mining may brutalize the environment— creating slag heaps, causing land cave-ins and underground fires, and polluting streams with culm and acid wastes—strip- and auger- mining are by comparison responsible for a much wider range of surface destruction. Land rehabilitation following these mining practices has been trivial, and mining regions have generally been left in an unproductive and unaesthetic state, subject to serious erosion and physical instability.

If the spillover costs of strip- and auger-mining were absorbed by the coal producer and passed on to the consumer, including charges to restore the stripped land to a usable or stable condition, the cost advantage of surface mining would be greatly decreased.

Taconite: Low-Grade Iron Ore

Increasingly, as the demand for natural resources rises because of growth in population and industrial output, lower-grade sources of supply will have to be developed. To bring these deposits to commercially acceptable quality, extensive processing is required, in which the desired mineral is separated from waste materials. If the disposal and pollution problems created by such operations are unaccounted for in the market system, the costs

---

* Economists have been extravagant in devising terms to indicate a cost shift from the producer to another segment of the economy. Essentially the same meaning is associated with the terms "side effects," "external diseconomies," and "social cost."

of obtaining raw material from lower-quality deposits will be understated. A case in point is iron ore produced from taconite.

As the higher-quality iron-ore deposits in the Great Lakes region and other areas of the United States have been used up, the steel industry has shifted to foreign ores from Quebec and Labrador, and from Venezuela, and to lower-grade domestic ores. One domestic source of low-grade iron ore is taconite, an extraordinarily hard rock that underlies much of the region north of Lake Superior. In taconite, the iron is held in tight bond with the rock and requires extensive processing before it can be separated and put into a form that can be used in the blast furnace. The Reserve Mining Company, an ore-processing firm jointly owned by Republic Steel and Armco Steel, has invested over 300 million dollars in a taconite-processing plant at Silver Bay, Minnesota, on the north shore of Lake Superior.

The Reserve Mining plant has an annual output of over ten million tons of pelleted iron ore of higher average iron content than that currently shipped from the Lake Superior ore mines. Before the Reserve product is ready for the blast furnace, however, the hard taconite rock has to be crushed to an extremely fine consistency, and the iron in the rock, which averages less than 25 percent, has to be withdrawn by magnetic separation, filtered, formed into pellets, and hardened by baking. Since making one ton of pellets containing 65 percent iron requires 3.14 tons of taconite, over two tons of waste are generated for every ton of ore. It is at this point that the market system fails, as in the case of surface mining, to record the full costs of the resource's production.

In 1951, when the Reserve Mining Company constructed its ore-processing plant on the north shore of Lake Superior, and changed the name of Beaver Bay to Silver Bay, few people were concerned about environmental damage to the area; most, instead, looked forward to the stimulating economic effect of the large investment in this somewhat depressed region. The state of Minnesota was anxious to have its declining iron-mining industry shored up by the development of low-grade ore processing, and the federal government had not yet become sensitive to environmental damage. As a result, Lake Superior was selected as a free, bottomless pit in which to dump the plant's powder-fine waste —nearly 25 million tons a year. The rock dust was sluiced into the lake, where it was expected to settle benignly to the bottom.

But the taconite wastes have not stayed in place. They have fanned out from Silver Bay for hundreds of miles and have made parts of this cleanest of the Great Lakes murky with suspended rock dust. The resulting aesthetic degradation is but one of the unaccounted costs shifted to the public in producing iron ore from taconite. In addition, the taconite wastes have created a translucence that blocks the sun's rays and modifies the biotic climate. A new underwater world has been created, which is hardly friendly to existing aquatic life.

If the full costs of upgrading lower-quality ores and employing surface-mining practices are imposed on the producers, including expenditures for the environmentally acceptable disposal of wastes and the rehabilitation of the mined areas, the prices of both resources and finished products will be raised. Although higher prices are not likely to excite enthusiasm among purchasers, something good can be said in their favor when they reflect more accurately the environmental costs of bringing a resource to market. First, shifting environmental costs to the consumer through higher prices places the burden where it belongs—upon those whose use of the product is responsible for the environmental damage—rather than upon the general public. Second, the "rationing effect" of the higher prices can generally be expected to reduce consumption of those commodities whose production endangers the environment, thus moderating pressure upon the more scarce resources at the same time that environmental damage is held in check.

The Classical Resource Question—
Lagging Food Supply

There has probably never been a period in which predictions of disaster because of too little food have not caused some to fear the future. The present is no exception. For centuries the

struggle for survival was intense. Malthus simply dramatized this
struggle when he contrasted the population's potential growth
with man's capacity to produce more food. Malthus believed the
food supply to be dependent primarily upon the availability of
land; more food could be produced by bringing more land under
cultivation, but the yield would be held to a modest arithmetic
increase. Population, however, was likely to unleash stronger
forces and grow more dramatically. When the two rates collided,
as they were bound to do, mankind was of course the loser.

Although few will dispute the fact that the world has seen too
many famines and too much malnutrition, somehow a full-scale,
worldwide Malthusian disaster has been averted. Population
growth has seldom measured up to its full potential, and the food
supply has increased well beyond the limited contribution from
additional acres brought under cultivation. The Industrial Revolution that swept the advanced nations of Europe shortly after
Malthus' famous pronouncement affected both sides of the
man–land relationship, initially by somewhat moderating population growth and later by providing the foundation for innovations in agriculture. In the mid-twentieth century these changes
are still under way: increased use of agricultural machinery, new
insecticides, inorganic fertilizers, genetic improvements in plants
and animals, and the use of antibiotics in animal production—
all push the output of food well beyond the limits of the simple
man–land relationship of Malthus' time.

These innovations have at times been accompanied by serious
environmental consequences, particularly in the case of the lavish
use of inorganic fertilizers and modern pesticides and herbicides,
but none can gainsay the increased farm output per acre that has
resulted from their use. The United States has increased its agricultural output over the past thirty years at the same time that
it has decreased the area of land under cultivation by about 50
million acres. During this period it has provided large amounts
of food to other nations and has done much to alleviate hunger
abroad. A full-scale famine did occur in Bengal in 1943, but India
was kept from a similar fate in 1966 and 1967 by food from
the United States, grain shipments that exceeded the consumption
in the United States for those years.

What do these developments do to the Malthusian doctrine? If it hasn't received the death blow, it appears to be somewhat staggered. But the recuperative powers of the doctrine have always been great, and its more ardent followers have stubbornly based their faith on future developments. And, in fact, although the food output per acre has increased dramatically in the more advanced nations, this does not ensure that these advanced techniques are equally adaptable in the nations of greatest need. More than making available a new type of seed or an improved animal strain is required in order for the innovations to take hold in the lower-income nations. A complex set of new production arrangements must sometimes be introduced along with the innovation in order for it to be effective. The new miracle grains illustrate the great promise and problems of modern agriculture.

The "Green Revolution"

In 1970, Norman E. Borlaug was awarded the Nobel Peace Prize for his part in the development of "miracle" wheat, an integral part of the "green revolution" that has been under way for the past two decades. Borlaug, working for the Rockefeller Foundation's wheat-improvement program in Mexico, succeeded in crossbreeding a wheat plant that is unusually sturdy and is insensitive to the length of the day. As a result, this new type of wheat greatly extends the range of wheat cultivation—from the temperate zone to the subtropics and tropics. Wheat can now be grown successfully in Mexico, where cultivation was previously indifferent at best, and in other low-income countries, such as India and Pakistan, where the higher-yield grain will help raise dietary standards.

The early experience of India and Pakistan with this miracle wheat is impressive but not entirely conclusive. Output has increased, but data are available for only a few years, and production has been affected not just by the introduction of the new variety but by seasonal variations and by improved supporting practices—more fertilizer, better cultivation, and a larger area under cultivation. But in spite of some skeptics, the Rockefeller Foundation is confident that an annual output increase in wheat of

5 percent is well within the reach of India, and that self-sufficiency in this grain is merely a matter of time for both India and Pakistan.

Miracle rice, now well established in Ceylon, the Philippines, Vietnam, and the Middle East as well as in India and Pakistan, has had even more of an impact upon the food supply in hungry nations than the new wheat. Evidence of this is found in India's announcement early in 1972 that it was now self-sufficient in rice production. But cultivation of the new rice has not been confined to the hungry nations. Japan, formerly an importer of rice, is now a surplus producer, selling in the world market. Output has increased so much that the Japanese government has found it necessary to pay farmers not to produce rice. Meanwhile, the United States, which has recently become the world's largest exporter of rice—in part because of its easy credit terms for purchasers—has reduced acreage allotments for rice in this country.

The increased output of rice has eased the pressure upon the food supply in the poorer countries, but it has also produced something of a rice glut in the world market. For those nations, such as Thailand and Burma, that depend on others to purchase their surplus rice, the lower price and the decreased market can only be a cause for serious concern. For these exporting nations, the gains from greater rice production are in part diminished by the smaller return from world sales.

The promise is great that in the near future, while hunger may not be totally eliminated, we will vastly improve our chances of banishing large-scale starvation. Moreover, protein deficiency —the hunger that afflicts low-income nations and parts of wealthier ones as well—may also succumb to the geneticists' skills soon. Already the isolation of a protein-carrying gene, "opaque-2," promises that plants may be bred to carry a larger protein complement, thereby making increased protein available both from the enriched plants themselves and from animals fed on the new grain. When this development is realized, one of the world's primary causes of malnutrition will be a candidate for extinction.

The spread of the high-yield grains to the lower-income nations is not likely to lay to rest the Malthusian specter, but the greater agricultural output could give more time to bring population growth under control. Unfortunately, in certain areas the new abundance of food has created a climate that has worked against population-limitation programs. What some hail as the best opportunity mankind has had to erase the threat of famine and ease the world's hunger ironically could be lost if the remarkable gains in food production divert attention from the continuing need to check rising population.

References and Readings

Barnett, Harold J., and Morse, Chandler, *Scarcity and Growth: The Economics of Natural Resource Availability*. Baltimore: Johns Hopkins Press, 1963.
> A comprehensive study of natural-resource availability made by comparing resource price movements with those of other prices. Undertaken before the "environmental crisis," the study largely ignores the issue of the social costs of resource use in the American economy. Nonetheless, it makes an important contribution. It was sponsored by Resources for the Future, a research organization supported by the Ford Foundation.

Brown, Lester R., *Seeds of Change: The Green Revolution and Development in the 1970's*. New York: Praeger, 1970.
> An informative account of the results of the introduction of the "miracle" types of wheat and rice, and an appraisal of their likely future effects.

Cochrane, Willard W., *The World Food Problem: A Guardedly Optimistic View*. New York: Thomas Y. Crowell, 1969.
> A careful examination of the relationship between world population growth and food production, and of the impact of foreign-aid programs and a consideration of appropriate polices for developing countries.

Landsberg, Hans H., *Natural Resources for U. S. Growth—A Look Ahead to the Year 2000*. Baltimore: Johns Hopkins Press, 1964.
> A condensation of a larger resource study by a research team of Resources for the Future. The study finds no evidence of ". . . any general running out of resources in this country during the remainder of this century." The forecast is based on an examination of the expected needs and supplies of the major raw materials used by the United States industrial system.

Malthus, Thomas R., "Population Growth and Poverty," in *Readings in Economics*, ed. by Paul Samuelson, sixth ed. New York: McGraw-Hill, 1970.
    This very brief passage from Malthus' famous works contains the propositon that population has the potential of increasing geometrically, the food supply can only increase at a lower rate. For a more extended presentation of this view, the study from which this excerpt was taken should be consulted: *An Essay on the Principle of Population*, eighth ed. (London: Reeves and Turner, 1878). Malthus also considered the population issue in his *Principles of Political Economy*, second ed. (New York: Augustus Kelley, reprinted 1951), especially in Book I, Chapter 4.

Meadows, Donella H., *et al.*, *The Limits to Growth*. A Potomac Associates/Club of Rome Book. New York: Universe Books, 1972.
    The subtitle of this book is *A Report from the Club of Rome's Project on the Predicament of Mankind*. The predicament of mankind, according to this report, is more or less imminent disaster if the present rates of population growth and industrial output are not checked. The conclusions are supported by a series of generally unconvincing computer simulation models.

Spengler, Joseph J., "Malthus's Total Population Theory: A Restatement and Reappraisal," *Canadian Journal of Economics and Political Science*, XI (1945), pp. 83–110, 234–264.
    A comprehensive scholarly examination of the views of Malthus; a highly significant contribution.

——— *Population Economics: Selected Essays of Joseph Spengler*, ed. by Robert S. Smith *et al*. Durham, N. C.: Duke University Press, 1972.
    A collection of the scholarly articles of a leading American economist specializing in population. The article on Malthus cited just above is included.

Chapter Four

Economic Growth—Friend or Foe of the Environment?

To stop growing now would be to commit suicide now for fear of remote death.—Henry Wallich [1]

Japan is very much alive; but it is still a question whether this . . . country is in the process of committing a kind of spiritual hari-kari in pursuit of G.N.P.—John Oakes [2]

On December 15, 1970, President Richard Nixon was five minutes late for the unveiling of the Department of Commerce's new GNP clock, and by the time he arrived it had passed the trillion-dollar mark by 2.3 million dollars.

Technicians at the Department of Commerce tried to turn the clock back at the last minute, but—like the inundated sorcerer's apprentice—could not check the steady tick of dollars. Actually, however, 1970 didn't tick off dollars too well; indeed, the last quarter's dollars that brought the economy up to the trillion-dollar mark were the flabby inflation kind, rather than being firmly based on added output. And although the Department of Commerce's GNP clock ticked its way to a record, it didn't represent much of an improvement in national well-being.

[1] *The New York Times* (February 12, 1972).
[2] *The New York Times* (November 30, 1970).

Figure 4.1. Gross National Product for the Years 1960–
1970, Shown in Current and Constant Dollars *

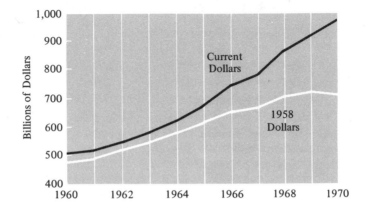

* Department of Commerce.

Economic Growth and GNP

Economic growth, usually denoted by changes in Gross National Product, is a simple concept but a difficult phenomenon to measure. The approach to measurement is straightforward: Gross product is all *final* output in the economy.* But many statistical twists and turns are necessary before this output concept can be expressed numerically. Since the variety of goods and services produced in an industrial economy is diverse, it is impossible to comprehend and compare a nation's output in physical terms. There is also no convenient way to sum goods and services—pianos, haircuts, beefsteak, appendectomies—without submerging their physical dissimilarities in a universally applicable unit of measure. The monetary unit—the dollar—serves

* Final output is used to prevent the overstatement of GNP that would result from counting a product, say an automobile part, more than once as it moved from the supplier through the assembly stage to the final purchaser. In like manner, money transfers such as welfare payments and gifts, that do not result from the creation of output, are excluded in order not to overstate GNP.

this purpose and makes possible the computation of gross national product, but its use also makes it necessary to insulate the GNP figure from changes in the value of the monetary unit. If this is not done, national output will be recorded as higher than is justified during periods of rising prices and as lower than is correct during deflationary periods. For the most part, in recent years eliminating this price-level effect has involved deflating the monetary unit, but when GNP estimates are extended backward, to the 1930's for example, upward adjustments are required to compensate for the lower price level during the Great Depression. Figure 4.1 shows the difference between expressing GNP in current and in constant dollars; the latter method, eliminating the effect of changes in prices, reveals that GNP declined in 1970.

GNP and the Environment

Recent concern for the quality of the environment has highlighted one shortcoming of national-income accounting and of concepts such as GNP: their failure to make adjustments for those additions to economic output that cause environmental deterioration. In computing GNP, output is output and no final dollar value is excluded—unless it is illegal, like fraud, or immeasurable, like housewives' services. This is a crippling weakness of the use of such concepts as a measure of economic well-being, but in itself does not justify opposition to economic growth.

The Causes and Costs of Economic Growth

Although economic growth may be difficult to measure, it is simple enough to identify as an increase in the nation's output of goods and services over a given period of time. The annual basis for GNP growth measurement makes it inevitable that the growth achievement of one year will be compared with that of other years. As a result, growth statistics provide the raw material for more than economists; they are also grist for the mills of the politicians and news commentators. Nor does the irresistible game of growth comparison stop at national boundaries; growth-rate comparisons between nations—the U.S.S.R. with the United States, for example—at times lead to the most agonizing examination of national achievement. That such comparisons conceal incompatible ingredients, and of course involve measurement difficulties, has done little to diminish the attention they attract and the anxiety created in the nation that places second in the "growth race."

Issues in Growth Measurement

Expenditures to improve the environment raise a familiar but unresolved problem in the measurement of gross national product. If resources are purchased and used in the market economy, the expenditure is counted as an addition to gross national product, even if the outlay has been made to maintain a given level of productivity of the system (as by repairing storm damage or by treating sickness) rather than to increase the output of goods and services.

No distinction is made in national-income accounts between market outlays to correct environmental abuses and those to produce more goods and services; both add equally to gross national product, although obviously what the expenditure is for makes a great difference in what GNP represents—a fund of goods and services or the attainment of a given quality of life. If we compare two periods of equal employment, one in which no resources are used to abate pollution or otherwise correct environmental disabilities and the other in which improvements are made in the quality of life, we see that the output of goods and services becomes a trade-off for the quality of life. None of this shows up in the statistics of national-income accounts.

But the problems in measuring growth do not negate the fact that most people, confronted with the opportunity of having either more goods and services or less, will opt for more. And so it has been with nations, sometimes with equal narrowness of purpose. In the pursuit of greater growth, many contributing factors have been identified and studied: the size, skill, and age distribution of the population; the length of the workweek; the techniques of production and the kind and amount of capital equipment provided the working force; the quality and abundance of material resources; the size of the production units; the priority of economic output compared with other goals; and the social climate within which production is carried out. Obviously, growth is subject to many influences, some of which are intangible and difficult to appraise. From the broad gamut, however, a number of influences deserve elaboration because of their critical and changing effect upon economic growth.

Large-Scale Production

As the size of a nation's industrial establishment and the extent of its market for economic output increase, large-scale production techniques can be employed that lower the per-unit cost of output. Lower unit cost can be translated directly into increased output—growth—the production of more of a given product with the same amount of resources. Very small nations, those limited in market and capital and labor, have more difficulty in bringing to bear the large investment in capital equipment that is the necessary prerequisite of the technologically and economically efficient steel mill, or auto plant, or transportation system, and for the development of other manufacturing activities that can be adapted to mass-production techniques. Moreover, once a large-scale operation has been initiated within one of the larger nations, a cost level is established that makes the operation of smaller, higher-cost installations difficult both in that nation and in the smaller nations.

Large-scale production is an important contributor to a country's economic growth, but it is easy to overemphasize its influence. Its effect is mainly confined to the development period, when the economy moves from small to moderate size. The economies of large-scale production do not continue indefinitely in response to increasing market demand. When an industrial installation reaches a certain size, large-scale advantages are exhausted, and further additions to productive capacity are best made by duplicating the optimum-size installation, rather than by building larger and larger plants. Correspondingly, as larger nations increase in population and economic output, the by-products of industrial growth and concentration—wastes, spatial congestion, and encroachment upon the aesthetic use of resources—more than offset the decreasing number of instances in which new applications of large-scale techniques contribute to the growth rate.

Technology

Part of the contribution of technology to growth stems from large-scale production—technological processes such as the assembly line that cannot be undertaken on a small scale—but other technological innovations may be employed by either the large or the small firm. Whether limited to large-scale production or not, technological innovations—inventions and discoveries— usually attract the most attention among the various growth factors. This is not because technology is the most important single cause of growth. Improvements in education and training and increases in the size of the population have been regarded as more important, consistently accounting for over 50 percent of the increase in growth down through the years. But the effects upon output of changing technology are somewhat more apparent and considerably easier to manipulate than either education or population, especially in the short run.

Improvements in technology are inseparably linked to investment and capital creation in the market economy. As a result, innovation is sought for more than its contribution to an expanding growth rate; it is also coveted as a source of investment opportunities, to sustain a high level of income and employment in the economy. The investment process is one of the more volatile elements in the behavior of the economy, at various times absorbing different amounts of resources in creating capital and responding to different forces in providing greater or less stimulus to the economy. Because of this, it is one of the prime levers of control that the federal government attempts to manipulate through such devices as investment tax credits, corporate tax rates, modifications in the interest rate, depreciation policy, and subsidies for research and development. Whatever its stimulus, however, capital formation consists in the construction of the machinery and equipment that underpins the economy's output.

The importance of capital creation in raising output is well illustrated by the developing nations. Underdeveloped countries may turn to almost any field to strengthen their fund of capital, as is indicated by the high return on investment in such economies, but the mature industrial state has already taken advantage of all but the most recent innovations. As an economy matures, the industrial structure and the available opportunities for capital creation also undergo change, creating different productivity patterns. If an underdeveloped country can draw upon the backlog of technology in more advanced nations, its opportunities for productive investment are greatly enhanced. During the post-Civil War period, the United States was able to take advantage of importing technology only to a limited degree.

From the pre-Civil War beginnings of industrialization in the United States until just short of the twentieth-century, roughly from 1850 to 1890, the annual productivity increase averaged about 1.5 percent. (The productivity rate is only a part of the growth rate; the latter reflects many other factors, as has been indicated.) The productivity rate didn't change appreciably until the years between World War I and World War II, when it rose to 2.1 percent. The really significant change has followed World War II, however. Since then, the annual productivity rate has averaged over 3 percent, a rate that when combined with other growth-enhancing factors can be expected to double the nation's output in approximately twenty years.

The Environmental Impact of the Changing Structure of American Industry

The major sources of American economic growth in the past have been agriculture, mining, manufacturing, and construction—industries that have flourished under increasing energy and capital inputs and that have been heavy resource users and heavy waste producers. The future will find these industries continuing to grow, but at a decreasing rate. Gradually, smokestacks and assembly lines will become less dominant in the American economy and an increasing part of the nation's resources will be devoted to government and to the service industries: motels and television repair, doctors' services and legal aid, research in the problems of youth and nursing care for the infirmities of age. Already in the early 1970's, nearly 60 percent of the labor force is employed in service activities. However, the impact of the expansion of the government sector and the service industries goes well beyond a simple shift in employment and investment opportunities. The change in industrial structure will reach to the heart of the economic system, gradually but greatly affecting the economy's productivity and therefore its growth rate, the stability of the nation's income and employment, and the pressure of pollution upon the environment.

If the past is a guide, the so-called service economy will be more stable than the industrial economy. Government employment and service activities are subject to fewer cyclical and seasonal fluctuations than are industrial operations, and the service industry in general is less the domain of the large-scale corporations. If this trend holds, not only will economic stability in the American economy increase in the future, but there is the possibility that the role of the large corporation will decline, curtailing centralized decision-making in the market economy. The shift from high-productivity manufacturing industries to a larger service sector will dilute the overall growth rate, but this effect may eventually be reversed by adapting productivity-increasing techniques to the service industries. In the immediate future, however, the continuation of high economic growth will depend largely upon the established high-productivity industries.

As long as the government's share of resource employment remains relatively unchanged from year to year, its effect upon growth will probably be largely neutral. Increasing the share of resources committed to government will reinforce the stabilizing effect exerted by a larger service-industry sector, and the enlargement of the government sector may depress the growth rate even more than does the expansion of the service industries. Since government undertakings generally are not made more efficient by innovations or new techniques, as is frequently the case in manufacturing, less growth is likely to occur when the government sector is larger. But if the government's use of resources changes and its effect upon growth is not reflected in the national-income accounts, comparisons of annual output figures will be increasingly unreliable. The economy will benefit (or lose) just as much, however, whether the government contribution can be determined or not.

Whatever the impact of the structural changes in the economy upon the growth rate, the relative decline of the heavy natural-resource-using, waste-producing industries in our economy will allay the increasing pressure upon both the environment and the supply of natural resources. But before this structural realignment takes place, in the years immediately ahead, the environment will encounter increased waste discharges from a growth-oriented industrial system. Economic growth has raised the output of waste by-products in many areas beyond the absorptive capacity of the environment. In an earlier time of lesser pollution loads, the environment could heal the scars of growth by-products, but now its natural resilience and recuperative powers have been overrun and impaired.

Zero Economic Growth

Zero economic growth—no increase in economic output—is frequently urged in various forms to ease the pressure upon the environment. But zero economic growth is more than a prescription for saving the environment. In its broader conception, it is a rejection of the materialistic basis of American society. On both scores it has much appeal and some persuasive impact.

Obviously, the American economy can be pushed to greater outputs of coal, petroleum, timber, and other natural materials without encountering disabling costs or serious shortages, but the inexorably increasing stream of goods and services has carried with it a heavy burden of waste by-products, at first unheralded, and as yet largely uncounted in the pricing processes of the market economy. Only yesterday—ten years ago—these problems were minor by comparison; today they are mounting progressively.

Why not, then, return the genie of productivity to the bottle? If economic growth is the cause of the environmental deterioration, why not check the rate of growth before the next twenty years brings more than twice as many tin cans, three times as many junked cars, $2x + n$ suppurating auto exhausts, and a six-pack of empties for every highway billboard?

Why not? Because to turn off growth is to turn off more than the output excesses of an affluent society and to do more than moderate the degradation of the environment. To shut off growth, to fall back to a zero rate, output per capita must be held in check. A zero growth rate does not require that productivity-enhancing techniques be outlawed, only that increases in productivity must be diluted by decreases in man-hours of employment. The object is a "steady-state" economy, not a stagnant economy, and it is presumably achieved by means of an unchanging national-output fund that limits any net improvement in the overall living standard of the nation to more leisure—the thirty-five-hour week, for example, instead of the forty-hour week—but no increase in goods and services.

More growth does not necessarily mean higher per-capita income. A certain amount of growth is required to keep a larger population from suffering a lower living standard. Increases in the population have been an important reason for the larger output in the American economy and have been largely responsible for the long-run growth increase. If the zero-growth goal is interpreted to apply to *aggregate* annual output rather than *per-capita* annual output, a zero growth rate can be achieved with an increasing population only through decreasing the standard of living. The fixed output has to be spread over the larger population. Correspondingly, zero economic growth per capita does not hold the pollution load constant if the population increases, since the larger population requires more goods and services, thereby increasing the pressure upon the environment.

Zero Economic Growth and the Disadvantaged

A change in one's income position, say from the disadvantaged lower fifth of the population to a middle-income group, could take place under the constraint of zero growth, but only through redistribution of part of the frozen output fund, which would have to be withdrawn from others gainfully employed. Simultaneously, under the steady-state economy, a reduction in the aggregate hours of work in the economy would be necessary. Otherwise, the increase in productivity represented by upward occupational mobility—shifting from a lower- to a higher-output job—would allow growth to creep into the system as a result of the drive for self-improvement by the disadvantaged.

By contrast, at the present time improvement in the lot of the disadvantaged is not limited to increased productivity from upward occupation mobility. Welfare outlays, supported by progressive taxes, shift income from the upper- to the lower-income groups independently of any changes in the productivity of the lower-income groups. An important source of the welfare outlays is the productivity increases of those in the higher tax brackets, although the middle-income ranges provide a greater overall tax contribution. A policy of zero economic growth would discourage this income shift from those in our society who have more to those who have less. The fiscal dividend may illustrate this point.

The Fiscal Dividend

Revenues for welfare programs and other government undertakings are dependent on the size of the tax base, and economic growth provides a built-in increase, a "fiscal dividend," in the yield of existing taxes without requiring any modification in the rates or coverage of the tax structure. Under normal rates of economic growth, the fiscal dividend in the early 1970's will be about 15 billion dollars annually; as the next decade approaches, it can be expected to rise above this figure because of the compounding of the GNP growth rate. If there is no significant increase in GNP or if the tax base is reduced, the fiscal dividend will of course fail to materialize. In addition, sharply increasing expenditures will consume the fiscal dividend. Zero economic growth would wipe out the fiscal dividend and the programs that might be supported by this easy money—"easy" because the costs of collecting the fiscal dividend are negligible and taxpayer opposition to the higher tax yield is minimal compared with the usual reaction to new tax levies. The fiscal dividend raises revenue by withdrawing a portion of the increase in income (GNP), not by decreasing a fixed income through higher tax rates, which would lower living standards.

The way the fiscal dividend occurs—as a tax on the growth increment—makes it especially suitable for providing for the disadvantaged in our society. As a nation's income increases, its capacity to forgo private consumption in order to divert money to public purposes also increases; its tax base enlarges, and not only does a given tax rate yield a larger amount of revenue, but the economy that has attained a higher level of per-capita economic output can support a larger drain of output from private consumption and investment into public consumption and investment. Developing nations, in contrast, are hard pressed to meet the public needs through expansion of the public sector. The developed economy finds its consumption and capital needs less urgent and can more easily spare resources from the private sector.

Zero economic growth would achieve environmental protection by stopping the increment of economic output in order to check the accompanying increment of environmental abuse. But in the large number of cases where the output increment is large enough to more than pay for the necessary environmental rehabilitation, zero economic growth avoids a direct solution of the problem at the same time that it curtails the capacity of the economy to cope with any pollution load—growth-induced or otherwise.

Increasing the resources devoted to environmental protection and rehabilitation can take a number of public and private avenues. In the public sphere, the federal water-pollution-control program illustrates one approach—that of grants-in-aid by the federal government to municipalities to assist in the construction of water-pollution-abatement systems. Such federal undertakings have a better chance of success in the competition for a generous share of the budget if a high level of economic growth provides a substantial tax base and a large built-in fiscal dividend.

The private sector too will have an easier time of meeting stiffer pollution controls, as in the case of air-pollution regulations, if the growth rate is high. The cost of installing and maintaining precipitators, for example, must be borne either by the private firms involved or shifted to consumers through higher prices. (In rare cases, it may be possible for a firm to shift these costs elsewhere in the economic system, to resource suppliers, for example, but this is likely only for relatively short periods pending adjustment.)*

In cases of both public and private action to protect the environment, the essential point is that economic resources need to be withdrawn from the production of other goods and services in order to be used in neutralizing the destructive effects of industrial wastes. Whether the approach taken is a government subsidy to pay for pollution-abatement systems or higher consumer prices to cover the costs of such corrective action, the ultimate source of the funds for the diversion of resources is the economy's output. Obviously, economic growth—increasing output—makes it easier to divert these resources.

The economic growth that is triggered by technological innovation may be turned to the advantage of the environment. In the private sector, two aspects of growth enhancement from innovation aid the environment. First, more productive techniques promise a higher return on investment—otherwise they would not be undertaken—and if successful can better finance the charges for pollution abatement, and second, technically and

---

* The Environmental Protection Agency has concluded on the basis of a selective study that 7 out of 18 industries will pass air-pollution-abatement costs on to the consumer, 3 will recover enough salvageable materials to offset abatement costs completely, and another 7 will absorb part of the costs. (One of the 18 industries—sulfuric acid—was not completely analyzed.) See *The Economics of Clean Air: Report of the Administrator of the Environmental Protection Agency to Congress* (Washington, D.C.: Government Printing Office, 1971), pp. 1–7.

economically a new plant can be more easily designed to eliminate pollution at much lower charges than older facilities can be
adapted to abatement practices. In the same way that the contribution to air pollution by the automobile could be vastly decreased if all cars were to be replaced next year, new factories
meeting stiffer pollution standards that replace older installations
represent a net gain for the environment. Economic growth
generated by technological change reduces the cost of achieving
this.

But growth qua growth is difficult to justify. The trouble with
economic growth is that too often in the past it has meant bigger
neon signs, aluminum beer cans, higher billboards, and longer
skirts—output that a substantial portion of the population considers a questionable allocation of economic resources. If growth
had to be of this kind, we might well conclude that the alternative of increased leisure and less output served a higher social
purpose. But the forces that have directed resources into the
production of socially innocuous or socially pernicious goods
and services can be redirected to build into the economy a comprehensive system of environmental protection. We are not
doomed to an endless repetition of our past follies.

Where the federal government has exerted the greatest impact
upon resource allocation—defense and space—there is certainly
no evidence of failure to stimulate vast technical undertakings by
private industry. Indeed, the mutuality of interest that seems to
have developed between the federal agencies and congressional
committees on the one hand and the contracting firms on the
other is nothing if not excessive. Protection of the environment
should not involve such a high public-subsidy cost or such
overprotection of industry as in the case of the military-industrial
complex, and the public benefit should be greater.

Fine Tuning the Economy: Zero-Growth-Rate Department

The question of what prescriptions to follow in promoting
the goal of a zero growth rate can only create a certain unease
in the mind of the economist, quite aside from the issue of the

legitimacy of the goal itself. In part, the goal is more complex and difficult to attain than appears at first because of its strong impact upon national employment as well as upon output. Since the federal government following World War II accepted the responsibility of maintaining a high level of employment and income in the United States, economic growth has been a handmaiden of this policy. To stimulate economic growth was to ensure full employment and higher living standards. While fiscal and monetary policies have been directed toward these ultimate ends, growth was the central core of their attainment, and hardly a book or article on macroeconomic policy in the immediate postwar period neglected to point out its contribution to the discussion of the growth issue.

Something approaching a growth cult arose in the United States, and eventually produced its own small reaction. Alvin Hansen quietly remarked on the overemphasis, to be followed not so quietly by John Kenneth Galbraith and the London economist E. J. Mishan. Hansen and Galbraith made much the same point: that growth in some areas of the private sector of the economy had reached the trivia stage—planned obsolescence, as in motorcar tail fins, and a proliferation of gadgets—while the public sector suffered underdevelopment, as shown by poor educational facilities and inadequate recreational opportunities. Mishan went further; he questioned the desirability of narrow economic growth as a social goal. On the whole, however, this healthy reaction has had little effect. Growth, although mentioned less frequently in book and article titles, persists as a prime goal of national economic policy.

The relative importance of the contributions of the private and public sectors to gross national product is shown in Figure 4.2, which details personal-consumption expenditures (individual purchases of goods and services), government purchases, and gross private investment (the dollar value of resources used in creating domestic capital, unadjusted for depreciation). It is the contention of such critics as Hansen and Galbraith that rising GNP justifies larger expenditures in the public sector than have generally been made.

Since most economists have viewed growth as a means to the

Figure 4.2.   United States Gross National Product by
Sector, 1930–1971 *

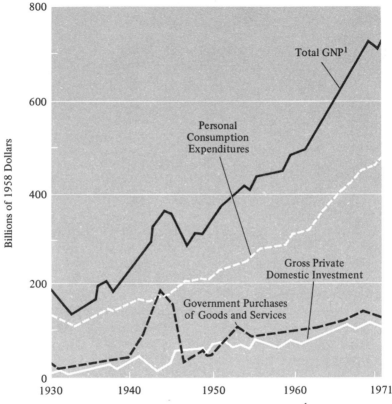

Billions of 1958 Dollars

Total GNP[1]

Personal
Consumption
Expenditures

Gross Private
Domestic Investment

Government Purchases
of Goods and Services

800

600

400

200

0
1930   1940   1950   1960   1971

[1] Excludes net exports

end of full employment and high income, little attention has been
given to the question of how to stop growth at the same time
that the good things that go along with it are not also reduced.
Until recently those advocating a no-growth goal would have
been dismissed simply as well-meaning but heroically naïve

* *Environmental Quality: Third Annual Report of the Council on Environmental Quality* (Washington, D.C.: Government Printing Office,
1972), p. 66; data from Council of Economic Advisers, *Annual Report*, 1971.

cranks—which they are. But now further examination is required. How does the economic system cut back on the rate of growth? To increase employment and output in the economy, there are numerous fiscal and monetary knobs and levers that can be pushed and pulled: government expenditures and taxation; commercial-bank interest rates and Federal Reserve money-market activity; accelerated depreciation arrangements and investment tax credits; increased private and public funds for research and development, and greater outlays for education and training.

Not all of these controls have the same bite, and some work with delayed and uncertain impact. Do we simply push and pull in one direction for growth and in the other direction for no-growth? This might achieve no-growth, but it will bring something else as well—such as unemployment. Take investment, for example, which is considered by many economists to be a key factor in employment and output. With expanding investment opportunities, growth, employment, and income remain high; with decreasing investment opportunities, growth sags and employment and income also suffer. Investment is influenced by many factors: the interest rate, technological innovation, expectations, the period of depreciation, to name but a few. Modification of such factors may be undertaken, but primarily in order to keep the full-employment economy from building up harmful pressure through higher prices. Cutting back on investment opportunities and the factors that stimulate investment is likely to be attempted only when the price-level gauge shows dangerous inflationary pressure. Curtailment of growth, a much less accepted goal, would hardly provide an equivalent incentive to restrict investment.

If the policy goal is zero growth *plus full employment and high income*, investment reduction as a means of checking growth is not worth much. Curtailment of investment is appropriate as long as inflationary pressure is widespread, but it is not an approach that can be followed in other situations without seriously endangering jobs and living standards. If we cannot simply reverse the investment lever and similar controls, what can be done to control growth? As was indicated earlier, the only acceptable policy consistent with other traditional social goals—such as full employment but *not* high income—is to decrease hours of work to prevent productivity enhancement from raising the aggregate output.

Labor and the Growth Rate

The normal union bargaining tactic is to include shorter hours as a part of the contract-negotiation package, or the employer may be compelled to make such an hours concession in order to keep his work force in the face of competitive employment opportunities elsewhere. The extent of the adjustment in hours of work, and how quickly this adjustment takes place, depend upon a complex interaction of market forces—both in the market in which labor and other resources are hired and in the market in which firm's products are sold. These forces affect the product price, the productivity of the labor force, the relative bargaining strength of the employer and the labor group, and especially labor's scale of preference for leisure in comparison with other elements in the bargaining package, such as improvements in wages and working conditions. The market mechanism resolves these diverse forces and minimizes conflicts by causing changes in product prices and resource prices without the intervention of a formal administrative organization.

Zero economic growth would require that the market decision be modified by an increase in the leisure of those employed beyond what they have traditionally chosen. To attain zero economic growth, a minimum-leisure law would establish an upper limit on hours of work, to keep output from rising if productivity increased. Faced by such a leisure requirement, some industries and firms would be better able to meet the limit than others—because of the uneven distribution of productivity-enhancing innovations and dissimilar labor-capital ratios—just as some firms find it possible to pay more than the present minimum wage without difficulty. But there is an important difference between the application of a minimum-wage law and a minimum-leisure law: The minimum-wage law establishes a wage floor that affects mainly the less productive industries and occupations; a minimum-leisure law, by contrast, would have some effect upon most of the economy, but the greatest impact would fall upon its more innovative sections.

Environmental Protection and Economic Growth

The zero-economic-growth approach to environmental protection freezes economic output in order to forestall the undesirable by-products of increased production. It views environmental damage as the inescapable consequence of production and considers the benefits of additional GNP to be outweighed by the environmental damage it creates. Ignoring the complex social issues raised by zero economic growth, it proposes to prevent the incremental damage to the environment from greater output by imposing a ceiling upon economic growth. In actuality, however, output is not all bad for the environment. Production of Wankel engines and lead-free gas, for example, may improve the environment. Some output may be environmentally neutral, and most output increases the capacity of a nation to meet its economic needs. Among these needs, environmental protection can be assigned whatever priority is desired. A wealthy nation can better afford to clean up its atmosphere and its waters, to withhold some natural areas from commercial development, and to dispose aesthetically of its solid wastes, whereas a poorer nation has less flexibility and must use a larger share of its output to meet the basic food-and-shelter needs of its population.

This does not mean that all economic activity is equally desirable. Some is clearly more environmentally damaging than others—such as the public investment in the Cross-Florida Barge Canal and the private investment in the Disney Productions' Mineral King development in the High Sierras. What is needed is selective control of these environmentally questionable undertakings and the allocation of an increasing share of economic growth to environmental protection—pollution abatement, wilderness preservation, waste-disposal systems, and the like—not retreat to economic restraint.

References and Readings

Commoner, Barry, "Economic Growth and Ecology—A Biologist's View," *Monthly Labor Review*, XCIV (November 1971), pp. 3–13.
> Commoner's position, which he has stated repeatedly in articles and books, is that the increasing output of synthetic products is the main cause of pollution. He does not subscribe to the zero-economic-growth position, however.

Daley, Herman E., "Toward a Stationary-State Economy," in *Patient Earth*, ed. by John Harte and R. H. Socolow. New York: Holt, Rinehart and Winston, 1971.
> A strong statement against the goal of economic growth, suggesting that additional GNP may cost more than it is worth and that "a policy of maximizing GNP is practically equivalent to a policy of maximizing depletion and pollution."

Denison, E. F., *The Sources of Economic Growth in the United States and the Alternatives Before Us*. New York: Committee for Economic Development, Supplementary Paper No. 13, 1962.
> A comprehensive examination of the causes of economic growth and the measurement of the relative contribution of various factors to growth in the United States over recent decades.

Fuchs, Victor R., *The Growing Importance of the Service Industries*. New York: Columbia University Press, 1965.
> A National Bureau of Economic Research project examining the trend toward a larger service sector in the United States economy, with some analysis of its significance for economic growth.

Heller, Walter W., "Economic Growth and Ecology—An Economist's View." *Monthly Labor Review*, XCIV (November 1971), pp. 14–21.
> An article by a former chairman of the Council of Economic Advisers which suggests that growth should be more carefully directed rather than checked. He believes that internalizing the costs of environmental damage—requiring that the producer absorb the full costs of water pollution, for example—will stimulate the development of industrial processes that do not harm the environment.

Jarrett, Henry, ed., *Environmental Quality in a Growing Economy*. Baltimore: Johns Hopkins Press, 1966.
> A collection of articles that are generally questioning, if not critical, of the vigorous pursuit of economic growth.

Mishan, E. J., *Technology and Growth: The Price We Pay*. New York: Praeger, 1969.

> A broad-scale criticism of the growth goal and the tendency to identify wealth and welfare. Mishan has repeated his position in a number of books and articles, of which this volume is a more popular version.

Morgenstern, Oskar, "Qui Numerare Incipit Errare Incipit," *Fortune*, LXVIII (October 1963), pp. 142–144.

> This article is a very brief condensation of Morgenstern's book *On the Accuracy of Economic Observations*, which calls much-needed attention to the errors frequently concealed in growth rates, national-income statistics, and other commonly-accepted measures of economic activity. The title of the article translates as, "He who begins to count begins to err."

Phelps, E. S., ed., *The Goal of Economic Growth*, rev. ed. New York: W. W. Norton & Company, 1969.

> A collection of articles expressing various views of the growth goal and examining various aspects of the topic.

Rostow, W. W., *The Stages of Economic Growth: A Non-Communist Manifesto*. New York: Cambridge University Press, 1960.

> A somewhat controversial historical interpretation of the causes and stages of economic growth.

PART II

Economic Decision-Making

Chapter Five

The Market Economy
and Its Operation

*As every individual . . . endeavours as much as he can both
to employ his capital in the support of domestic industry,
and so to direct that industry that its produce may be of
greatest value; every individual necessarily labours to ren-
der the annual revenue of the society as great as he can. He
generally, indeed, neither intends to promote the public interest, nor knows how much he is promoting it. . . .[H]e
intends only his own gain, and he is in this, as in many other
cases, led by an invisible hand to promote an end which was
no part of his intention—Adam Smith* [1]

In the mystique of the marketplace, Adam Smith's proposition that the public interest is best served by the unabashed
pursuit of self-interest has become a familiar defense of the
private-enterprise system and the distribution of income that is
generated under this form of economic organization. In order to
justify widely differing economic rewards, however, whether in
a market economy or in a collectivist planned economy, the inequality must contribute in some important way to the attainment of socially desirable goals. One such goal, according to
economic orthodoxy, is the maximization of economic output
consistent with existing resources. This economic output, in
turn, is considered optimum if its composition is determined by

[1] *The Wealth of Nations,* Book IV, Chapter 2.

an unconstrained expression of consumer choice in the market-place. This is a big order—especially since the attainment of this optimum in the market economy occurs without benefit of a formal administrative organization or conscious control. The consumer, far from being the forgotten man of modern industrial society, is presumed to be a real mover and shaker in the market system's operation.

Consumer Sovereignty

To speed Adam Smith's invisible hand in its good work, not only must the consumer be knowledgeable and decided in his choices, but there must be nothing that interferes with the economic system's response to the signals he gives. Then his scale of preferences is the driving force behind the businessman's decision; merchants and manufacturers compete for his favor and he rules the ordering of production priorities with his distribution of dollars.

Some economists accept this conception of the market system more fully than others. Some subscribe to the assignment of sovereignty to the consumer primarily as a handy oversimplification in introducing a discussion of decision-making in the market economy, admitting later that this view of the system's operation is badly distorted. Here it will be acknowledged at once that the consumer is considerably less than the system's monarch and that there are indeed limitations to his exercise of power. The interferences with the ideal operation of the market system will be discussed in detail in this chapter and will be further explored in other chapters showing how the way the market economy operates affects environmental problems. Meanwhile, however, an examination can be made of the idealized operation of the economy, in which it is seen as responding largely to the consumer's signals.

How the System Works

By showing that he likes turtleneck sweaters rather than togas, bland beer rather than stout, or television rather than opera, the

American consumer establishes sets of preferences that the producer must work within to attract the purchaser's dollar. Preference without purchase is a hollow achievement at best from the standpoint of the producer. (Shortly after World War II, the Chrysler Corporation attempted to adapt its cars to the preferences revealed in a consumer survey. The message of the survey was clear: The consumer wanted a short-wheelbase, low-horsepower, conservatively styled automobile. When it came to buying, however, the message was quite different. Chrysler's sales seriously trailed those of its competitors, whose cars had design features almost the reverse of those shown as preferred, in the survey.)

The kinds of signals that the consumer can give the producer (here understood to include the whole range of suppliers, manufacturers, wholesalers, and retailers) are more effective in some cases than in others. This has contributed to the controversy surrounding the concept of consumer sovereignty, the defenders at times looking at one part of the system's operation and the critics viewing another. If the consumer's purchase is a commodity or service that is well known and uncomplicated, for example a loaf of bread or leaf-raking, there is no difficulty in evaluating either the quality of the product or the amount needed. Moreover, if the good or service is frequently purchased, the consumer's signal is almost always clear and specific. The situation is quite different, however, when the consumer is confronted with a highly technical or complex good or service that is infrequently purchased—such as a heating system for the home or the services of a heart specialist. In such cases, the consumer is hardly king, exercising his own wisdom of choice; instead, he meekly accepts the judgment of others—his contractor or general practitioner—or exercises a kind of stumbling random selection.

The temptation to compare the working of the market system with that of the political system is irresistible, but it is justified only so long as it is recognized that the analogy has serious limitations. The economist David McCord Wright draws the following parallel:

> In effect, the capitalist market can be looked upon as a perpetual election to decide what shall be produced. Money forms the

votes, advertising the campaign literature; and the election returns, determining which businesses shall stay in operation and which shall go out, are set by profit and loss.

Sooner or later this economic election serves to eliminate the more unwanted products and to guide producers into uses which people can be persuaded to pay for. It functions in the following way. If there are too many people making bicycles, the price of the bicycle will tend to fall and eventually some of the bicycle makers will shut down. . . . People make mistakes, changes may not offset each smoothly or may lag, and there may be a consequent depression. Nevertheless, the analogy with political democracy is exceedingly strong even to its imperfections.[2]

As devices for receiving the diverse expressions of individuals and organizing them into a single uniform choice, the market system and the elective process have much in common. The final decision both in the market and in an election is narrowed to a limited range of choice, and the individual, whether consumer or voter, is presumed to hold the ultimate decision-making authority. A further similarity is the less-than-complete authority that the individual is able at times to exercise in both systems.

No matter how well the market system responds to the purchase decisions of the consumer, however, it departs greatly from the democratic principle of one person–one vote. In the market "election," the consumer's "votes" are directly proportional to his money expenditures; a rich person can "outvote" a poor person and channel resources into production that satisfy needs that are trivial compared with those of the poor, since the market is indifferent to need. Under such circumstances, it is hardly likely that the market decisions will coincide with what people believe to be an ideal distribution of goods and services in a democratic society.

Questions of equity generate disagreement. Conservatives tend to come closer to approving of the income distribution and resource allocation produced by the market mechanism than do liberals, who generally favor greater use of the tax and spending powers to adjust what they consider inequities. As a result, even

[2] From *Capitalism* by David McCord Wright, p. 46. Copyright 1951 by McGraw-Hill Book Company. Used with permission of McGraw-Hill Book Company.

if the market system operates efficiently in following the dictates of the consumer, it still will not gain the approval of those who believe its decision-making is overly concentrated in the pocket-books of the upper-income groups. The invisible hand in its amoral response to the consumer's dollar promotes a public interest of a quite narrow kind.

The Market—An Oversimplified View

If we temporarily confine our examination of the market system to the area in which the consumer is able to make his choices known in a clear and unequivocal way, this idealized operation of the economy can be described by a flow chart, as in Figure 5.1. The consumer, as befits a sovereign, is at the top of the circular-flow diagram, and the system responds to his bidding. As illustrated, it is closed system: The expenditures by the consumer are made possible by income from employment or resource ownership. The chart is like a cutaway model of a machine showing its internal mechanism; important external features have been ignored. As it stands, the consumer's role in resource allocation—the so-called *micro*economic function—has been overemphasized. But if the cutaway section is built back to full scale by addition of streams from the banking system and the government injecting money into the circular flow, the diagram can also describe *macro*economic activity, such as overall changes in the economy's employment and income. Since our interest here is with the micro allocative function of the market system, the influence of the banking system and the government is disregarded in the model. Even though our attention may be limited to the micro functions of the market system, however, it is time to correct the notion that the market system works with the flawless simplicity that our model suggests.

The Decline in the Consumer's Authority

Although the consumer has never exerted the influence over producer's decisions that he is assigned in the doctrine of consumer sovereignty, his authority has declined with society's increasing affluence. Affluence has expanded the range of the consumer's choice well beyond the familiar necessities of life to a glittering array of complex products. Technology is in large part responsible; it has filled the home with sophisticated equipment --automatic dishwashers, microwave ovens, air conditioners-- that most consumers do not understand much beyond starting and stopping. Moreover, expanding consumer markets and the financial rewards from their exploitation have created an industry of persuaders, which has presided over large expenditures for television time and space in newspapers and magazines. As a result, the consumer decisions have become less and less independent judgments.

Figure 5.1.   The Circular Flow: A Simplified Pricing
System

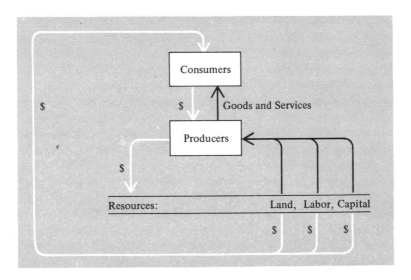

Andreas Papandreou, economist and exiled Greek cabinet minister, describes the erosion in consumer control in the American system as follows:

... [T]he modern industrial system serves ends which to a large extent are shaped by its own requirements. Ultimate ends are no longer independent of the profit-through-growth or growth-through-profit requirements of the modern corporate giant. This no longer raises only questions of efficiency, but the much more basic question of effectiveness. Had we been able to define ultimate ends—the ends of the consumer and the state—independently of the influences of the industrial system, we would have been in a position to establish almost certainly that these ends are not served by it. The fact is that we cannot even do that. The economic process has become irrational *de profundis*. . . . Technically, but only technically, the market mechanism still allocates resources to uses. But consumer sovereignty is no longer present [3]

At the same time that the interaction of affluence and technology has confronted the consumer with increasingly difficult decisions, the skilled persuaders have created differences where there were no differences, glamor where before there was only mundane similarity, need where there was but curiosity. Take cigarettes, for example. It is hardly of any social importance whether Marlboro or Virginia Slims excels in sales, but it is a considerable social and economic disutility that economic resources are devoted to persuading consumers to choose one over the other.

Paradoxically, one of the most lucrative opportunities for "creative" advertising in the market economy occurs when the products involved are nearly identical. Only a few can be convinced that a product clearly inferior for a particular use—say Epsom salts as compared with penicillin in the treatment of gangrene—should be accorded preference in purchase, but if the product differences are slight, like those between most proprietary headache remedies, it is possible through advertising to inflate trivial differences or endow particular brands with superiorities that override the consumer's rational judgment. Indeed, this area of "creative" advertising—unencumbered as it is by a strong regard for factual considerations—provides the greatest opportunity for the persuaders' talents. So effective is the advertising industry's power of persuasion that at times even the professionals may be taken in, if a study by the Mayo Clinic of the

---

[3] Papandreou, Andreas G. *Paternalistic Capitalism.* University of Minnesota Press, Minneapolis. © 1972, University of Minnesota. Pp. 77–78.

effectiveness of the prescription drug Darvon is to be believed. This drug, represented by Eli Lilly and Company as a super-strength pain-killer and widely prescribed by physicians, has been found by Mayo Clinic research to be less effective than aspirin and hardly superior to an inert placebo.

Running to Stay in the Same Place

Partly because it is so effective, advertising may lead to all producers in an industry adopting much the same program in order to protect their market positions. One firm's increased sales from advertising may call up similar outlays by other firms in order to recoup their share of the market. Like the Red Queen in *Alice Through the Looking Glass,* who found it took all the running she could do to stay in the same place, the advertising industry devotes much of its talent to keeping one firm from getting ahead of other firms in the industry. Benefit to the consumer or society, or indeed to the firms purchasing the advertising, is either nonexistent or transient, but it provides the advertising industry with a continuing source of income.

If advertising and other latter-day encroachments upon the invisible hand prevent it from guiding the market in the public interest, including protection of the environment, *laissez-faire* as a policy loses much of its appeal. Market intervention, such as that to protect labor and the consumer, becomes necessary to prevent the producer from making decisions affecting the environment without answering for the consequences. In addition, since in many cases damage to the environment does not show up in either producer costs or consumer prices, adjustment of both may be necessary to bring market decisions in line with the public interest. We need to take a closer look at what price can and cannot do in selected environmental areas.

The Adequacy and Inadequacy of Price

Prices perform some functions very well. In response to scarcity, a higher price for resources, commodities, or services coerces the consumer into purchasing less; with lower prices, a more abundant supply will find an expanded market. The market, with no centralized direction or control, carries on an unending process of adjustments that correct for changes in demand and supply. It works well enough so that it is not unusual to hear the statement, "You can't repeal the law of supply and demand." Actually, the law can be largely circumvented, but the warning is justified; intervention that neutralizes the market's rationing function may bring both unexpected and undesired results.

Normally the market rations or allocates the existing supply of a good or service among those who are willing and able to pay for it. By imposing price control such as that of the Nixon new economic policy, however, prices may be kept below what the market would establish, in effect disconnecting the market's rationing mechanism. Now too many purchasers will try to buy too few goods because of the lower-than-market price. If prices are held below the market level for very long, the consequences may be quite far reaching: It may be necessary to replace the market's rationing mechanism with another system of allocation control, black markets may develop where prices are higher and goods easily available, and an extensive administrative organization may be required to perform the functions previously carried out more or less automatically by the market.

Prices—Servant of the Public or of Private Interests?

"Prices" and "costs" are sometimes used as if they applied to different things. This is not the case. What is the seller's price is the buyer's cost, and any difference is in the eye of the beholder. For society, however, there are important instances in which the price or cost of a product does not pay for all the unwanted consequences of its production, such as pollution, waste of a resource not purchased, and aesthetic degradation. The shift of these burdens or costs to the public was identified as "spillover costs" or "social costs" in Chapter 3 and illustrated by surface mining and taconite production. Not only the extractive industries are responsible for such cost shifts to the public, however, although their occurrence in the mining industry may be more apparent because of the physical destruction of the land. Unseen and difficult-to-detect by-products of industry and agriculture, such as mercury, DDT, and lead, may be a more important source of environment concern.

As industry and agriculture burden the environment with new chemical wastes, the validity of market price is impaired in its function of recording the full costs of production. Where social costs are not covered by the producer, the final price of some economic output does not measure fully what society gives up to obtain such things as highways, motorcars, hybrid corn, and cotton. To adjust for this deficiency, market prices would have to be raised to cover costs that are not borne by the consumers of these products. It is easy to point out the need for this kind of adjustment, but to attain it is quite another problem. Existing institutional arrangements through which such adjustments can be undertaken provide only a kind of *ad hoc* use of tax and zoning authority. Obviously, until the market mechanism imposes the full social as well as private cost of resource use, the decisions it generates will fall short of protecting the environment.

Prices Can't Do Everything

The market mechanism can't at the same time encourage both economic development and the conservation of natural resources, stimulate all kinds of private economic activity and maximize the social welfare, promote unrestrained economic growth and protect the environment. To assume that the market system can accomplish such a wide variety of tasks, some of which are conflicting, is to endow it with an omnipotence it cannot hope to achieve. Limited largely to the movement of prices upward and downward in response to scarcities and surpluses, market adjustments may conserve resources by directing economic usage away from the depleting, exhaustible resource. At other times, however, scarcity may simply accentuate the drive to harvest the depleting resource because of its higher price. These totally different results, conservation in one case and depletion in the other, are largely dependent on whether the higher resource price encourages a shift to substitute resources. If substitutes can be found for the higher-priced resource, as petroleum or natural gas for coal, a rise in the price of coal will lead to shifts to the use of other resources and conservation of coal. If the price of a resource is already well above or well below other resource prices, however, no substitution of other resources is likely to be encouraged by a moderate price change. The price of a resource may be either too high or too low to encourage the use of other products in its place. The exploitation of the whale is a case in point.

The Plight of the Whale—a Migratory Resource

Increased pressure upon the whale in recent decades has come about in part because there are few close competitors of whale products. Although whale products have risen in price, they are still too cheap to be undercut by many substitutes. The whale contributes in a minor way to the food supply of some nations, but unlike the whaling era of the past, when whale oil provided the main source of illumination, today its contribution to human welfare is at a much lower level. The primary demand for whale products comes in the production of pet foods, fertilizers, lipsticks, and lubricating oils. All these uses can be satisfied as well or better by other materials, but—unfortunately for the whale —not at a price that is competitive. As a result, the market system continues to send out signals that bring the whale closer to extinction.

Already some whale species are dangerously near the point of extinction and the supply price for whale products has not risen sufficiently to call forth relief by substitute materials. In large part this has been because of the modernization of the whaling industry. The rugged and romantic ways of Captain Ahab in his compulsive pursuit of the white whale have been replaced by a whaling technology of terrifying efficiency: Exploding harpoon heads, electronic tracking devices, factory-ship processing at sea, fast pursuit vessels, and modern navigational aids. Too big to hide, too slow to escape the hunter, the whale cannot avoid being eliminated at the present rate of kill—unless the dictate of the market is set aside.

This largest mammal suffers a special vulnerability, biologically and economically, because it is a migratory resource. It cannot be constrained in herds like livestock, conserved, and declared the property of the capturer; it wanders the seas at will and is the legal property of any intercepting whaler. As its numbers diminish, the pressure for harvest increases. The success of one whaler reduces the prospects of competitor whalers and forces upon all the most aggressive harvesting practices, increasing annual kills and destroying the resource base of the industry. Record-breaking kills occurred in the 1950's and 1960's at the same time that the overall whale populations were greatly reduced.

The whaling nations of the world, in a show of concern for the "conservation and rational utilization" of the world's whale resources, signed the International Whaling Convention in 1946 and established a world supervisory commission. This commission, which one might have expected to divert the industry from its self-destructive path, appears to have operated largely as a cover for the continued pursuit of the short-run commercial objectives of the more active whaling nations, primarily Japan and the Soviet Union. The United States, no longer a whaling nation of any importance but a major market for whale products, has somewhat slowed the whale's exit from the seas by placing it on the endangered-species list and prohibiting the importation of its products into the United States. But more interference with the market than this will have to take place before the destruction is stayed.

Forests—a Multiple-Purpose Resource

Unlike the whale, which faces extinction if its numbers fall below a critical population threshold, forest resources can be severely depleted and later restored through careful reforestation. Both are victims of a narrowly focused market economy, however. A forest is a different thing to different people. To a timber merchant, it is board feet of sawtimber or the raw material of plywood; to a recreationist, it is the necessary environment for hunting, fishing, hiking, and camping; to a conservationist, it is protection of the topsoil, a habitat for wildlife, and provision of natural resources for the future. In seekng to appeal to the widest possible clientele, the United States Forest Service and other federal agencies administering natural-resource programs have frequently advanced the objective of multiple-purpose resource use. According to this view, the public interest is best served by not limiting forest use to the production of sawtimber alone or restricting the purpose of a dam simply to stopping floodwaters. Camping and hiking in national forests and fishing and water skiing in the impounded waters of a flood-control dam are benefits that do not seriously interfere with the main purpose of the federal project.

In the economic analysis of a government flood-control project, for example, the main benefit of the dam—that of preventing floods—would be augmented by the multiple-purpose benefits. Obviously, the more extensive the multiple-purpose benefits, costs being otherwise the same, the greater the project's contribution to the public welfare.* Unfortunately, in the analysis of a government project it is not always possible to establish accurately the economic value of such multiple-purpose benefits, and the market's appraisal may not be of much help. The market evaluation is confined within a narrow focus of monetary gain and takes no account of the benefit of a resource use that is not expressed in dollar terms. To the market, Yellowstone Falls has an economic value that is more easily estimated for hydroelectric power production than for its scenic grandeur, since no price has been established for this unique value while a price for kilowatts is readily available.

When some project benefits are recorded in dollar terms by the market, as the sale of forest products, and others are not,

* The multiple-purpose issue is much more complicated than has been represented here. In some cases, for example, a primary project purpose, such as flood control, that is of limited worth will be bolstered by multiple-purpose uses that are also of modest benefit, at the same time that important social costs are ignored. Such an approach to multiple-purpose project design obviously does not enhance the public interest.

such as environmental protection, those unrecorded are all too often swept aside as uneconomic and unimportant. But the fact that the market fails to record the value of a benefit does not mean that it is either uneconomic or unimportant. It is not whether a product or service is recorded by the market that determines whether it is economic or not, but its usefulness and scarcity. If it satisfies these conditions, it is economic, and Yellowstone Falls obviously satisfies these conditions easily and importantly in areas other than power production. But time and time again, the market is accepted as the final arbiter of the value of resource use, largely because of the persuasiveness of a neatly quantified numerical value. Logging, for example, will continue to threaten the canoe country in northern Minnesota, Algonquin Park in Canada, the redwoods in California, the Big Thicket in Texas—regions in which lumbering is destructive of other values, economic and noneconomic, in these unique and scarce wild remnants of ecological balance.

The market in its obsession with monetary gain not only extends commercialism into areas that would serve society better without development, but assigns control of a resource to the most profitable use of that resource. Normally, this accords with society's scale of preferences, since the uses paying more for a resource are responding to signals from consumers that they desire this resource output more highly than others. But this overstates the case for the market. Take the logging practice of clear-cutting, the removal of all trees and undergrowth irrespective of age, presumably to promote reforestation of tree species that require unshaded conditions for optimum growth.* Since these species, such as the Douglas fir, provide an important source of lumber and plywood in the United States, there is strong market support for their cultivation, while the alternative practice of selective cutting affords a broader use of

* Former Secretary of the Interior Walter J. Hickel points out in his account of his short tenure in the Nixon Administration that clear-cutting, although it may be a response to the reforestation needs of certain tree species, is substantially cheaper than selective cutting and more frequently practiced by the timber industry when logging federal lands than when logging its own holdings.

the forest, but with lower and more delayed return to the forest owner.

Private Versus Public Benefits in Forestry Practice

The benefits of clear-cutting are largely private—higher returns to the timber owner—whereas selective cutting provides broader nonmarket benefits: reduction in soil erosion, preservation of wildlife habitat and wildlife populations, less stream pollution, and more forest cover for camping and hiking. Although the forest owner may also gain from these broader benefits, the monetary rewards of clear-cutting are at times irresistible to all but the most socially motivated timber owner. Public policy is a different matter, however. The private incentive to clear-cut is understandable, but for the United States Forest Service to condone the widespread use of this practice on federal lands—the public's domain—is a simple perversion of values. In the logging industry, such policies come about because the professional forester finds it necessary to adopt or at least operate under the profit-and-loss constraint of his employer. For this set of values to be imposed on the management of public forest lands, however, shows a misplaced emphasis upon federal monetary revenues from timber sales at best or the capture of the Forest Service by the logging industry at worst.

Wetland Wasteland?

To the market system, a marsh or wetland is a place to dispose of old tires and wrecked cars, dump rubble, and carry out what is euphemistically called "sanitary landfill," which means spreading garbage and other wastes with a layer of soil on top. With enough fill, the marsh may be completely eliminated, creating reasonably firm land and encouraging economic development. Airports are frequently constructed where there were once wetlands, as in the case of the Kennedy and LaGuardia terminals in New York, and the market value of the created land is pure joy to the developer and city planner. Progress, according to the calculus of the market, has taken place: A swamp, considered mainly a source of mosquitoes and miasmatic mists, has been transformed into a valuable economic asset. But such reasoning is unjustified. As in the case of clear-cutting, the market mechanism falters and fails to record the substantial social benefits of wetlands simply because these benefits are not bought and sold.

Far from being a wasteland nuisance, a wetland is enormously productive of aquatic life, birds, and waterfowl. Salt marshes and estuaries serve as the spawning grounds of fish, oysters, mollusks, and other sea creatures—many of which have substantial market value—as well as providing nesting areas for waterfowl and other birds. The varied life that can originate only in the dilute saline waters of the estuary, the intermingled salt and fresh waters, fans out after birth to the deeper reaches of the sea, and in the case of the migratory birds, ranges across the continents. Some of these creatures eventually return to land as commercial catch, providing employment and output of obvious economic value; others afford intangible, but no less economic benefits. As much as two-thirds of the fish consumed by man starts life in wetland areas or depends for food upon other aquatic life that originates there. As a result, wildlife populations far removed from the wetlands owe their abundance and their survival to the protection of the wetlands. In the circle of biotic interdependence, the destruction of a salt marsh or estuary, which passes uncounted by the market mechanism, may be unknowingly recorded later in a diminished fish catch on the Grand Banks off Newfoundland or the Georges Bank fishing grounds of New England.

This is not all. The destruction of a wetland area is almost always irreversible. Unlike depletion of the soil or the logging of a forest, both of which can be restored by appropriate measures, once an estuary is filled in with garbage and refuse, or paved over with airport runways, or fouled with sewage and industrial wastes, it is irretrievably lost. Wetlands are fragile and vulnerable to the wastes and development pressures of our industrial society. Although they make up the merest fraction of our total land area, they are largely unprotected and generally held in low regard. But if they are to perform their essential biotic function, these areas can stand very little alteration. At times, a change in water level is enough to modify their character, and the spread of silt from land erosion may choke out much of their highly concentrated aquatic life.

The Texas Wetlands and the Whooping Crane

Texas, which has more of most things than other states, including coastal wetlands, provides an extreme example of market bias, where trivial commercial gain has been permitted to endanger further a threatened species—the whooping crane. Reduced over the years to a threshold population of less than a hundred, and struggling to survive, the whooping crane nests in northern Canada and winters in the Aransas National Wildlife Refuge on the Texas coast. For many in the nation who follow the progress of the whooping crane's flight in spring to its nesting ground and its later return to Texas, it is not just curiosity about the survival of a large, somewhat overspecialized bird that holds their attention. The whooper is a remnant of wild America, a frail link with an age in which man lived in a closer and more dependent relationship with nature; for some, the whooping crane is a symbol of this calmer, less materialistic time as well as a test of whether there is room in our industrial society for other than the values of the marketplace.

But the question is bound to be asked, "How much is such a symbol worth?" The market mechanism has no way of answering this question, of course, but the state of Texas during the governorship of John Connally responded with a unequivocal, "Not very much." For the most part the whooping crane was not seriously endangered by commercial operations in its federal refuge—oil rigs work nearby without much disturbance—until Texas permitted dredging operations to move in close to the refuge, effectively reducing the whooper's habitat area and impairing its food supply by silting. It is ironic that the dredging operations that have pressed in upon the crane, one of the most scarce species in North America, have been for the purpose of gathering one of the most abundant and cheapest road-building materials of the Texas coast—oyster shells. In effect, the market system has given a decision on the whooping crane. It has, with the aid of the Texas state government, decreed that the saving in secondary road-construction costs by the use of oyster shells justifies endangering the whooping crane.

Why Not Use the Market to Protect as Well as to Exploit?

Why not compete with the developers for such diminishing resources as wetlands, scenic areas, and wildlife habitat? Why not buy the oyster shells and leave the shore undisturbed? Actually, there is a conservation organization that does just this—the Nature Conservancy. Instead of attempting to persuade the public and the politicians that the government should intervene to protect the remaining wild regions of North America, the Nature Conservancy removes some of these areas from the danger of exploitation by buying them and preventing development. Within the limits of its financial resources, the Nature Conservancy is quite effective.

But in spite of operating within the framework of the market economy, the approach of the Nature Conservancy suffers from an obvious difficulty—limitation of finances. For the most part the sources of financial support of such an organization are the dedicated conservationists in the upper- and middle-income groups. In spite of tax incentives for donations to nonprofit conservation organizations, private contributions have been no match in the market for the developers. Moreover, the market approach to preservation runs headlong into the issue of public and private goods.

Although one interpretation of market behavior may be that resource conservation is explicitly rejected when instead of contributing to an organization such as the Nature Conservancy, one buys a product from a business firm that extends its commercial operations into a wetlands or wild area, this view misses the essential difference between most reactions to private and to public goods. The preservation of a marsh or wild area from commercial development is a public good; private individuals benefit, of course, but there is no way an individual can gain only for himself, as in the case of a private good such as an estate or home. As a result of this fundamental difference, a contest between private and public goods for the consumer's dollar is bound to be quite one-sided.

One may be highly in favor of preserving wetlands and preventing the commercial development of wild areas, but find private contributions an inappropriate means of achieving this as long as others can benefit equally from the areas without any contribution. Instead, zoning or public purchase of the resources to forestall commercial development may be considered by most individuals to be both more effective and less inequitable in burden than purely private action. For the individual of average income, it is totally unrealistic to pit public-interest contributions against self-interest expenditures, especially since protecting natural areas can be achieved as well or better by means that do not involve the uncertainty and inequity of private contributions.

Can the Market Really Serve as a Vehicle of the Public Interest?

Certainly not in the overall and automatic manner assumed by Adam Smith, but on a more modest scale, the market mechanism can be controlled so that it directs resources toward predetermined social goals, such as reduced industrial air and water pollution. The market mechanism is a fairly blunt instrument of control, however, and although its capacity to modify economic activity is considerable, it takes the form of encouraging or discouraging a resource use without the opportunity for very refined adjustments in between.

Biasing market decisions for or against certain resource uses or industrial processes is usually viewed with at least apprehension by most economists because of past experience with market intervention. Instead of furthering the public interest, too often the market mechanism has been rigged in favor of a special group, such as the farmers through the agricultural price-support program, manufacturing industries through the tariff, or the petroleum industry with the oil-depletion allowance.

These interventions benefit special interests at the expense of the public, and in the cases here specified, not only does a misallocation of resources occur that reduces the nation's general economic welfare, but the benefiting groups—large-scale farmers, manufacturers, and the petroleum industry—are not found among the more needy in the United States. The federal subsidy programs in agriculture, for example, generally represented as a means of assisting the poor farmers, are much more effective in making the rich farmers richer. Although Congress tried to correct this inequity in the early 1970's by passing legislation to prevent the payment of an annual subsidy of more than fifty thousand dollars per farmer, corporation farms and the larger landholders easily bypassed this limit by subleasing portions of their acreage and hiring others to collect the subsidies for them.

From the time of Adam Smith, economists have cautioned against the subversion of the public interest by business firms enlisting the aid of government to reduce the area of competition or to gain subsidies at public expense. Warnings of the danger of consumerism to the system are seldom heard, presumably because of a closer identity between "consumer" and the "public" interest, but producer complaints against price controls and restraints upon profits arise whenever such policies are imposed or considered. Usually, however, the consumer has not exerted anything like the influence in bending the market to his advantage that the producer has. The reason is not hard to find. For most individuals, what happens to their income is more important than what happens to only a part of the things upon which it is spent. This is not to say that consumer protests and boycotts are inevitably ineffective, but they are based on an unstable coalition of different interests and are almost always short-lived.

Producer pressures, by contrast, reflect strong and stable economic interests—makers of watches, producers of petroleum, or growers of artichokes. The producer interest, which extends to those who work in a particular industry as well as the owners, easily outweighs the consumer interest. Even to the artichoke addict, for example, an increase in the price of this delicacy is hardly as important as it is to the grower. For the consumer, the price increase marginally reduces purchasing power, but for the producer, a price increase raises income significantly. As a result, Washington lobbies find the conditions necessary for their growth and survival in furthering the interests of the producer, not the consumer. But this is not to say that market intervention can benefit only the producer.

Society's Carrot and Stick

Subsidies and taxes can persuade the producer to modify his behavior in many ways, and zoning can banish it from certain areas. Financial grants from the government may be used to encourage the producer to undertake industrial-waste treatment instead of polluting rivers and streams or burdening municipal-treatment plants. Taxes can be designed to make untreated-waste disposal a financial burden to the producer.

By imposing taxes that are equivalent to the social costs that the producer shifts to society, market prices would be made to reflect full production costs more accurately. Taxes collected because of pollution, for example, could be used to construct waste-treatment facilities and check environmental damage. More importantly, however, a tax on pollution would serve as an incentive to change the polluting process, since the producer would be rewarded by lower taxes for improvements in environmental protection and penalized by higher taxes for environmental damage. The tax approach has certain clear advantages: It reallocates costs where they belong, provides funds for abating pollution, and encourages process change to eliminate the pollution. Process change to reduce pollution is ideal, since it conserves resources otherwise used in treatment plants and talents otherwise devoted to administering and collecting taxes.

For these reasons, the "stick" appears to be a better choice than the "carrot," although a subsidy program of grants to municipalities for the construction of waste-treatment plants has been the foundation of the federal government's approach to the water-pollution problem. The federal subsidy has been available only to municipalities, however, *not* to industry. This is an important difference. An entirely different set of ethical considerations and economic consequences is raised by a grants program to private industry. When industry is subsidized to build treatment plants, other methods of coping with pollution, such as the modification of the industrial process, are discouraged and a questionable income transfer from the public to private industry takes place. In the grants program to municipalities, the transfer is essentially neutral—from one public to another public.*

Whether subsidies or taxes are employed to protect the environment, they carry a coercive impact different from the somewhat similar concessions made by states and localities to persuade businesses to locate operations in their territory. To attract industry, tax concessions, guaranteed loans, and rent-free sites have been employed, resulting in significant income shifts from public to private. Promotion of pollution control by taxes or subsidies does not involve this kind of income transfer. A subsidy to encourage pollution control is income-enhancing for a firm only by contrast with the tax approach. Since a grant for pollution abatement is not directly income-creating or cost-reducing, while free rent and guaranteed loans are, the grant may be considered essentially neutral. A tax on pollution is clearly income-decreasing, however, and imposes a burden upon the producer that previously slipped through the market mechanism and was borne by the public.

More will be said about the options of pollution control in later chapters, and there will be additional discussion of the economic and ethical limitations of the market system in the next chapter, on benefit-cost analysis. But although less than perfect in operation, the market should not be underrated as a mechanism for achieving protection of the environment. Consumer choice can direct resources away from some environmentally damaging products, such as leaded gasoline, throwaway bottles, and high-phosphate detergents. For the most part, however, more than good intentions expressed through consumer choice will be

---

* This is an oversimplification. Actually, a federal grant to a municipality involves a subsidy to industry in those cases where industry uses the municipal plant to dispose of its wastes but does not pay its full share of the costs of treatment. Where the municipal plant depends heavily upon property taxes, as opposed to user charges, for operating revenue, industry gains at the expense of other property owners when its tax rate is lower.

required to check the deterioration in our environment. Guiding the operation of the market by zoning, taxes, subsidies, and other controls is necessary to superimpose broader social objectives on the more narrow consumer-producer interests.

References and Readings

Friedman, Milton, *Capitalism and Freedom*. Chicago: University of Chicago Press, 1962.
> A collection of essays by one of the most ardent advocates of the uninhibited operation of the market system. Friedman, a professor of economics at the University of Chicago, is not only convinced of the superior economic efficiency of the market system; he finds it a necessary condition for political freedom as well. See Chapters 1, 2, and 10.

Galbraith, John Kenneth, *The New Industrial State*, second rev. ed. Boston: Houghton Mifflin, 1971.
> Galbraith has repeatedly criticized the concept of consumers' sovereignty in his various writings. Chapter 19 of this work contains one of the later expressions of his views on this issue.

Lindblom, Charles E., "The Rediscovery of the Market," *The Public Interest*, IV (Summer 1966), pp. 89–101.
> Ultraconservatives such as Milton Friedman and Frederick von Hayek have implicitly identified the market system with private enterprise and *laissez-faire* economic policy. Professor Lindblom, of the Yale University economics department, examines the implications of the increasing reliance upon the market mechanism for resource allocation in collectivist states.

Mishan, E. J., *The Costs of Economic Growth*. London: Staples, 1967.
> This book is primarily a criticism of the economic-growth objective, but in the process it repudiates the notion of consumer sovereignty. Mishan holds that the "want-creating" function of the market in wealthy nations has become more important than its "want-satisfying" function. See especially pp. 109–12.

Papandreou, Andreas G., *Paternalistic Capitalism*. Minneapolis: University of Minnesota Press, 1972.
> Papandreou believes that a managerial elite, rather than the consumer, is responsible for decision-making in the American economy—a paternalism likened to that of the autocratic Big Brother.

Polayni, Karl, *The Great Transformation*. New York: Farrar & Rinehart, 1944.
> A study of the emergence of the market system following the Industrial Revolution, and its impact upon ideas and institutions. A somewhat controversial classic in interpretative history.

——— "Our Obsolete Market Mentality," *Commentary*, III (February 1947), pp. 109–17.
> Polayni believes that the emergence of the market system since the Industrial Revolution has led to an overemphasis upon materialism that has had a stultifying influence upon institutions and social values. He argues for the return to a broader value system.

Schwarz, William, ed., *Voices for the Wilderness*. New York: Ballantine Books, 1969.
> A selection of papers from Sierra Club conferences on wilderness preservation. The articles illustrate the range of values that are neither articulated nor protected in the normal operation of the market economy. "The Economic Aspects of Conservation," the paper of John B. Condliffe, professor of economics emeritus from the University of California, addresses itself directly to this issue. Other articles examine the problems of preserving the wilderness, and the gains and setbacks in this struggle.

Van Tassel, Alfred J., ed., *Environmental Side Effects of Rising Industrial Output*. Lexington, Mass.: Lexington Books, D. C. Heath and Company, 1970.
> An excellent collection of articles on areas of environmental abuse that are not compensated for in production costs under the market system.

Chapter Six

The Public Sector:
Benefit-Cost Analysis

STUART, FLA.—*When the U.S. Army Corps of Engineers began work on a flood control project some 20 years ago, alarmed townspeople tried to halt it. They feared ruination of their picturesque river, the St. Lucie. But the Corps assured residents its project would enhance boating, swimming, and fishing, and the project went ahead.*

The people were right and the Corps was wrong.—The Wall Street Journal. [1]

In what turned out to be a futile attempt to induce Florida to stand firm in the Democratic column in the 1960 presidential election, John F. Kennedy promised to support the Cross-Florida Barge Canal project, an undertaking of extended history but uncertain validity.

The state of Florida went Republican in 1960, but Kennedy nonetheless made good on his pledge and a feasibility study was ordered in 1961. This was hardly the first federal involvement with a canal across Florida. During James Monroe's administration, in 1824, such a canal was proposed as a means of improving mail service between New Orleans and the East Coast and avoid-

[1] Tom Herman, "Embattled Corps—Army Engineers Draw Increasing Critical Fire for Disturbing Nature," *The Wall Street Journal* (January 6, 1970), p. 1. Reprinted with permission of *The Wall Street Journal*.

ing pirates from the West Indies. Later, in 1850, the War Department authorized a survey for a possible canal route, but the undertaking was interrupted by the Civil War. Finally a survey was made between 1909 and 1911, and a report issued in 1913 found the investment in the canal, set at $15,538,055, entirely unjustified on military and commercial grounds. During World War II, when the Atlantic submarine menace was at its peak, a cross-Florida canal was urged as a protected route from the Gulf to the East Coast.

Congress authorized the canal in 1942—by a vote margin of one—and the Army Corps of Engineers estimated the benefit-cost ratio for the project to be 0.18 to 1, a return of eighteen cents for every dollar invested, certainly one of the lowest benefit-cost ratios in recent times. This is *not* an 18-percent return on investment, but a payoff that would *lose* eighty-two cents for every dollar invested. Clearly, without the war emergency, the Cross-Florida Barge Canal had no economic justification according to the Army Corps' feasibility study. The canal was not built during the war; instead, a pipeline for oil transportation was constructed in less time and at lower cost, but the World War II congressional authorization for the canal was not rescinded and it was the basis of the Kennedy Administration project. Since it was not wartime, however, the earlier benefit-cost ratio of 0.18 to 1 would hardly justify appropriating federal funds for such a project. According to the conventional standards, benefits should at least exceed costs.

Fortunately for the advocates of the canal, the project had been refigured in 1958, and the total of such benefits as "transportation savings," "recreational boating," and "commercial fishing boat passages," raised the benefit-cost ratio to 1.05 to 1 —hardly impressive, but not ludicrous. Still, the economic feasibility of the project was marginal and not likely to stand comparison with that of other projects in the competition for appropriations. Moreover, the ratio went from bad to worse when it was brought up to date in 1962 using the interest rate then generally employed by the agencies for analysis of 2⅝ percent instead of the earlier 2½ percent, and when higher construction costs were acknowledged. It dropped to 1.01 to 1. Nevertheless, the project was reported to Congress in the fiscal 1962 budget hearings. But the ratio was too low, so a restudy was ordered.

The restudy added two new categories of benefits, flood control and waterfront-land enhancement, and the benefit-cost ratio was refigured for a hundred-year project life as well as a fifty-year period. The result was predictable: The benefit-cost ratio moved upward, to 1.2 to 1 for fifty-year life and to 1.6 to 1 for one-hundred-year life. Construction started March 1, 1964, and somewhat less than eight years and 70 million dollars later, President Nixon brought the project to a halt when it was one-third completed—a decision that recognized the mounting concern for the environment and the appalling ecological havoc produced by the construction of the Cross-Florida Barge Canal in a natural area of unusual beauty and wildlife abundance.

Benefit-Cost Analysis

What is benefit-cost analysis—a charade, as it appears to be in the foregoing case, or rigorous economic analysis?

In most applications, it is neither. A product of the American political system, benefit-cost analysis must respond to a number of masters: Congress, administration, and bureaucracy and at times its loyalty may be divided and its integrity compromised. Benefit-cost analysis came into being with the passage of the Flood Control Act of 1936, in which it was established as policy that "the Federal Government should improve or participate in the improvement of navigable waters or their tributaries, including watersheds thereof, for flood-control purposes if the benefits to whomsoever they may accrue are in excess of the estimated costs. . . ." The wording "benefits to whomsoever they may accrue" is considered important in justifying a broad conception of project worth, beyond those benefiting directly. Originally applicable only to the civilian functions of the Army Corps of Engineers, primarily its flood-control projects, the use of benefit-cost analysis in areas of environmental impact has spread to a number of federal agencies engaged in capital planning for water-resource development.

Those responsible for the federal development of benefit-cost analysis were a mixture of engineers, economists, and administrators. When the academic economists discovered benefit-cost analysis in the late 1950's, they saw it as a means of answering the question of whether resources should be used in the public or the private sectors of the economy. With full employment in the postwar period and preoccupation with the goal of economic growth, directing resources to their most productive use was an important means of promoting growth. The benefit-cost analysis had been initiated in the depression period, however, and on the whole, the federal agencies found in it another purpose—comparing projects competing for congressional appropriations. Other things being equal, the project with the higher ratio of benefits to costs, say 2.5 to 1 as compared to 1.8 to 1, would be favored, and the project with the lower benefit-cost ratio would be put off until a later time for congressional authorization.

Almost to a man, however, those economists who examined the federal use of benefit-cost analysis in the late 1950's and early 1960's emphasized the fact that with full employment in the economy, the opportunity cost of a federal project was the loss of private-sector output that would occur when resources were shifted from the private to the public sector of the economy. The guns-or-butter analogy of the war period became flood control-or-butter to the academic economists, and they urged a tightening of analytic standards to prevent what they considered to be lower returns from the uses of resources in the public sector.

For the academic economist, investment in the public sector was a trade-off for investment in the private sector. The cost of a flood-control project, for example, thus becomes the loss of output in the private sector from the shift of resources from that sector. The nature of the trade-off can be illustrated by "production possibility" or "transformation" curves, such as those shown in Figure 6.1.

Figure 6.1 indicates the theoretical ranges of investment in a public and a private economic activity, with two sets of fixed amounts of resources. The curves show the various combinations—from all flood control and no urban development to all

Figure 6.1.   Trades off of Flood-Control Investment for
Urban Development

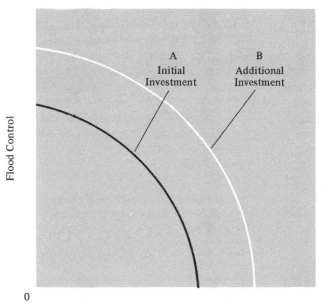

Urban Development

urban development and no flood control—that can be obtained
with the two sets of resources. A larger fund for investment
moves the transformation curve upward and to the right, but
does not modify its shape significantly. The curve is slightly
concave to the origin (O) on the assumption that as more investment takes place in one sector, the loss in the other sector is
greater. In other words, as more flood-control projects are
undertaken, the loss from urban development forgone is dis-
proportionately greater and the gain from flood-control investment is correspondingly diminished. This nonproportional return relationship may be related to diminishing returns * when

* The term "diminishing returns" is not solely the property of the economist. It has found its way into the language of the editorial writer, the
politician, and the butcher. In noneconomic usage, the term generally points

the production possibility curve is used to illustrate the output of two commodities in the private sector; it involves somewhat broader considerations when applied across the public and private sectors.

The broad philosophical rationale behind benefit-cost analysis is that federal projects are economically unjustified if they cost more than the benefits they create are worth. As a general principle, this proposition is a simple truism; before it means anything, the nature of costs and benefits must be specified. For

---

out a decline in some kind of response, such as tax receipts from higher excise rates or the attention span for longer television commercials. For the economist, however, diminishing returns has a very narrow and precise application: the effect upon output from holding constant one factor of production, such as machinery and equipment, and adding more of another factor, such as labor. Under such conditions, output per unit of labor, the so-called variable factor, initially rises as more labor is applied to the fixed factor until an output peak is reached, where the variable–fixed factor relationship is optimum. This is the point of diminishing returns, because further additions of the variable factor will cause a falloff in output increases per unit of labor. (Total output will continue to rise, but at a decreasing rate, and average output will fall.)

The economist's diminishing returns can be conceptualized by reconstituting the curves in Figure 6.1 to portray varying amounts of two commodities, say refrigerators and air conditioners, instead of flood control and urban development. The convexity of the curves expressing different refrigerator–air conditioner combinations results from diminishing returns in the production of each item as the output of it from existing, fixed facilities is increased. As more resources are devoted to refrigerator production, cutting back on the output of air conditioners, refrigerator production initially rises at an increasing rate until the point of diminishing returns is reached and then rises more slowly until the greatest possible refrigerator production occurs, with the existing resources all devoted to making refrigerators. Maximum refrigerator output is indicated by the contact of Curve A with the vertical axis. An identical production function is illustrated for air conditioners. When increasing amounts of resources are allocated to air-conditioner production, output initially increases rapidly, slows its increase, and finally reaches a maximum when Curve A touches the horizontal axis. All resources are devoted to air-conditioner production when Curve A reaches the horizontal axis; in between, varying combinations of refrigerators and air conditioners are produced. Curves A and B are usually called production possibility curves because they represent the possibilities or options of producing different combinations of products; Curve B depicts the same factor relationship as Curve A when larger amounts of resources are employed.

the federal agencies, this involves either using the private market to determine the benefits and costs employed in the analysis or broadening the concepts to take account of factors that are generally not acknowledged in the market mechanism. The market standard will be examined first.

The Private Market as a Standard for Public Projects

Why is the market economy, with the price signals it gives, considered an appropriate guide for public projects? In large part, the answer may be much the same as that given by George Mallory when asked why he climbed Everest: "Because it's there."

This answer will not please those who find in the market economy the embodiment of organizational efficiency and a value structure with which they identify. In addition to the inadequacies of price discussed in the previous chapter, the market economy has certain structural weaknesses and ethical biases that make the market standard an inappropriate guide in some cases of project choice. In its structure, the market economy is at times prevented from attaining the economist's optimum of the lowest resource cost for a given output because of well-recognized impediments. These impediments range from moderate restraint to strong monopoly control by producers and labor groups, and hinder the flow of resources into areas desired by consumers. At the same time, the consumer's inadequate knowledge, hardly improved by advertising, prevents his choices and market prices from achieving the efficiency ideal. Market prices —signals of what to produce and appraisals of product worth —do not convey the same message when reflecting the background of monopoly and consumer ignorance that they do in a competitive economy with informed consumers.

The Market Standard and Social Goals

Even if the economy is briskly competitive, full of consumers alert and vigilant in protecting their interests from encroachment by the producers, the market actions are responsive only to private goals. There is no way—save by monetary contributions to social causes or the purchase boycott of products that carry unwanted side effects—to express through the market mechanism an individual's social choices. There is of course the opportunity to choose between products, such as phosphate and nonphosphate detergents. But a boycott—such as the refusal to buy lawn furniture to protect Pacific Coast redwood forests—is not likely to attract many participants without efficient organization and inspiring leadership. Both are scarce.

Where the appropriate social policy is nondevelopment, the market system is simply inept. How does one express opposition in the market to the exploitation of copper deposits in the Superior National Forest in northern Minnesota or to the Disney Productions' proposed recreational development in the California Sierras' Mineral King Valley? Unlike the rare jukebox designed with an option to purchase silence, the market system provides few opportunities for direct expenditures to buy undeveloped resources.

Income and Ethics

The decisions of the market system reflect not only the imperfections of its structure, but also the underlying distribution of consumer income. As a result, it is possible that a market economy could be virtually free of hindrances to its efficient operation as reflected by minimizing production costs and still reach decisions that are socially questionable.

In overcoming the effects of an inequitable distribution of income upon an economy's allocation of resources, the government may choose to tax the upper-income groups in order to subsidize mass transportation and public housing. In periods of full employment, both of these public investments will reduce private output and, according to conventional market indicators, will involve an opportunity cost represented by the output loss in the private sector of the economy. As a result of the tax upon the upper-income groups, the output forgone in the private sector may be Cadillacs and summer homes, for example, hardly submarginal resource uses, and the *private* opportunity cost involved is unlikely to be equivalent to the *social* opportunity cost. Social welfare may be enhanced by a trade-off of Cadillacs and summer homes for mass transportation and public housing, but by standards of the market alone such a resource shift would be vetoed.

Benefit-Cost Analysis and the Environment— the Federal Agencies

The standards employed by the government in making budgetary decisions have an important effect upon the protection of the environment, quite aside from how they affect the choice of programs devoted to environmental protection. Increasingly, government projects—such as many of those initiated by the Army Corps of Engineers and the Bureau of Reclamation of the Department of the Interior—are in conflict with accepted conservationist-environmentalist values. Policy analysis that favors these kinds of projects makes it harder to achieve environmental protection. Some project benefits and costs cannot be expressed as readily as others in monetary terms. Pollution-abatement benefits, for example, are at best incompletely accounted for in the market whereas the economic benefits of flood-control projects are well covered by the market's appraisal of property values, providing a reasonably complete measure of the project's economic worth. Since projects devoted to environmental protection are likely to be justified largely by the kinds of benefits that are *not* well covered by the market, benefit-cost analysis subjects these projects to a kind of double jeopardy: first, when the basis for project selection favors those activities that may involve environmental injury, and again when these standards make it difficult for the environmental-protection program to compete with other demands for federal funds.

For the most part, environmental-protection programs are heavily loaded with aesthetic considerations and other so-called intangibles, benefits that are real and important to society, but that are not automatically recorded in the market economy. Other federal programs may produce social costs that are not recorded in the project's benefit-cost ratio because, once again, the market does not take account of some detrimental externalities, just as it does not record some beneficial externalities. The result is a built-in analytical bias against some kinds of programs and in favor of other kinds of programs. This bias becomes more serious when the benefit-cost technique is extended broadly throughout government.

Opportunity Cost and Public Investment

All but economists define cost as the amount of money given up in order to obtain possession or use of resources. Economists, although frequently chided for their preoccupation with money matters, insist on looking behind the dollar sign to the "real costs" of production. Real costs are the resources used in obtaining economic output, and the opportunity cost of this output is what could have been produced if the resources were used for different economic objectives—the turtlenecks-or-togas trade-off. Sometimes the impact of government projects on resources in the private sector is described as if the opportunity cost of such projects were the reduction of output by such firms as International Business Machines or Xerox, but unless the method of financing the government project curtails the use of resources in particular areas—as was assumed above in the case of the output of Cadillacs and summer homes—only those private firms whose hold on resources is weak, and whose own return on investment is low, will find the government's pull upon resources to be overpowering. Unless the mobility of resources in the private sector is obstructed and production factors are unable to break out of pockets of low return, the expansion of the government sector—or any part of the private sector—will take place at the expense of marginal firms and marginal industries in the economy, those barely covering costs. The foregoing assumes full employment, where increasing output in one section of the economy causes the withdrawal of resources from another section of the economy.

If there is unemployment, again assuming resource mobility, no opportunity cost for resource use arises, since output may be increased by reemploying idle resources. For this reason, it is sometimes noted that resource use by the government in periods of depression has a money cost but no real cost because no alternative output is lost. This does not mean, however, that because some output is superior to no output, project choice is unimportant in a depression. Even though the opportunity cost is zero, obviously a project that yields a higher return is to be preferred to one with a lower return.

The Interest Rate for Project Analysis

For the federal agency engaged in constructing large-scale capital projects, success is a low interest rate. A low interest rate holds down the cost of capital and at the same time the future benefit stream is discounted less than with a higher rate, thus leading to a higher benefit-cost ratio. Since *the* interest rate of the private market turns out upon inspection to expand into a number of different rates, depending upon the risk involved and the nature and duration of the debt instrument—such as government securities, corporate bonds, installment-purchase paper, and real-estate mortgages—the federal agency is confronted with a choice of what interest rate to use.

Ideally, the rate chosen would measure the alternative output forgone in the private sector of the economy, but the capital market is imperfect and the prime rate of interest—the lowest-risk rate in the private market—may at times be greatly influenced by attempts to control the level of employment and income in the economy. From late 1970 to early 1971, for example, the prime rate in the United States ranged from 8½ percent to 5½ percent, largely as a result of credit policies of the Federal Reserve System. Interest-rate movements in the private sector of the economy have the effect of encouraging or curtailing capital formation, increasing capital creation with lower rates and holding back its formation as the rate increases. There are other factors, of course, that may be of equal or greater importance in capital creation, such as technological innovation and rising demand, but interest-rate changes will influence investment decisions in the manner indicated, along with these other factors.

As the interest rate in the private market fluctuates, it raises or lowers the opportunity cost of using resources from the private sector for public projects. If the market interest rate had been used by the government as the cost of capital in project analysis from 1969 to 1971, not only would the interest charge in the benefit-cost ratio have fluctuated widely during this period, but it would have been considerably higher than the rate employed by most federal agencies.

Project Interest Rates

In the period from 1946 to 1962, federal agencies undertaking water-resource projects generally employed an interest rate based on the average long-term federal bond rate, which ranged between 2½ and 3 percent. (The rate was increased to 3¼ percent in 1962 and to 4⅝ percent in 1969.) The effect upon project justification of a rate lower than the market opportunity-cost rate is shown in a study by Robert Haveman of 147 Army Corps of Engineers projects in the South.[2] Haveman has computed benefit-cost ratios for the 147 projects using two different standards of analysis: first, an interest rate of 2½ percent and a project life of fifty years, and second, an interest rate of 5½ percent and a project life of a hundred years. As indicated in Tables 6.1 and 6.2, even though the project life has been increased to a hundred years with the higher interest rate—thereby extending the benefit stream over a longer period of time—the number of projects out of the 147 total falling below unity (a benefit-cost ratio less than 1) is sixty as compared to one project when the interest rate used is 2½ percent and the project life is fifty years.

The defense of the use of the low, long-term federal bond rate as the interest-rate standard for project evaluation has been based on the contention that this is the cost of capital to the government. Nongovernment economists have generally been critical of this approach and have considered it an inadequate

[2] Robert H. Haveman, "Postwar Corps of Engineers Program in Ten Southern States . . . ," in *Essays in Southern Economic Development*, ed. by M. L. Greenhut and W. T. Whitman (Chapel Hill: University of North Carolina Press, 1964).

Table 6.1 Distribution of 147 Water-Resource Projects
Constructed in Ten Southern States from 1946 to 1962 by
Benefit-Cost Ratio When Future Benefit Streams Are
Evaluated by a 2½-Percent Rate of Interest * †

Benefit-Cost Ratio	Number of Projects	Federal Funds Committed ($000)	Percent of Total Federal Funds Committed
.60–.79	0		
.80–.99	1	$94,600	3.58
1.00–1.19	25	477,694	18.07
1.20–1.39	31	568,757	21.51
1.40–1.59	22	187,082	7.07
1.60–1.79	21	514,953	19.47
1.80–1.99	7	91,123	3.45
2.00–2.49	17	450,032	17.02
2.50–2.99	7	97,866	3.70
3.00–4.99	12	148,751	5.63
5.00 or more	4	13,123	.50
Total	147	$2,644,001	100.0

* The length of project life is assumed to be fifty years unless specifically stipulated to be less by the Corps.
† Robert H. Haveman, "Postwar Corps of Engineers Program in Ten Southern States . . . ," in *Essays in Southern Economic Development*, ed. by M. L. Greenhut and W. T. Whitman, (Chapel Hill: University of North Carolina Press, 1964), p. 465.

measure of the cost of capital. The federal government is in the unique position of being able to borrow in the money market at a low rate because its securities represent the lowest risk of any credit instrument. In addition, unlike other borrowers, the Treasury Department can call upon the Federal Reserve System under some circumstances to provide a market for its securities at low-rate funding. As a result, the spread between private-bond and government-bond rates is maintained.

In private investment there is generally a close connection between the risk of the business venture and the costs of financing; the private firm borrows money for a particular purpose that is the basis of the lender's decision to advance funds. In

Table 6.2   Distribution of 147 Water-Resource Projects
Constructed in Ten Southern States from 1946 to 1962 by
Benefit-Cost Ratio When Future Benefit Streams Are
Evaluated by a 5½-Percent Rate of Interest.* †

Benefit-Cost Ratio	Number of Projects	Federal Funds Committed ($000)	Percent of Total Federal Funds Committed
.60–.79	18	$399,153	15.10
.80–.99	42	761,017	28.77
1.00–1.19	35	642,210	24.29
1.20–1.39	12	179,245	6.78
1.40–1.59	9	110,322	4.17
1.60–1.79	8	293,475	11.10
1.80–1.99	6	93,813	3.55
2.00–2.49	6	143,583	5.43
2.50–2.99	3	7,549	.29
3.00–4.99	6	4,186	.16
5.00 or more	2	9,448	.36
Total	147	$2,644,001	100.0

* The length of project life is assumed to be one hundred years unless specifically stipulated to be less by the Corps.
† Robert H. Haveman, "Postwar Corps of Engineers Program in Ten Southern States . . . ," in *Essays in Southern Economic Development*, ed. by M. L. Greenhut and W. T. Whitman, (Chapel Hill: University of North Carolina Press, 1964), p. 465.

federal fund raising, there is a separation between project risk and government borrowing. The low interest rate on federal bonds is not the result of risk-free projects—a public power project, for example, may actually represent a greater economic risk than a private electric utility—but reflects the unparalleled credit rating of the federal government. There is no reason for the federal government not to take advantage of this position in borrowing money; it does not follow, however, that this borrowing rate is appropriate for project analysis—especially if the objective is to duplicate the standard of the private market.

Although the most obvious impact of the interest rate upon project evaluation is as a measure of the opportunity cost of capital, a high or low rate affects more than project rejection or approval. The rate of interest used in project evaluation also influences the design of the project and the timing of its construction. The higher the interest rate, for example, the less favored are capital-intensive projects, the greater the advantage held by projects of short duration, and the more favored the project with an early payoff.

Joseph Stalin and the Rate of Interest

By now, the cry may be "Enough!" So the interest rate is important, but whoever thought otherwise? Well, Joseph Stalin thought otherwise, along with the Marxist planners who sought to keep the Soviet system free of capitalistic taint by outlawing the payment of interest or profits. Since, according to Marxist doctrine, all value is created by labor, the Soviet system could not justify paying capital a return. But capital was an especially scarce productive factor in the early years of the Soviet Union, and it had to be rationed to different industries by the planning authorities. Normally, the rate of interest would provide a guide to the use of this scarce capital, directing it to areas where the return would be highest and where return would be earlier rather than later.

In the Stalin era, the use of the zero interest rate coincided with Soviet planning blunders called "gigantomania"—the design of capital installations beyond economic scale with benefits at times too long delayed. A campaign against gigantomania was undertaken by the central authorities, and the use of what was really a surrogate interest rate helped ensure against such planning errors. Since the Soviet planners could not charge an interest rate for the use of capital without violating Marixst principles, they simply required that a capital investment pay off its original cost within a given period of time. Thus a payoff period limited to five years was equivalent to an interest rate of 20 percent, ten years equaled an interest charge of 10 percent, and so on.

As late as 1958, however, Nikita Khrushchev complained of the Soviet planning bias for large-scale, distant-yield capital investments. The August 24, 1958, *Pravda* quoted him as saying,

"We built the 2,300,000 kilowatt Lenin Volga Hydroelectric Station in seven years. . . . But with the same money we could have built in less time several thermal plants with a total capacity of 11,000,000 kilowatts. True, the electric power from thermal plants is more expensive, but on the other hand they will supply power to our factories much earlier. . . ."

Assuming that the appropriate rate of interest could be developed in a command system of planning such as the Soviet Union, its use in establishing the present value of future benefits and costs of capital installations would bring about the optimum economic apportionment of capital between, say, distant-yield hydro developments and earlier-yield thermal plants.

At the present time, different interest rates or their equivalents are used in the Soviet Union, with the rate for large investments as high as 10 percent and for less intensive capital investment even higher. Since for practical purposes there is no private sector in the Soviet Union, the opportunity cost of capital is other public investment forgone. The use of different rates of interest avoids this test and grants a preference to those industries permitted to finance at the lower rate.

The Discount of Project Benefits and Costs

To most people, a dollar now is worth more than a dollar later, and the later the dollar the lower its value for those who have a "time preference" for the present. A small segment of the population, such as those nearing retirement and in need of income later, may have a time preference for the future, but they are considerably outnumbered by those who want to spend now and pay later. This is another way of saying that future benefits and costs have to be discounted (decreased) in order to convert them to present worth—and the more distant the benefit or cost and the higher the rate of discount, the lower the monetary value placed on the future stream of benefits or costs.

The use of a high rate of interest in benefit-cost analysis leads to a greater discount of benefits and costs than a low rate, as well as higher capital costs. As a result, a high interest rate lowers the benefit-cost ratio compared with the ratio based on a lower rate.

Period of Analysis

The Soviet planners in effect raised or lowered the interest charge for a capital investment by decreasing or increasing the payoff period. By permitting payoff over a longer period of time for some projects, they charged these projects less for the use of capital. A somewhat analogous situation occurs in federal water-resource planning in the choice of the "period of analysis." The period of analysis is the length of time—40, 50, 85, 100 years—that it is assumed the government project will remain a viable economic undertaking, yielding benefits and bearing costs. Costs are spread over the time period selected, with annual charges lower for longer periods and aggregate benefits greater for more extended periods.

A longer period of analysis affords the project more time to cover costs and obtain a better-than-unity benefit-cost ratio, but the advantage of the longer period of analysis is largely dependent upon the use of a low rate of interest. As indicated in Table 6.3, with a 3-percent interest rate, when the benefit-cost ratios for Shasta Dam with a fifty-year life and with a hundred-year life are compared, the ratio is noticeably higher for the longer period. The benefit-cost ratios recorded in Table 6.3 are for the California Central Valley Project (CVP) and for the major parts of this project that can be evaluated separately. The CVP is a gigantic water-resource investment project planned by the federal Bureau of Reclamation for irrigational development of the Central Valley region of southern California, involving moving water from the Cascade Mountains of northern California to as far south as Bakersfield. In the middle 1960's, most federal agencies, including the Bureau of Reclamation, adopted a period of analysis of a hundred years, making it somewhat easier for a project to attain an acceptable benefit-cost ratio. The ratio-raising effect of the longer time period falls off sharply, however, as indicated in Table 6.3, when the interest rate rises. (The computations in Table 6.3, although based on the Bureau of Reclamation project, are part of an independent study by a group of University of California economists.)

Table 6.3 Benefit-Cost Ratios for the Central Valley Project and Separable Features *

Item	Time Period	Interest rate			
		3%	4%	5%	6%
1. "Basic" CVP features; without adjustment for surplus crops	50 years	1.21	1.03	0.89	0.77
	100 years	1.45	1.16	0.96	0.81
2. "Basic" CVP features; using adjusted world prices for price-supported crops	50 years	0.72	0.61	0.53	0.47
	100 years	0.85	0.69	0.57	0.49
3. Shasta Dam; including maximum net benefits attainable along Sacramento channel, but excluding all works south of the Delta	50 years	1.16	1.00	0.86	0.76
	100 years	1.38	1.11	0.93	0.80
4. Delta-Mendota and Contra Costa canals and Friant Division; without Shasta but including allowance for opportunity cost of water use forgone in the Delta	50 years	1.22	1.05	0.91	0.79
	100 years	1.47	1.18	0.99	0.84

* Joe S. Bain et al., *Northern California's Water Industry* (Baltimore: Johns Hopkins Press, 1966), p. 558. Published for Resources for the Future, Inc. by The Johns Hopkins Press.

Taxes and Federal Projects

For the most part, federal installations pay no taxes and there is no inclusion of this item on the cost side of the benefit-cost ratio. In those cases where market prices are the measure of benefits—such as electricity rates and agricultural-product prices—no adjustment is made for the increase in prices due to taxes included in the final price. In other words, benefits, but not costs, are raised by taxes. No argument can be made for deducting taxes from the market price in determining benefits, since the final price, whatever the ingredients, represents the market appraisal of the value of the project's output, but by ignoring taxes as a cost factor, the benefit-cost analysis falls short of duplicating market conditions.

By understating the costs of the public project in comparison with those of the private firm, such as an electric utility, the benefit-cost ratio may justify a shift in resources from the private to the public sector of the economy as a result of the different treatment of taxes rather than because of a higher return in the public sector. A further upward bias of the benefit-cost ratio of the public project may occur from the failure to include taxes as a cost in those cases where economy of scale is important, such as hydroelectric plants where the cost of a kilowatt of electricity is less for a larger plant.

The Secondary-Benefit Issue

Secondary benefits are economic activities generated by a project in addition to the value of the project itself. In the case of an irrigation project, for example, the primary project benefit is the market value of, say, grapefruit that is grown on the irrigation project, whereas the secondary benefit is the net increase in dollar value of the economic activities stemming from the project's grapefruit production: canning, transportation, increased service, and so on.

The secondary-benefit measure is a somewhat elastic gauge of project worth, capable of accommodating different standards. The key to the impact that secondary benefits have upon the

benefit-cost ratio is how "net" is interpreted. If secondary benefits are cast in terms of the national economy, only project output
that raises national income is considered a benefit. If, however,
"net" is interpreted to apply to the region in which the project
is located, then activity that involves resources employed elsewhere at much the same reward—grapefruit canning instead of,
say, artichoke canning—will be counted as a project benefit.
Again, full employment is assumed.

In the past, secondary benefits have not played an important
role in benefit-cost analysis. Only the Bureau of Reclamation
has made much use of this means of augmenting project ratios,
largely because of the help secondary benefits can afford an
otherwise low benefit-cost ratio. Economists generally have
viewed the inclusion of secondary benefits in the benefit-cost
ratio as more of a kind of low cunning than a justifiable addition.
And yet some kinds of investments produce more productivity-
enhancing waves throughout the economy than others. For example, the greatest impact in underdeveloped countries of secondary benefits stems from the social-overhead capital investments:
transportation systems, power production, and other basic industries that provide a foundation for further economic output.
But the United States is far removed from the status of a "developing" nation, and the Bureau of Reclamation, the main champion
of the use of secondary benefits, is more concerned with grapefruit than with social-overhead capital.

Agency Analysis: A Less-Than-Arm's-Length Operation

The federal agencies are primarily responsible for the benefit-cost studies that contribute importantly in determining
whether the projects obtain congressional appropriations. Sometimes a number of federal agencies are involved in a particular
project. A comprehensive project of either the Bureau of Reclamation or the Army Corps of Engineers, for example, will likely
incorporate hydropower production as a benefit and affect the
aquatic life of the river that is damned. As a result, analyses by
the Federal Power Commission and the Fish and Wildlife Service

will be integral parts of the benefit-cost study. These "outside" agencies may be less dedicated to the advancement of the project than the sponsoring agency, and in some cases, will furnish appraisals that decrease rather than increase the benefit-cost ratio. The Fish and Wildlife Service frequently finds itself in the "spoiler" role when a project has an adverse effect upon the recreational opportunities of an area, but it is an unusual case where its reservations lead to the rejection of a project.

In the preparation of the benefit-cost study by the agency, those undertaking the analysis cannot adopt the posture of the disinterested scientist. They are agency employees, fully aware that the continuation of the agency's function depends upon projects with adequate benefit-cost ratios. Pressures within the agency to produce high benefit-cost ratios may be more or less evenly distributed from the lowest agency analyst worried about the continuation of his job to those in the policy-making hierarchy anxious not to be considered disloyal. In each case, the price of conformity may involve some "flexibility" in the analytical approach to project evaluation.

The need to modify benefit-cost analysis has been pressed upon the federal agencies employing this technique by critics within and without the federal government. Bureau of the Budget directives, reports of panels of experts, congressional hearings, and extended review in academic studies have all questioned agency practices. Moreover, in 1972, the Water Resources Council undertook a comprehensive reexamination of benefit-cost-analysis practices in a series of public hearings and written reports on such questions as the appropriate discount rate, the legitimacy of regional benefits, consideration of environmental issues, and the like. Since the membership of the Water Resources Council is made up of the secretaries of Interior, Agriculture, Defense, Health, Education, and Welfare, and other departments employing benefit-cost analysis, the Council is obviously capable of undertaking policy modifications if it desires. Whether the secretaries will overturn the practices of the agencies in their departments, however, is another matter. In the past, the agencies have not been immune to such assaults upon their analytical practices, but they have generally been successful in countering them with protective bureaucratic maneuvers. The constraint of a higher interest rate, for example, may be set aside by the admission of more secondary or regional benefits, or as will be shown in the next chapter, by excluding project costs that are not recorded in the private market.

Table 6.4   Recent Federal Interest Rates for Economic
Analysis and Repayment *

Fiscal Year	Project Formulation— B/C Ratio and Cost Allocation (percent)	Repayment— Water Supply Act of 1958 (percent)
1963	2.875	2.936
1964	3.000	3.046
1965	3.125	3.137
1966	3.125	3.222
1967	3.125	3.225
1968	3.250	3.253
1969	4.625 [1]	3.256
1970	4.875	3.342

* B. P. Blenn, *A Guide to Using Interest Factors in Economic Analysis of Water Projects* (Washington, D.C.: Government Printing Office, 1970), p. 14.
[1] Applies to latter half of year.

References and Readings

Bain, Joe S., *et al.*, *Northern California's Water Industry*. Baltimore: Johns Hopkins Press, 1966.
    An unusually comprehensive application of economic analysis to a regional water problem, in which benefit-cost analysis plays an important part.

Dorfman, Robert, ed., *Measuring Benefits of Government Investments*. Washington, D.C.: The Brookings Institution, 1965.
    A collection of articles ranging widely over the field of benefit-cost analysis.

Harberger, A. C., *et al.*, eds., *Benefit Cost Analysis 1971: An Aldine Annual*. Chicago: Aldine-Atherton, Inc., 1972.
    A collection of journal articles on the application of benefit-cost

analysis to a wide range of different kinds of investment projects and expenditure programs, including health and medical services, recreation, housing, and transportation as well as the usual area of water resource development.

Haveman, Robert H., *The Economic Performance of Public Investments; An Ex Post Evaluation of Water Resource Investments*. Baltimore: Johns Hopkins Press, 1972.

> A study sponsored by Resources for the Future that attempts to determine how well selected projects fulfill the original benefit-cost evaluation. The results suggest that on the whole projects tend to underachieve on benefits and overrun on costs.

Laycock, George, *The Diligent Destroyers*. New York: Ballantine Books, 1970.

> A strongly critical appraisal of the federal agencies, such as the Army Corps of Engineers and the Bureau of Reclamation, that undertake projects that cause environmental damage. Some attention is given to the use of benefit-cost analysis in justifying such undertakings.

McKean, Roland N., *Efficiency in Government Through Systems Analysis*. New York: John Wiley & Sons, 1958.

> One of the clearer explanations of the theory and application of benefit-cost analysis.

Subcommittee on Evaluation Standards, *Report to the Inter-Agency Committee on Water Resources—Proposed Practices for Economic Analysis*. Washington, D.C.: Government Printing Office, 1958.

> The federal handbook on benefit-cost practices more or less used as a guide by federal agencies.

Subcommittee on Priorities and Economy in Government, Joint Economic Committee, *Benefit-Cost Analyses of Federal Programs*. Washington, D.C.: Government Printing Office, 92nd Congress, 2nd Session, 1973.

> This Joint Committee Print includees the results of a survey of the evaluation practices of federal agencies in decision-making and a compendium of papers on various aspects of benefit-cost evaluation issues.

Chapter Seven

Benefit-Cost Analysis in Action— The Middle Snake River Hydroelectric Project

> *Let the Snake flow free ". . . for the way the river sings, the way its birds fly, the way the light plays upon its rocks in a grand pattern of form and color, for its exquisite harmonies."—The Sierra Club* [1]

> *The flat water reservoir would provide more recreation for more people than the present river with its dangerous rapids and fast moving water.—William C. Levy, Federal Power Commission examiner.* [2]

In the fall of 1805, when Lewis and Clark neared journey's end with only the Snake and Columbia rivers between them and the sea, this wild river system was the economic base of the Nez Percé, the Flathead, and the Chinook Indians. Captain Clark's journal describes the river's abundance:

I took 2 men and set out in a small canoe with a view to go as high up the Columbia river as the 1st fork . . . large scaffols of fish drying at every lodge, and piles of salmon lying, the squars

[1] Quoted in William C. Levy, *Presiding Examiner's Initial Decision on Remand, Projects Nos. 2243 and 2273* (Washington, D.C.: Federal Power Commission, February 23, 1971), p. 40.
[2] *Ibid.*, p. 38.

engaged prepareing them for the scaffol. a squar gave me a dried salmon. . . . This river is remarkably clear and crouded with salmon in maney places, I observe in assending great numbers of salmon dead on the shores, floating on the water and in the Bottom which can be seen at the debth of 20 feet.[3]

Today, the Indian still casts his net for the salmon as it swims up the rapids and leaps the falls to spawn in the reaches of the Snake and other tributaries of the Columbia. But the Snake and the Columbia no longer provide a passage to the sea impeded only by rapids and falls. In many places these rivers are raised high above their original banks, plugged by concrete masses that direct the water through generating equipment and frustrate the salmon in its return to the place of its birth. Below Hells Canyon Dam the Snake is still wild, a white-water river in a canyon where the banks are sometimes nearly vertical, but these rugged, unspoiled areas are marked for destruction as the Pacific Northwest raises its consumption of power. And the Indian—once dominant and unchallenged in his use of the river—now finds his fishing "rights" in dispute.

The white man's power plants have blocked much of the salmon's return to spawning waters in spite of fish ladders around the dams and attempts to trap and propagate salmon in areas where the spawning waters have been destroyed. And because the run of the salmon has decreased, the Indian's interception of the returning salmon competes with another of the white man's commercial interests—the West Coast salmon industry, which harvests the salmon in the Pacific Ocean, where it reaches its growth. The Indian is caught in the middle—between the use of the river for power production and its use for spawning to keep the ocean-salmon industry profitable.

By the middle of the twentieth century, the Columbia River system was laced with hydro dams, and a conflict over the use of the little remaining free-flowing river arose between those who wanted it free of more dams, to save a remnant of its original natural wildness, and those who saw the river system primarily as a series of sites for power plants. The Pacific Northwest's need

[3] *Original Journals of the Lewis and Clark Expedition, 1804–1806,* ed. by R. G. Thwaites, Vol. III (New York: Dodd, Mead, 1905), p. 122.

for more power has promoted a number of plans to harness the Middle Snake, which is the undeveloped reach of approximately 150 miles from Hells Canyon Dam to Lewiston, Idaho. The plans are extensive: dams for power and dams to check the turbulence of the peak-power water release upon the river, mechanical aerating equipment embedded in the river to restore the oxygen lost when the water is impounded behind the power dam, devices to trap and transport migrating fish around the man-made obstructions, and hatcheries to substitute for the lost spawning areas of the inundated river.

By conventional market standards, hydroelectric generation is the cheapest and cleanest method of power production. Its primary capital cost, for the dam and turbines, is the main expenditure; little outlay is necessary for operation and maintenance, and none for fuel. At the same time, no unwanted by-product, such as heat discharge or air pollution, accompanies the generation of hydroelectricity. Hydroelectric generation would be the ideal solution to the country's increased power needs in those areas where suitable sites are available if not for one disadvantage—the damming of free-flowing rivers to produce electricity grossly degrades the character of some rivers. It causes the accumulation behind the power dam of a large area of slack water that is lowered and raised in response to the needs for power, generally exposing an unseemly shore area. It may substitute flat-water use—boating, panfishing, water-skiing—for fast-water use—white-water canoeing, game fishing, wilderness travel. The opportunity cost of flat-water use is thus fast-water use. Obviously, how much we need of one depends upon how much we have of the other, but as a nation we are just becoming aware of this choice, and the market standard may be more a hindrance than a help in achieving the appropriate distribution.

Hydroelectric Power and the Pacific Northwest

Unlike the rest of the country, where most power installations are thermal plants, the Pacific Northwest has been largely dependent upon hydroelectric power. Until recently, the Columbia River and its tributaries have provided ample sites for power dams, and these rivers have been studded with power plants. Figure 7.1 shows the extent to which the Columbia River system has become a captive of the power industry. By comparison with other regions, the Pacific Northwest is deficient in coal resources, although abundant coal and oil shales are close by in the Rocky Mountain region. Now, however, sites for hydro-electric development are very scarce in the Columbia River system and plans for future power are based almost entirely upon nuclear-thermal generation.

Delays in bringing nuclear power plants into production have caused a shift to coal-fired thermal plants, however, and the vast gas and petroleum resources that will be available to this region if the Alaskan North Slope deposits are developed may consider-ably change the competitive position of these fuels. The planned North Slope-to-Edmonton Canadian gas pipeline may offer at least a partial solution to the region's need for additional power without significant air pollution. Natural gas is a virtually pollu-tion-free source of fuel for thermal power. The question is mainly whether the natural-gas pipeline through Canada will be completed in time to influence the plans for the Pacific North-west's future power production, which are presently committed to atomic plants at the rate of roughly one plant per year, largely relegating existing hydro plants to peaking output.

The Middle Snake River as a Power Plant

Before the Pacific Northwest power grid turns entirely to atomic power for future production, one of the last free-flowing stretches of the Snake River has been measured for hydroelectric development. The Snake River has its inception at the foot of the Teton Range in Wyoming and works its way through Idaho and Washington, where it finally joins the Columbia on the way to the sea. For a part of its course, from the Boise River to Lewiston, Idaho, the Snake serves as the boundary that separates Idaho from Oregon and Washington in the region of the Payette and Nezperce national forests—largely undeveloped and mostly semiwilderness.

This section of the river—the Middle Snake—is the last rem-

Figure 7.1. Hydroelectric projects of the Columbia River Basin *

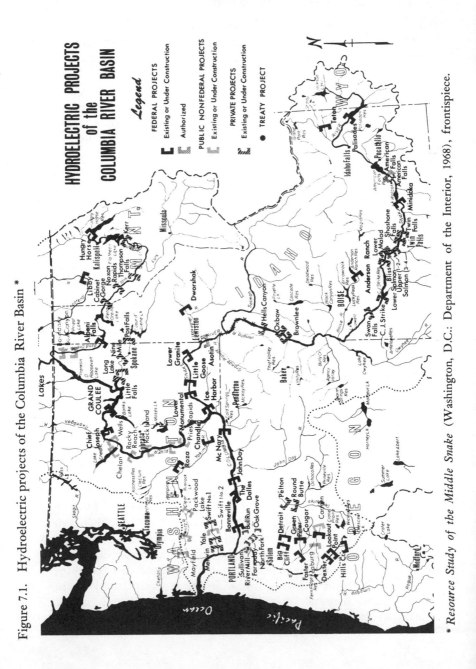

* Resource Study of the Middle Snake (Washington, D.C.: Deparment of the Interior, 1968), frontispiece.

nant of the wild river that Lewis and Clark traveled in the final
days of their westward journey. The Upper Snake, in contrast,
is smothered with hydro dams—fifteen in operation or under
construction from the shadows of the Tetons to the Hells Canyon
site. Below the Hells Canyon plant to the unconstructed but
authorized Army Corps of Engineers installation at Asotin, the
Snake runs free of man-made obstructions, and the steelhead
trout and the chinook and sockeye salmon that surmount the
many dams in the Lower Snake and the Columbia can spawn in
their birthplace—the Middle Snake and its tributaries: the Grande
Ronde, the Salmon, and the Imnaha.

But the Middle Snake is more than a breeding area for fish.
Along with the Salmon and limited portions of other tributaries, the Middle Snake is one of the last of its kind—a 150-
mile reach of wild, white-water river flowing through one of the
deepest gorges in the country, a sharp contrast to the slack, mill-
pond backwaters behind the many power dams on the rest of the
Snake and Columbia. Although the Middle Snake flows through
a gorge that is spectacularly steep in places, there are points of
access to the canyon floor, and wildlife of moderate abundance,
including cougar, elk, deer, and a variety of bird life, inhabit
the canyon. A power dam in the Middle Snake will not only turn
a river into a pond and endanger or eliminate the migratory and
resident game fish in the Snake; it will destroy a semiwilderness
area and its wildlife.

The Federal Power Commission
and the Middle Snake

The Federal Power Commission understands its primary function to be that of "assuring an abundant supply of electric energy
throughout the United States with the greatest possible economy and with regard to the proper utilization and conservation
of natural resources." [4] The FPC has interpreted this responsibility to mean the promotion of hydroelectric power wherever

[4] Section 202(a), Federal Power Act (16 U.S.C. 791–825).

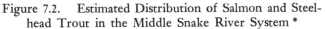

Figure 7.2.   Estimated Distribution of Salmon and Steelhead Trout in the Middle Snake River System *

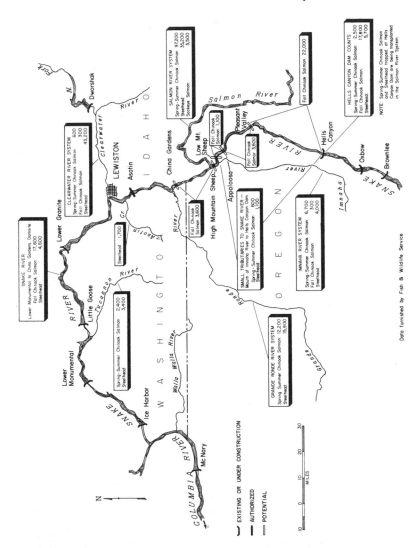

* *Resource Study of the Middle Snake* (Washington, D.C.: Department
of the Interior, 1968), data from the Fish and Wildlife Service.

possible. With an unyielding singleness of purpose, the Commission has promoted the development of hydroelectric power in the United States until there are few remaining economically feasible sites.

Middle Snake Power Sites

A brief inspection of Figure 7.1 shows how extensive is the network of hydroelectric power plants in the Pacific Northwest —the area is virtually saturated save for the reach of Middle Snake from Hells Canyon Dam to Asotin. This part of the river —shown in detail in Figure 7.2—affords the physical opportunity for four possible hydroelectric dams or combinations of dams: Appaloosa dam and Low Mountain Sheep reregulating dam; High Mountain Sheep dam and China Gardens reregulating dam; High Mountain Sheep dam without a reregulating installation; and Pleasant Valley dam and Low Mountain Sheep reregulating dam. (The main dam, such as High Mountain Sheep, is solely designed for power production, whereas the lower site, the reregulating dam, such as China Gardens, is a secondary source of power generation but mainly controls the flow of water downstream, decreasing the surges of the river that result from peaking power releases at the main dam.)

The Middle Snake: A Federal Interagency Struggle

The Federal Power Commission's involvement with the Middle Snake has been long and controversial. The dispute started quietly in the fall of 1954 when the Pacific Northwest Power Company, a private electric utility, filed with the FPC for a permit to construct a hydroelectric power project in the Middle Snake. Years later, on February 23, 1971, the FPC examiner recommended that a license be granted to build a hydroelectric dam in the Middle Snake. The license was issued to a consortium of public and private utilities, of which the Pacific Northwest Power Company was a leading applicant, but between the time of the original application and the 1971 decision, over 28,461 pages of transcript and 1,436 exhibits had been reviewed, and two court actions—one involving the United States Supreme Court—and numerous hearings had taken place. And still the issue is not resolved. The FPC can overturn the examiner's 1971 decision, and Congress can take action that will void it if it is upheld by the FPC.

In an early finding for the Pacific Northwest Power Company, the Federal Power Commission rejected a similar application by a public group, the Washington Public Power Supply Company (which subsequently joined forces with Pacific Northwest Power) and held against the Secretary of the Interior, who requested the postponement of licensing either applicant while the issue was studied further. Later, Secretary of the Interior Udall urged the FPC to recommend to Congress that the federal government construct the hydroelectric project, and still later—after successful court action—Secretary of the Interior Hickel withdrew the Interior Department's recommendation for federal hydro construction and went on record as opposing any Middle Snake power development.

In the meantime, however, the United States Circuit Court of Appeals of the District of Columbia, to which the Secretary of the Interior had carried his appeal of the Federal Power Commission ruling, upheld the Commission, and the Secretary of the Interior found it necessary to take the case to the United States Supreme Court. In 1967 this court reversed the FPC and addressed itself both to the question of whether the Middle Snake project should be federally sponsored and to the broader environmental issue of whether the project should be undertaken at all. In reaching this decision, there is little doubt that the Court's strong concern over the environment was greatly influenced by the famous conservationist Justice William O. Douglas, who wrote the majority decision.

The court held in part that

> on the Snake-Columbia waterway between High Mountain Sheep and the ocean, eight hydroelectric dams have been built and another authorized. These are federal projects; and if another dam is to be built, the question whether it should be under federal auspices looms large. Timed releases of stored water at High Mountain Sheep may affect navigability; they may affect hydro-

electric production of the downstreams dams when the river level is too low for the generators to be operated at maximum production; they may affect irrigation; and they may protect salmon runs when the water downstream is too hot or insufficiently oxygenated. Federal versus private or municipal control may conceivably make a vast difference in the functioning of the vast river complex.

Beyond that is the question whether any dam should be constructed . . . whether preservation of the reaches of the river affected would be more desirable and in the public interest than the proposed development.[5]

The National Environmental Policy Act

Justice Douglas' majority decision was strongly reinforced by the National Environmental Policy Act, signed by President Nixon on January 1, 1970, which requires

all agencies of the Federal Government . . . [to] include in every recommendation or report on proposals for legislative and other major Federal actions significantly affecting the quality of the human environment, a detailed statement by the responsible official on (i) the environmental impact of the proposed action, (ii) any adverse environmental effects which cannot be avoided should the proposal be implemented, (iii) alternatives to the proposed action, (iv) the relationship between local short-run uses of man's environment and enhancement of long-term productivity, and (v) any irreversible and irretrievable commitments of resources which would be involved in the proposed action should it be implemented.

The National Environmental Policy Act imposes upon the Federal Power Commission and all other federal agencies the specific obligation to minimize environmental damage, especially where the impact is irreversible, as in the case of power development in the Middle Snake. The Environmental Policy Act broadens the criteria for determining the desirability of hydro-electric-power production. No longer is hydroelectric-power development to be decided solely on whether the power can be

5 Udall v. FPC, U. S. Supreme Court *Reports,* 18 L ed 2d 869.

marketed, which was the basis for the original FPC approval in the case of the Storm King project, Consolidated Edison of New York's development that uses the top of Storm King Mountain overlooking the Hudson River for a storage reservoir. Conservationists contested the Storm King development on environmental grounds and the New York Supreme Court held that Federal Power Commission certification for such projects must include consideration of the project's environmental impact. Responding to a different New York case in late 1972, the FPC accepted the responsibility for undertaking environmental-impact studies by its own staff rather than relying upon those applying for project certification.

The introductory statement of the FPC's *Presiding Examiner's Initial Decision on Remand* (1971) acknowledges the environmental obligation and asserts unequivocally that "all environmental questions have been fully covered in the record by competent and responsible witnesses." [6] But given a 1971 decision that is essentially the same as that of fifteen years before —to build a power dam in the Middle Snake—it can reasonably be questioned whether the admonition of the Supreme Court and the requisites of the Environmental Policy Act were really influential in the decision reached.

The Four Plans for Power

The issue faced by the Federal Power Commission examiner was not simply that of dam or no dam in the Middle Snake. If he decided in favor of a hydroelectric development, he was faced with a choice of sites. The Department of the Interior's *Resource Study of the Middle Snake*, made following the Supreme Court decision, identifies four sites in the Middle Snake, each with a different generating capacity and different environmental effects. The installations at the four sites are also subject to variations, which include pump generators to return water above the Appaloosa and Pleasant Valley dams, but only the four basic plans will be considered here.

[6] William C. Levy, *op. cit.*, p. 6.

Plan 1: Appaloosa and Low Mountain Sheep

Table 7.1.   Plan 1: Appaloosa and Low Mountain Sheep *

Output: 2,500 megawatts

Benefits: $56,463,000 annual equivalent

Power		$49,267,000
Fish and wildlife enhancement		6,590,000
Resident fish	$ 189,000	
Anadromous fish	$6,401,000	
Recreation		406,000
Flood Control		200,000
	Total	$56,463,000

Costs: $20,770,000 annual equivalent

Federal investment		$16,083,000
Annual operating		4,687,000
	Total	$20,770,000

B/C ratio: 2.72/1
Interest rate: 3¼ percent
Project life: 100 years

* Data from *Resource Study of the Middle Snake* (Washington, D.C.: Department of the Interior, 1968), Part VI, pp. 3–6.

The Appaloosa project (see Table 7.1) consists of two dams and two power plants. The main power installation located at Appaloosa contains six 350-megawatt generating units plus one 400-megawatt unit that is located in the reregulating dam at Low Mountain Sheep. The combined output for the complex is 2,500 megawatts. Compared to other sites, such as Plans 2 and 4, the Appaloosa complex preempts a relatively short stretch of the Middle Snake. Because it lies above the Salmon and Imnaha rivers, the project would interfere less with the migration of salmon and trout than would a dam at High Mountain Sheep, which would cause massive fish destruction. The Appaloosa development would impair spawning of anadromous fish* in the area of the

* Anadromous fish, such as salmon and steelhead trout, are born in fresh water and migrate to the sea, where they grow to maturity, later returning to the river of their birth to spawn.

Snake River below Hells Canyon Dam, but this is the last stop of the migrants in any case. Fish that reach this point cannot ascend beyond Hells Canyon Dam and those that can be trapped are artificially propagated in hatcheries. Additional fish loss would undoubtedly take place because of the obstruction of the Appaloosa dam, but it is contended by the Interior *Resource Study* that the Appaloosa project would actually enhance the fish population of the Middle Snake.

A unique feature of the Appaloosa power project is a multi-level intake system to permit water to be withdrawn from five different levels of the reservoir in generating power. By selecting water from a lower level, the Middle Snake below the Appaloosa dam could be cooled, thereby improving fish habitat during the summer and fall. Since the oxygen content in water decreases at lower temperature levels, however, it would be necessary to reintroduce oxygen into the cooler water by aeration. This would be achieved by injecting air into the reregulating area from a network of pipes beneath the surface of the river.* A look at the map (Figure 7.2) is enough to show that the Middle Snake inherits moderately low-quality water from the slack-water storage areas of Brownlee, Oxbow, and Hells Canyon dams. The combination of slack water and high phosphorous and nitrogen content has produced floating algal slimes in the storage areas, which further deplete the oxygen supply when the algae die.

Because it would restore the oxygen content and improve the temperature of the water so that it is more hospitable to fish life, the Appaloosa project is assigned an annual benefit of $6,590,000 for fish and wildlife enhancement.† The Appaloosa

---

* The aeration process is not without risk to the fish that it is designed to protect. By forcing air into water under pressure, aeration may increase dissolved nitrogen in the water beyond the saturation level, resulting in fish killed by embolism. This has become increasingly frequent in areas below dams in the Pacific Northwest.

† The FPC examiner disputes the inclusion of $6,401,000 as an anadromous fish benefit from water-temperature control. He says, "The use of these figures is not justified. We cannot assume improved water quality and more spawning downstream in the face of past history of deterioration as each new dam is constructed. Moreover, the assignment of any specific

pool would destroy a spawning area for approximately 44,500 fall Chinook and lesser numbers of spring Chinook and steelhead, requiring the construction of collection and hatchery facilities at the reregulating dam in order to compensate for their loss. The capital cost of these facilities is estimated at $22,600,000, with an annual operating cost of $1,018,000. (These costs are not included in the figure in Table 7.1.) In addition, the Appaloosa pool would displace and therefore eventually destroy an estimated 960 deer and 1,840 game birds. Other wildlife losses are neither estimated nor evaluated, but they would obviously be of equivalent magnitude.

At an interest rate of 3¼ percent and a project life of a hundred years, this gives Appaloosa the highest benefit-cost ratio of the four projects—2.72 to 1. The project is also assigned the highest annual equivalent for recreational benefits of any of the plans, although the difference among projects is not great. Flood-control benefits—the value of property that would be saved from destruction by checking high river flow—is the lowest of all the benefits and relatively unimportant. All the plans are roughly the same in this category, except Plan 4, the Pleasant Valley project, which is less than half that of the others.

John Krutilla, senior research associate for Resources for the Future and a leading water-resource economist, reached quite different conclusions. He testified at the FPC hearings on the basis of a detailed analysis of the four plans in terms of 1967 prices that the Appaloosa project was the least desirable economically. Employing a 9-percent rate of interest, which he considered a more realistic measure of the opportunity cost of capital, Krutilla found only Plan 2, High Mountain Sheep and China Gardens, to be economically feasible—that is, an investment in which the benefits exceed costs—and this only by totally disregarding the destruction of the river's natural character.

---

number or dollar amount is pure speculation—'a calculated guess.' " (*Ibid.*, p. 35.) The examiner's refusal to accept the anadromous fish benefits in the Appaloosa project eliminates this site as a possible choice for licensing at this hearing.

Plan 2: High Mountain Sheep and China Gardens

This combination of dams would produce the greatest power output of any of the plans, 3,100 megawatts (see Table 7.2),

Table 7.2. Plan 2: High Mountain Sheep and China Gardens *

Output: 3,100 megawatts

Benefits: $61,329,000 annual equivalent

Power	$60,748,000
Fish and wildlife enhancement	none†
Recreation	336,000
Flood Control	245,000
Total	$61,329,000

Costs: $24,275,000 annual equivalent

Federal investment	$18,705,000
Annual operating	5,570,000
Total	$24,275,000

B/C ratio: 2.53/1 (acknowledged as misleading)
Interest rate: 3¼ percent
Project life: 100 years

* Data from *Resource Study of the Middle Snake* (Washington, D.C.: Department of the Interior, 1968), Part VI, pp. 14–15.
† Very large adverse effects on anadromous fish.

but it would virtually eliminate the large anadromous fish population that spawns in the Salmon and Imnaha rivers unless a satisfactory fish passage around the dams were devised. The Federal Power Commission had previously concluded that fish passages could be constructed around dams that would permit the Columbia-Snake River fish populations to be maintained without serious depletion. Later, however, fishery authorities determined from the experience of Hells Canyon Dam and other installations that fish-passage structures are generally unsatisfactory. As a result, attempts to maintain fish passage beyond China Gardens, High Mountain Sheep, and Hells Canyon Dam have been abandoned and instead, those fish that could be trapped would be subjected to artificial hatchery propagation. Such procedures are costly and necessarily result in a decrease in the fish population as compared with natural conditions.

The High Mountain Sheep and China Gardens project provides—as does Plan 1—multilevel intakes to the main dam's generating turbines, and mechanical aeration of the downstream discharge, but the extraordinary disorienting effect of blocking off access to the Salmon and Imnaha rivers, quite aside from the questionable efficiency of the trapping devices, is likely to have harmful effects upon the fish populations. The benefit-cost ratio of 2.53 to 1, which is based on a 3¼-percent interest rate and a hundred-year project life, does not reflect the adverse effect upon the migratory fish population of this reach of the Snake—one of the most productive aquatically of the whole Columbia-Snake system. The harmful effect of the project upon the fish population is acknowledged, but not included as a cost in computing the 2.53-to-1 ratio. In 1965, the net value of the Columbia River anadromous fish run was estimated at $13,805,000, with the Snake and Salmon rivers responsible for the largest single runs of spring Chinook and steelhead as well as fall Chinook (see Figure 7.2).

With or without fish passages, eventual total loss of the Salmon River and Imnaha River anadromous fish population can be expected. Spawning waters for 48,000 fall Chinook would be eliminated by the reservoir pool, and 1,450 deer and 2,570 upland game birds would be lost through inundation of habitat. The fishery loss is impressive, estimated by the Fish and Wildlife Service at 2,104,000 angler-days and 5,745,300 pounds of commercial fish harvested annually.

Although the destructive impact of the High Mountain Sheep –China Gardens project upon the migratory fisheries was not accounted for in the benefit-cost ratio, there is no doubt that the pressure from commercial and sports fishing interests was an important factor in the FPC decision not to consider development of this site in spite of the examiner's conclusion that it provided "greater power benefits than Pleasant Valley or Appaloosa with re-regulation at Mountain Sheep." [7]

[7] *Ibid.*, p. 12.

Plan 3: High Mountain Sheep Without China Gardens

The High Mountain Sheep project without the reregulating dam at China Gardens produces somewhat less than half the power of Plan 2—1,400 megawatts instead of 3,100 megawatts (see Table 7.3). Based on an interest rate of 3¼ percent and a

Table 7.3.   Plan 3: High Mountain Sheep Without China Gardens *

Output:	1,400 megawatts	
Benefits:	$36,525,000 annual equivalent	
	Power	$35,944,000
	Fish and wildlife enhancement	none†
	Recreation	336,000
	Flood control	245,000
	Total	$36,525,000
Costs:	$13,557,000 annual equivalent	
	Federal investment	$10,377,000
	Annual operating	3,180,000
	Total	$13,557,000

B/C ratio: 2.69/1 (acknowledged as misleading)
Interest rate: 3¼ percent
Project life: 100 years

* Data from *Resource Study of the Middle Snake* (Washington, D.C.: Department of the Interior, 1968), Part VI, pp. 19–24.
† Very large adverse effects on anadromous fish.

project life of a hundred years, Plan 3 has a benefit-cost ratio of 2.69 to 1, which is somewhat higher than the ratio for Plan 2, with the dam at China Gardens, but as in the former case, this ratio is acknowledged to be deceptively high because it does not account for damage to the migratory fish population. Although a dam at High Mountain Sheep does not seal off the Salmon River tributary from the Snake, the extraordinary water turbulence below the dam would be seriously disruptive of the fish life. In fact, the absence of the China Gardens dam and after-bay makes it more difficult to aerate the water below the High Mountain Sheep dam, even though aerating devices are a part of the equipment of Plan 3. Flow surges of water during the production of power for peak demand could therefore be expected to reduce the oxygen content of the water below the power plant as well as to cause significant temperature fluctuations. As a result, the construction of Plan 3 would be likely eventually to eliminate all anadromous fish using water upstream from China Gardens. Much the same wildlife habitat loss as in the case of Plan 2 would result from Plan 3.

Plan 4: Pleasant Valley and Low Mountain Sheep

This complex of two dams is one of the smallest of the four plans, measured either in reservoir storage or power production (see Table 7.4). The original plant at Pleasant Valley would yield 1,700 megawatts of power and the Low Mountain Sheep reregulating dam would produce 400 megawatts. Ultimately, however, the capacity of Pleasant Valley–Low Mountain Sheep could be raised to 3,200 megawatts, including a provision for

Table 7.4 Plans 4 and 4A
Plan 4: Pleasant Valley *

Output:	1,700 megawatts	
Benefits:	$44,544,000 annual equivalent	
	Power	$44,165,000
	Fish and wildlife enhancement	none
	Recreation	305,000
	Flood control	74,000
	Total	$44,544,000
Costs:	$18,987,000 annual equivalent	
	Federal investment	$15,021,000
	Annual operating	3,966,000
	Total	$18,987,000

B/C ratio: 2.35/1
Interest rate: 3¼ percent
Project life: 100 years

Plan 4A: Pleasant Valley–Low Mountain Sheep *
(The Pumped-Storage Addition to Plan 4)

Output: 400 megawatts

Benefits: $11,504,000 annual equivalent

Costs: $6,721,000 annual equivalent

B/C ratio: 1.71/1
Interest rate: 3¼ percent
Project life: 85 years

* Data from *Resource Study of the Middle Snake* (Washington, D.C.:
Department of the Interior, 1968), Part VI, pp. 24–29.

pumped storage.* Since the usable storage behind the Pleasant
Valley dam is limited, however, Plan 4 does not incorporate
devices for downstream temperature control or oxygen restoration.

Although the storage capacity of the Pleasant Valley pool is
too small to afford significant downstream temperature control,
the impounded waters would suffer oxygen loss at the lower
levels, and algal bloom on the surface waters would occur during
the summer. The algal bloom would impair the use of the
Pleasant Valley pool for recreation as well as eliminate much of
the resident fish population of this reach of the Snake. The loss
of high-quality stream fishing—smallmouth bass, trout, salmon—
is estimated at 15,000 angler-days, and could only in part be com-
pensated for by hatchery production of reservoir-tolerant fish,
generally considered inferior by the dedicated angler.

The adverse effect of the Pleasant Valley dam complex upon
anadromous fish would involve the destruction of the spawning
grounds for a moderately large number of fish—44,500 fall
Chinook and smaller numbers of spring Chinook and steelhead
trout. (In the absence of the Appaloosa dam, the Pleasant Valley
dam simply obstructs the same fish run higher in the Middle
Snake; see Figure 7.2.) But in comparison with Plans 2 and 3,
which involve dams at High Mountain Sheep, fish destruction

* Pumped storage provides for the return of waters above the generating
dam during off-peak periods, for reuse during later peak periods.

would be less with the Pleasant Valley development and down-stream recreational opportunities would be relatively unaffected. The creation of the Pleasant Valley pool would inundate wild-life habitat, however, and it is estimated that 500 deer and 960 upland game birds would be lost as a result. Other wildlife losses of equivalent magnitude would occur under this plan.

The spawning loss from the Pleasant Valley reservoir could be mitigated by building collection facilities in the Low Mountain Sheep reregulating dam at a capital cost of $22,600,000 and an operating cost of $1,018,000 annually. A cost for the loss of wild-life habitat can be assessed on the basis of the days of hunting forgone, but since this is but a partial measure of the worth of wildlife in the natural setting of the Middle Snake, such an es-timate is an understatement. Neither of these costs is included in the figure in Table 7.4.

The Fish and Wildlife Service, which is responsible for the determination of losses that result from the destruction of game species and their habitat, is concerned almost exclusively with the opportunities for hunting and sports and commercial fishing. But there is a vast army of outdoor enthusiasts who do not hunt or fish—hikers, canoeists, nature photographers, bird watchers, and simply scenery lookers—that would value the sight of a bald or golden eagle on the wing as much as the hunter prizes a Hun-garian partridge in the bag. As a national asset, the general out-door use of the Middle Snake may far exceed its hunting and fishing value. But such general uses are not so easily measured or so well represented in the bureaucratic system.

The Middle Snake as Wilderness

Within the past decade, the federal government has established the Bureau of Outdoor Recreation in an attempt to assess the future demand for outdoor recreation and provide for its fur-therance. The Bureau of Outdoor Recreation contributed a re-port to the Department of the Interior's *Resoucre Study of the Middle Snake*, but its analysis had none of the impact of the

Fish and Wildlife Service's assessment of angler-days forgone and mitigation costs for fish loss. The Bureau of Outdoor Recreation treats the loss of the free-flowing Middle Snake as follows:

> The cost of giving up recreational values not replaced by the project are not reflected in overall project costs because benefits of the recreation use of the free-flowing river were not evaluated in monetary terms. The increment of value reflecting the higher quality of the recreation experience provided by the free-flowing river, as contrasted with reservoir recreation, is lost as are some of the broader intangible values. Because these undetermined and intangible values lost add to the economic cost of the whole project, they need to be adequately weighed in decisions concerning project development.[8]

It seems unlikely that this correct but essentially ineffectual observation had any real influence upon the FPC examiner. In the first place, the examiner appears to believe that a little bit of semiwilderness Snake River will go a very long way, and even if most of it is used for power production, there will still be portions sandwiched between dams that are sufficient to meet the need. If not, then there are other rivers nearby that are just as good—the Salmon, for example. In the second place, the examiner considers the public better served by reservoir recreation: It will accommodate more people with less danger. Obviously, a conflict of values difficult to compromise is involved between the position of the Federal Power Commission, dedicated to the development of hydroelectric power, and those taking a different view of the public interest. Indeed, the hydropower advocates find the suggestion that the last undeveloped reach of the Snake remain free of power plants nothing less than subversive.* The

[8] "Bureau of Outdoor Recreation Analysis," *Resource Study of the Middle Snake* (Washington, D.C.: Department of the Interior, 1968), p. 56.

* A dialogue between Floyd Dominy, at the time commissioner of the Bureau of Reclamation, and David Brower, former executive director of the Sierra Club and later head of the Friends of the Earth, presents the conflict in values of a power/irrigation advocate and a wilderness preservationist. Related against the background of a float trip down the Colorado River—which contains a number of Bureau of Reclamation dams and plans for more—Commissioner Dominy finds the river better off as a result of Reclamation's dams, and regards conservationists as little more than ob-

Bonneville Power Administraton, the federal agency with juris-diction over power production from the Bonneville Dam and other installations on the Columbia River, finds it difficult to con-ceive of the Snake River in terms of anything but kilowatts. In the Department of the Interior study, the Bonneville Power Ad-ministration report says:

> The Middle Snake Canyon location is extremely strategic in the Pacific Northwest water and power economy. To weaken this system by depriving it of the major remaining potential storage project of the Middle Snake River subverts and undermines the legislative policies and intent of Congress in its enactment of the Bonneville Power Act.[9]

The Bonneville Power Administration and—to only a degree less—the FPC examiner see the undammed area of the Middle Snake as an incompleted hydroelectric system, unproductive and wasteful; others, such as the economist John Krutilla, see this undeveloped region of the Snake as increasing in value if it retains its unique semiwilderness character, free of power develop-ment. Krutilla's position is that the Middle Snake canyon

> may have few, if any, close substitutes. Moreover, if the present environment is adversely altered, its reproduction is not pos-sible. In short, while rare natural phenomena can be reduced in supply, they cannot be expanded by the works of man. They represent irreplaceable assets not subject to reproduction. Now if the supply is thus fixed but the demand for the services of this asset increases, it is an irreplaceable asset with an increas-ing annual benefit.[10]

At the same time that the pressure to add hydroelectric in-stallations rises with the demand for power in the West, the

---

structionists. He boasts to Brower, "I'm a greater conservationist than you are, by far. I do things. I make things available to man. Unregulated, the Colorado River wouldn't be worth a good God damn to anybody. . . ." John McPhee, *Encounters with the Archdruid* (New York: Farrar, Straus & Giroux, Inc., 1971, p. 240.)

[9] "Middle Snake River Resource Study—Bonneville Power Administra-tion," *Ibid.*, p. II-4.

[10] John V. Krutilla, *Testimony* Before the Federal Power Commission on the Middle Snake Issue (Washington, D.C.: mimeographed, 1970), p. 29.

value of the Middle Snake as a semiwilderness area also increases. The changing worth of a commercially undeveloped
Snake can be shown by a variant of the familiar supply-and-
demand illustration. In the usual supply-demand relationship,
supply responds to price with increased offerings as prices rise
and reduced offerings as prices fall; demand conventionally
reacts in just the opposite way; a higher price discourages sales,
while a lower price increases purchases. In Figure 7.3, however,
the supply of semiwilderness cannot be increased in response to
higher prices or increased demand, as is indicated by the per-
pendicular supply lines at 1930 and 1973. The destruction of
wilderness is not reversible and the supply of wilderness does
not respond to price in the usual sense. Indeed, the supply of
wilderness over the years has continuously decreased, and in
1973 the Middle Snake had approximately 150 miles of remaining semiwilderness.

Although Figure 7.3 is hypothetical, it conforms to the his-

Figure 7.3.   Value of Snake River Semiwilderness over Time

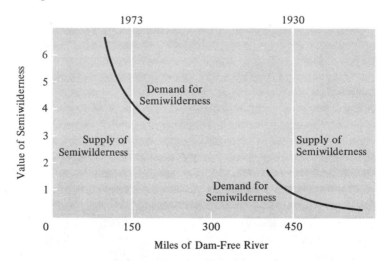

toric pattern of national development. It should be noted, however, that the vertical axis of Figure 7.3, sharply defined numerically, is not expressed in cardinal units that can be compared

with other value expressions, such as dollars, but is simply a scale indicating that a value of 5, for example, is greater than a value of 4. The demand curve for semiwilderness in 1973 is higher than that for 1930 because the increase in population and income in the later period causes a higher valuation to be placed upon a given amount of semiwilderness. More money and more people mean more demand for a resource. If the supply of a resource cannot be increased—as in the case of the dam-free portion of the Snake River—increasing income and population necessarily push up the value of the scarce resource.

How the "Costs" of Thermal Power Become the "Benefits" of Hydro

In the determination of the benefit figure in benefit-cost analysis, a few federal agencies have come to rely upon what is called the "alternate source" approach to the measurement of benefits. Normally, the benefit side of the ratio is computed from the market value of the commodity or service, such as the price of the agricultural crop raised on an irrigation project or the assessed value of the property protected from water damage by a flood-control project. In some cases, however, instead of computing benefits from the price of the product or service produced by the project, such as the expected kilowatt rates for a hydroelectric plant or freight rates for a canal development, the benefit figures of such projects are based on the *costs* of obtaining the same service by the most likely alternative source of supply. In the case of hydropower, the most likely alternative source of power is thermal generation.

The reasons for employing the alternate source approach to benefit determination are not completely apparent. The alternate source approach is obviously a substitute for the use of market data. The Federal Power Commission, which undertakes benefit cost studies of hydroelectric installations for the other federal agencies, uses the thermal alternative as a measure of the benefits of hydro production in part because the power-rate structure that is appropriate for the market of one plant may not be appropriate for another. Since the power rates vary in terms of amount and time of use, utilities with different customer composition and time distribution of sales will experience different revenue returns. But whatever the reason for its use, the alternate-source approach provides an extremely favorable frame of reference for the determination of project benefits.

Relying upon the cost of the most likely alternative for the measure of benefits means that there is little danger of understating the project's worth. In the case of hydropower, for example, the thermal alternative is almost always a higher-cost method of producing power. As a result, the alternate source approach builds in a benefit cushion that holds the benefit-cost ratio farther above unity than would be the case if the market rates of hydropower were relied upon to determine benefits. Consequently, the analysis is able to produce a higher benefit-cost ratio and thereby record greater justification for development of the project.

Benefits and Costs—An Exercise in Choice

In Plans 1 through 4, benefit-cost ratios for the Middle Snake hydro opportunities are recorded, in some cases with the stipulation that the ratio is "acknowledged as misleading" because no cost computation is made for extensive fish and wildlife destruction. These ratios were prepared for the Department of the Interior *Resource Study* under the direction of the Bureau of Reclamation, and all plans have benefit-cost ratios above unity, but Plan 1—the Appaloosa project—ranks first.

In benefit-cost analyses prepared by the Federal Power Commission staff for the use of the FPC examiner, only Plan 2—High Mountain Sheep with China Gardens—is able to produce power at a lower cost than the most economic thermal alternative. And when the costs of the loss of the free-flowing character of the Middle Snake are assessed against this project, costs computed by John Krutilla to range between $700,000 and $1,100,000 annually, the High Mountain Sheep–China Gardens development also fails to pass the test of economic feasibility.

Considering such environmental factors together with the marginal character of the projects, the FPC staff report to the examiner found *none* of the projects economically justified. The examiner did not accept the staff's reasoning, however, contending that "it should be emphasized that feasibility studies, however useful and detailed, remain speculative models of a future that eludes prediction. They are aids, not substitutes for decision-making." [11]

The Case of the Applicants

The consortium of private and public utilities seeking a license to build a power dam on the Middle Snake—the Pacific Northwest Power Company and the Washington Public Power Supply System—also presented to the Federal Power Commission examiner benefit-cost analyses, but employing different considerations from those of the Department of the Interior. The capital investment in the applicants' plans was less, and the benefit-cost ratios were below those of the Interior Department. The applicants' lower benefit-cost ratios, ranging between 1.426 to 1 and 1.194 to 1, are primarily the result of using a higher rate of interest to compute costs and discount benefits and a shorter period of analysis. Although the applicants employ a higher rate of interest and a shorter period of analysis, the benefit-cost ratio is kept above unity, mainly by employing lower construction-cost estimates and omitting major items of cost, such as those for downstream temperature control, oxygenation, recreation, and taxes.

Relying upon minimum design of facilities and low construction-cost estimates may appear to involve certain obvious hazards, such as later difficulty in meeting escalating costs. On the whole, however, the use of unrealistic cost estimates does not carry the same prospect of economic distress for the public project or the private electric utility that it does for other kinds of business activity. Public and private investments in power production are in large part insulated from some of the harsher forces of the

[11] William C. Levy, *op. cit.*, p. 28.

market process. The public project, once approved, will certainly be continued in spite of adjustments upward in cost and enlargement in the scale of the undertaking. Moreover, the private power utility, selling its service in a protected market during a period of rising demand, generally faces no problem of operating its equipment to near-capacity production.

In recent times, the demand for power has risen steadily at the same time that rates have been adjusted upward. There is no indication that this trend is likely to be reversed. In any case, the obvious remedy for the underestimation of costs is a rate increase—and in turn, by far the most persuasive justification to a utility regulatory commission for a rate increase is higher utility costs. As a result, in the strategy of obtaining a hydro license, there is nothing to lose and much to gain in understating costs —thereby ensuring an attractive benefit-cost ratio. Later, a petition for a rate increase can prevent the utility's experiencing financial distress.

The Middle Snake as a Wild River

The Wild and Scenic Rivers Act of 1968 obligates the Secretary of Agriculture and the Secretary of the Interior to determine whether a river should be recommended to Congress for inclusion in the National Rivers System because of its unique wild or scenic character. The secretaries of Agriculture and the Interior have urged Congress to include the Middle Snake in this protected category, and this action, together with the request for a moratorium for further study, persuaded the Federal Power Commission examiner to grant the license to develop the Pleasant Valley power site after a five-year moratorium. The FPC examiner's decision is subject to review by the full Commission.

If the designation of "wild river" is made permanent by Congress, this will not only eliminate the threat of power development at the four major sites, but will presumably prevent the development of the Army Corps of Engineers' project at the Asotin site near Lewiston, Idaho. The Asotin project has been authorized by Congress, but no appropriation has been voted and no date for construction has been established. Many of the problems for fish passage noted in connection with other dam sites in the Middle Snake would apply to a power development at Asotin.

Why Doesn't the Environmental Policy Act Protect the Middle Snake River?

In the Federal Power Commission hearing following the Supreme Court decision in 1967, the examiner was faced with deciding upon the reapplication by the Pacific Northwest and Washington Power group for a license of either the Appaloosa–Low Mountain Sheep or the Pleasant Valley–Low Mountain Sheep power site. The application for a license to develop the High Mountain Sheep site was abandoned by the applicants following the Supreme Court decision. In licensing power development for the Middle Snake in spite of the doubts raised in the Supreme Court decision and the increasing environmental concern indicated by the passage of the National Environmental Policy Act, the FPC examiner demonstrated a consistency that has little parallel either within the federal bureaucracy or among those outside the government who have examined this issue.

The Interior Department's *Resource Study*, although a massive document and the combined effort of a number of federal agencies, shows either an inability or an unwillingness to cope with the nondevelopment alternative. It is in fact a holdover from the period before the passage of the National Environmental Policy Act. Of the eight federal agencies that contributed to the study, only the Fish and Wildlife Service and the Bureau of Outdoor Recreation prepared material that indicated any recognition of the worth of the Middle Snake for any purpose other than power production. The other agencies—among them the Bonneville Power Administration, the Federal Water Quality Administration, and the Bureau of Reclamation have built up staffs talented primarily in promoting objectives that were either not threatened by power production on the Middle Snake or would be enhanced by this development. This was not the case for the Fish and Wildlife and Outdoor Recreation agencies.

As a result, "impact studies" by the agencies responsible for undertaking or cooperating in the project are seldom likely to provide either a very broad view of the public interest or disinterested analysis. Moreover, environmental impact studies require a range of talent that did not become available in the federal agencies through the passage of the National Environmental Policy Act. Time is required for recruitment of staff and development of methods of analysis. Until then, environmental factors in government projects will be acknowledged as extremely important, superficially examined, and generally disregarded—as occurred in the FPC examiner's review of the Middle Snake hearing on remand.

What Is the Economic Cost of Power Development of the Middle Snake?

Perhaps the most ironic aspect of the extended Middle Snake controversy is the failure to identify the economic cost of keeping the Middle Snake as a free-flowing river—especially in view of the use by the Federal Power Commission of alternate thermal costs as a measure of Middle Snake hydro benefits.

Obviously the supply of power in the Pacific Northwest is not limited to hydro production. Thermal generation is easily available at somewhat higher production costs and somewhat lower transmission costs, in terms of the traditional cost concepts of the Federal Power Commission. If power is not produced by Middle Snake hydro installations, it will be generated by other means —presumably thermal. The cost of not producing power by hydroelectric plants in the Middle Snake is therefore the difference between hydro costs and the thermal alternative—a trivial expenditure of resources to preserve the Middle Snake.

A free-flowing Middle Snake River does *not* mean less power for the Pacific Northwest. The Pleasant Valley installation licensed by the FPC examiner is designed to produce 1,700 megawatts of electricity. Adding 1,700 megawatts of thermal output instead of hydroelectric output to the Pacific Northwest grid would have an inappreciable effect upon power rates in that region. But adding a dam to the Middle Snake would involve a transcendent aesthetic change. There is no doubt about which is the greater cost.

References and Readings

Federal Power Commission, *Hydroelectric Power Evaluation*. Washington, D.C.: Government Printing Office, 1968.
> A useful description of the technical aspects of power production and some of the economic aspects of benefit-cost analysis.

Krutilla, John V., *Testimony* Before the Federal Power Commission on the Middle Snake Issue. Washington, D.C.: mimeographed, 1970.
> An excellent statement of the economic issues involved in power development of the Middle Snake River; it contains an unusually comprehensive quantification of recreation benefits.

Krutilla, John V., and Eckstein, Otto, *Multiple Purpose River Development: Studies in Economic Analysis*. Baltimore: Johns Hopkins Press, 1958.
> This book contains both an examination of the general issues involved in determining the worth of public investment and a series of case studies of government projects.

Levy, William C., *Presiding Examiner's Initial Decision on Remand, Projects No. 2243 and 2273*. Washington, D.C.: Federal Power Commission, February 23, 1971.
> The Federal Power Commission examiner's statement explaining his decision to license power production on the Middle Snake River.

Norton, Boyd, *Snake Wilderness*. San Francisco, Calif.: Sierra Club, 1972.
> This book is an impassioned plea for preservation of the Middle Snake. Chapter 3, "The Last Dam," traces the extensive bureaucratic and legislative maneuvering over the proposed hydroelectric development of the Middle Snake. Norton concludes, however, that the greater threat to Snake Wilderness is from the damming of the river to impound water for irrigation.

Resource Study of the Middle Snake. Washington, D.C.: Department of the Interior, 1968.
> A massive document made up of the contributions of various federal agences whose interests are affected by a hydroelectric project on the Middle Snake River.

Sander, Donald A., and Quint, Arnold H., *Initial and Reply Brief of Commission Staff Counsel—Pacific Northwest Power Company and Washington Public Power Supply System, Projects Nos. 2243/2273.* Washington, D.C.: Federal Power Commission, October 22, 1970.
This is the Federal Power Commission staff report recommending against power development of any of the Middle Snake River sites, for economic and aesthetic reasons. For two of these sites, Pleasant Valley–Low Mountain Sheep and Appaloosa–Low Mountain Sheep, the staff finds hydro generation more costly than alternative sources of power.

Subcommittee on Evaluation Standards, *Report to the Inter-Agency Committee on Water Resources—Proposed Practices for Economic Analysis.* Washington, D.C.: Government Printing Office, 1958.
A basic treatment of benefit-cost practices sometimes followed by the federal agencies.

PART III

Environmental Problem Areas

Chapter Eight

Energy—A Contest Between Demand and Supply

We in Colorado won't stand idly by while our environment is damaged for the sake of [providing power for] people in Los Angeles.—Lieutenant Governor John Vanderhoof of Colorado [1]

If you want to replace the internal-combustion engine with mass transit in our polluted cities, if you want to recycle aluminum and steel cans into useful products, if you are going to try to clean up the sewage and rivers and lakes, if you're going to clean the air, it will take enormous amounts of electricity.—W. D. Crawford, president of the Edison Electric Institute [2]

In 1970, the United States generated over 1.6 trillion kilowatt-hours of electricity—and still suffered brownouts and blackouts.

It is hard enough to comprehend 1,600,000,000,000 kilowatt-

[1] Comment on Four Corners power production before the Senate Interior Committee hearing at Durango, Colorado (May 27, 1971), quoted in Gladwin Hill, "Power Plant Resented in Colorado," *The New York Times* (May 28, 1971), p. 11.

[2] Quoted in John N. Wilford, "Nation's Energy Crisis: Is Unbridled Growth Indispensable to the Good Life?" *The New York Times* (July 8, 1971), p. 24.

hours of electricity, let alone the occurrence of an "energy cirsis" with this level of output. But the evidence is impressive: In recent decades, the use of electricity has doubled on the average of about every eight years, which converts to an annual growth rate in electricity use of about 9 percent, in contrast with total United States energy production increases of about 3.5 percent. The rapid rise in the use of electricity in the American economy has resulted from the development of industrial machines and household appliances that are more compact, powerful, and flexible in operation because of this power source, and from the more or less continuous elevation of illumination standards in the home, office, and factory. The curve of increasing electricity use may be flattening somewhat, but nothing resembling a downturn is likely to occur in the near future.

If the energy-growth relationships hold, electricity will soon supplant other forms of energy. But the one predictable aspect of such exponential rates is that they will moderate. The question that is less certain is when. In any case, an increasing share of the energy market for electricity does not mean that fossil fuels—coal, petroleum, and gas—or the newer energy sources will be displaced, but that conventional forms of energy along with new sources will be converted to electricity rather than used directly.

The Nature of the Energy Problem

What is frequently called the "energy crisis"—the increasing difficulty of energy sources, especially electricity, to keep up with projected needs—fits easily into the economist's framework of demand and supply. The American economy is a high-energy economy, and both domestic and industrial uses of energy have been stimulated by advances in technology, the high level of the nation's income, rising population, and economic growth. What has happened recently in the market for energy can be shown by a series of demand curves shifting from year to year in response to demand-increasing forces. For any given short period of time when incomes, technology, and consumers' preferences are likely to change little, the demand curve is a narrowly con-

Figure 8.1. Increasing Demand for Energy Over Time

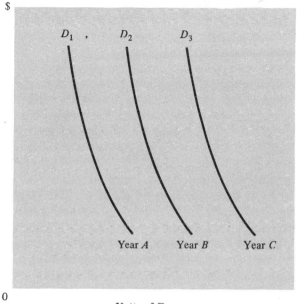

fined expression of consumers' reactions to changes in prices. Figure 8.1 shows a set of three demand curves of such consumers' reactions to energy prices for different time periods—Year . A, Year B, Year C. Although hypothetical, in an approximation to reality these curves have been drawn to show a somewhat limited reaction by consumers to changes in energy prices—consumption does not change greatly when energy prices move up or down.

The shorter the time period, the less opportunity there is for change to take place in energy demand. With time, however, both aggregate energy demand and the distribution of demand among energy sources may change, as in the increased use of electricity and petroleum compared with coal. Finally, when time is no constraint, industrial equipment can be redesigned and household practices modified to use either more or less electricity, with a consequent effect upon the demand curves. In Figure 8.1, this long-term effect is shown increasing energy demand over the time span covered from D_1 to D_2 to D_3.

Energy Demand and Price

The demand for energy is relatively insensitive to price changes, as shown in Figure 8.1, because outlays for energy by the industrial firm and the household are smaller than for most other important purchases and generally cannot be much changed without considerable time for redesign and rearrangement of practices and equipment. The precisely paralled sets of curves, Year *A* through Year *C*, are a reflection of the aesthetics of draftmanship, however, rather than a representation of the real world. In any case, the demand for energy over recent years has steadily moved to the right, as indicated, and at any given time has been relatively inflexible.

Energy Supply and Price

The supply of energy has shown an equal or greater short-run inflexibility, although nothing comparable to the complete inflexibility of supply described in Chapter 7 for the semiwilderness of the Middle Snake region. Some variation of energy output, increasing with higher prices and decreasing with lower prices, will take place over as short a period as a few months for such energy sources as coal, petroleum, and electricity. But any considerable increase in energy output involves more than working existing facilities and labor forces harder and longer. Additions to machinery and equipment must take place, and more labor must be recruited. When this is done, the supply curve will shift to the right, as shown in Figure 8.2 for S_2 and S_3.

Standing alone, these demand and supply curves are a convenient graphic summary of the reactions of consumers and producers to price changes, but the full message is not revealed until they are superimposed to show successively rising energy prices for the three time periods, Year *A*, Year *B*, and Year *C*. In addition to expressing graphically the forces that establish price in any given year, the intersections of demand and supply

Figure 8.2. Increasing Supply of Energy Over Time

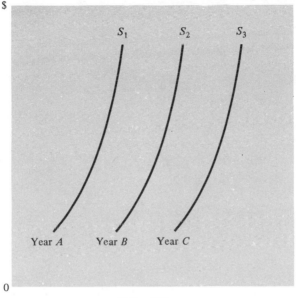

in Figure 8.3 can be connected (curve LR) to show what has happened to price over the years. If, as is the case in the energy market, demand has shifted to the right (increased) more than supply, the LR curve connecting the intersection points will tilt upward, indicating an increasing price over the long run.

Confirming this hypothetical demand-and-supply analysis, Figure 8.4 shows what has actually taken place in energy prices compared with an index of all commodity prices since the mid-1960's. Most authorities expect the sharp increase in energy prices in the years from 1969 through 1971 to continue in the immediate future because of the mounting demand for energy in relation to its lagging supply. Exactly how high these prices will in fact go and how long the upward movement will continue depends upon the forces that shape demand and supply. But how much the price of energy increases is of more than passing interest. The relative change in energy prices is a sig-

Figure 8.3. Increasing Demand and Supply of Energy
Over Time

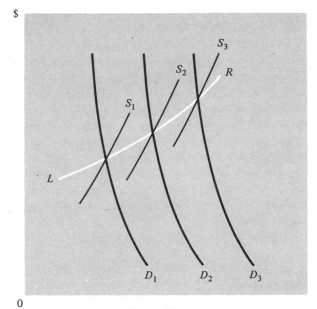

Units of Energy

nificant environmental indicator, reflecting the extent of the exploitation of energy sources and consequently, of pressure upon the environment. To understand the nature of the environmental pressures that accompany increased exploitation of energy sources requires more than analysis of demand and supply, however. We must look behind supply-and-demand curves to the sources of energy and the factors affecting the demand for energy. These sources are shown in Figure 8.5.

Petroleum

Warnings of resource depletion have seldom been so consistently premature as in the case of oil reserves. There are two reasons for this: First, not all potential oil fields have been ex-

Figure 8.4.   Price of Energy Compared to Wholesale
Prices for All Commodities *

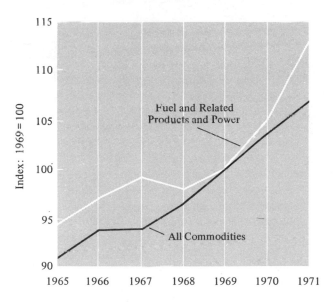

* The Chase Manhattan Bank, *Business in Brief* (October 1972); data from
U. S. Department of Labor.

plored by drilling, and second, frequent improvements in the
technology of the discovery and extraction of oil have periodically added to the known reserve supply of oil. Oil is unlike other
resources, such as timber, in that more than visual inspection is
necessary to determine the amount and quality of the supply.
An oil company normally undertakes exploration work to establish oil claims and to determine the approximate quantity and
quality of the deposit. Test drilling continues gradually over the
years as the oil is withdrawn, establishing the full extent of the
deposit only as it is used.

The prospect for future oil discovery in the United States
remains good even though many deposits have been exhausted.
Geologically, the rock type and structure of much of the United
States is conducive to the deposit of petroleum, and many of the
potential producing areas have not been intensively investigated.

Figure 8.5.   United States Energy Market Shares,
1950–1970 *

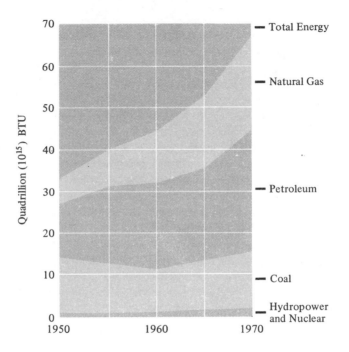

* Department of the Interior, *United States Energy: A Summary Review* (Washington, D.C.: Government Printing Office, 1972), p. 20.

Moreover, techniques of exploration continue to improve, so an area testing negative in one year may later reveal substantial deposits. Not only are potentially productive regions underexplored, but most of the commercially developed deposits and reserves are shallow. As techniques of drilling improve, exploration and extraction of oil at greater depths has taken place—as well as greater recovery of oil through the use of the injection of water or other substances in the depleting deposit to force the oil out of the parent rock. Nevertheless, at least one authority, M. K. Hubbert of the United States Geological Survey, has concluded that United States petroleum production is now in its peak period. We are not on the verge of running out of oil, but future

Figure 8.6.   United States Crude Oil Production, Discoveries, and Reserves *

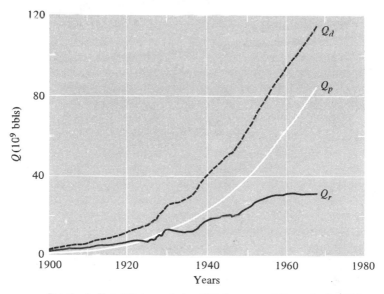

Data for the United States, exclusive of Alaska, on cumulative production (Q_p), cumulative proved discoveries (Q_d), and proved reserves (Q_r), of crude oil.

* M. K. Hubbert, "Energy Resources," in *Resources and Man*, W. H. Freeman and Co., San Francisco, California, 1969, published for the National Academy of Sciences, p. 174.

output is not likely to increase greatly, and over the years it will decline.

Although the concept of "proved reserves" understates the future supply of oil, only in the early 1960's did the upward trend in proved reserves flatten out, as shown in Figure 8.6. The decrease in proved reserves excludes the Alaskan discovery, a petroleum find of major proportions located on the North Slope of the Brooks Range whose exploitation has been delayed by actions of conservationists. If the Alaskan deposit is added to the trend line of Figure 8.6, the decline in proved reserves is reduced but not reversed—unless the Alaskan deposit turns out to be well beyond present expectations. The falloff in proved reserves and, more particularly, the need to go deeper for oil have been interpreted by Hubbert as evidence of an increasing scarcity of oil deposits:

> This decline [in oil discovered per foot of drilling] during the 30-year period since 1937 is particularly significant in view of the fact that the oil credited with having been discovered during this period represents the cumulative results of all of the advances in the techniques of exploration and production of the petroleum industry during its entire history up to 1967. This also was the period of the most intensive research and development in exploratory and production techniques in the history of the industry. The observed decline in the rate of discovery during this period is, accordingly, difficult to account for on any other basis than that undiscovered oil is becoming scarce.[3]

Alaskan and Offshore Oil

In addition to the Alaskan North Slope, with its extensive undeveloped deposits, the continental shelf remains largely unexplored, and is potentially the greatest domestic source of oil for the United States. The deposits under the continental shelf extend to great depths, however, and the technical problems, the costs, and the dangers to the environment from extraction are entirely different from those encountered in on-land production. Indeed, the technology of underwater oil extraction remains uncertain, as blowouts in Santa Barbara Bay and fires and spills in the Gulf of Mexico demonstrate. In the competitive struggle to exploit offshore oil deposits, the development of safeguards against fires and oil spills has frequently lost out in the rush for oil. In part because of lax federal enforcement of existing regulations, and inadequate controls in the early period of offshore exploitation, oil firms have been permitted to shift to society a part of the costs of production through damage to the environment.

[3] "Energy Resources," in *Resources and Man*, W. H. Freeman and Co., San Francisco, California, 1969, published for the National Academy of Sciences, p. 180.

Future Petroleum Production

Since energy output from fossil fuels has increased so dramatically in the past thirty years, and since petroleum and allied products have increasingly been substituted for coal, it is not reasonable to expect the growth in petroleum production to continue at its initially high rate. If we have reached near-maximum output of domestic oil, as some geologists believe, how far into the future will our reserves carry us? The future does not hold a specific "exhaustion date" for oil deposits, but well before the turn of the century the price of petroleum is likely to rise relative to that of other energy sources. More capital and labor will be required to bring crude oil to the surface and the quality of the deposits eventually will diminish. Increasingly, oil of foreign origin will supplant domestic crude oil in the American economy.

The Special Protection of the Petroleum Industry

The United States is not an economic island entire of itself—even though import restrictions shelter the United States petroleum industry from foreign competition. But the structure of the American petroleum industry contributes to a high-cost, inefficient operation that makes it difficult for it to compete with foreign oil. In the past, excess capacity in extractive wells has resulted in fields with wells producing as little as ten days per month, creating more capital facilities than were necessary to meet the country's needs. This excess capacity was in part the result of the competitive struggle to extract more oil from a pool or deposit shared with other producing concerns. To prevent wastage in extraction and to keep from spoiling the market for crude oil, however, certain states—such as Texas and Louisiana—imposed output restrictions on producers.

As well output is held down by state output restrictions in the primary oil-producing areas, unit cost rises and the petroleum industry is forced into the upside-down economics of maximizing costs and minimizing efficiency. But once having encumbered itself with excess capacity and higher costs, the industry finds it impossible to compete on a price basis with foreign imports, so it resorts to the political solution of restricting imports. Overcapacity seals the inefficiencies into the industry, imposes an uneconomic burden upon the consumer, and forgoes the opportunity to conserve the American crude-oil supply by importing foreign oil. The political solution of import quotas, preferred by the petroleum industry to the economic solution of competition, is available to the industry because of the effective political pressure it can exert upon the legislative and executive branches of the federal government, irrespective of whether Republicans or Democrats are in control. Nor are restrictions upon foreign trade the only way the industry exercises its political influence. The oil-depletion allowance is perhaps even better evidence of its power.

At the same time that oil-well output in the major producer states is held down by production quotas, the federal depletion allowance permits a deduction of 22 percent from corporate gross income in determining federal corporate taxes. This federal subsidy, also available in lower percentages to owners of other depleting resources, clearly encourages overexpansion of domestic production of petroleum and further shelters inefficient producers from the forces of competition.

Crude Oil by Conversion

Beyond domestic and foreign deposits of crude oil, other sources—shale, tar sands, and the liquefaction of coal—will provide abundant but somewhat higher-cost liquid fuel in the future. Other sources of energy may have a comparative advantage over petroleum products—such as natural gas in the pollution-free generation of electricity—but the automobile, the major user of liquid fuel, is likely to remain dependent upon petroleum products for many years.

The use of petroleum is locked into transportation, which accounts for about 85 percent of the industry's sales, and it will take a change in the internal-combustion engine, not in home heating and the generation of electricity, to effect any significant decrease in the demand for petroleum as a source of energy. In fact, in the near future the use of petroleum products for transportation can only rise; how much, depends upon population growth, national income, and consumer choice. But the expected longevity of the internal-combustion engine is a sufficient reason to anticipate the eventual production of petroleum from tar sands, oil shales, and coal, before the exhaustion of underground crude-oil deposits.

Tar Sands

Heavy-oil sands, or tar sands, are found mainly in the province of Alberta, Canada, with the Athabasca deposit of that region holding the greatest promise. The oils from tar sands are similar to those of the ordinary crude-oil deposit, but more viscous, making it impossible to collect the oil by natural flowage from wells. The reserves of oil from Alberta tar sands are estimated at slightly more than 300 billion barrels, and commercial production of petroleum from these sands has been undertaken on a small, pilot-plant scale. Commercial exploitation of oil from tar sands has been undertaken only by the Sun Oil Company in Alberta, but the apparent success of its operation justifies adding tar sands to the petroleum-reserve base.

Oil Shales

Unlike the deposits of tar sands, those of oil shales differ from conventional crude oil in both structure and chemical composition. Oil shales are solid in form and their chemical structure includes nitrogen and other impurities, which require costlier methods of refining. These materials, which are found mainly in North America, are far more abundant than the deposits of tar sands—so much so that petroleum demand well beyond the year 2000 easily can be supplied from the known sources in Wyoming, Colorado, and Utah.

The aggregate petroleum equivalent from the oil-shale deposits in these three states is set at the mind-boggling total of 1,430 billion barrels. (Henry R. Linden, director of the Institute of Gas Technology, accepts a considerably lower figure, 750 billion barrels of oil-shale crude, but believes that as a source of petroleum, oil shales are on the threshold of competing with conventional sources.) Utah has the largest deposit with an upward potential of 800 billion barrels, followed by Wyoming with 400 billion barrels and Colorado with 230 billion barrels. It should be emphasized, however, that petroleum production from oil shales requires extensive raw-materials processing and a modification of refining procedures. These changes of course mean higher costs and higher prices for petroleum—and a most serious waste-disposal problem by the extractive industry.

Coal

In spite of the fact that energy consumption in the United States has consistently increased over the past decades, coal—the most abundant of all conventional energy sources in the United States—has not maintained its position in the energy market. Partly as a result of the heavy war and postwar demand, coal output in the United States increased until 1947, when production abruptly turned downward. From that year until the early 1960's, the coal industry suffered a steady decline in output. Although it is currently experiencing a revival, the long-run economic prospects for coal are anything but secure. As a result, the Office of Coal Research has been established in the Department of the Interior in an attempt to bolster the faltering market by developing new uses for coal. The problems faced by the use of coal are dramatized by the Black Mesa–Four Corners case.

The Case of Black Mesa: Energy Export

The Navajo reservation at Black Mesa, Arizona, is the site of a massive strip-mining operation of the Peabody Coal Company and the focus of a controversy between the coal-mining and power interests and conservationists. Black Mesa is a forbidding, erosion-scarred plateau about three-hundred miles north of Phoenix, Arizona, which is part of the twenty thousand square miles of the Navajo Reservation and the location of enough anthracite coal to provide 13 million tons a year for at least thirty-five years. The coal is ground fine and mixed with water for pipeline transport 275 miles to the 1,500-megawatt California Edison Mohave generating plant on the Colorado River, a hundred miles south of Las Vegas in the southern tip of Nevada. The Mohave plant is one of six huge thermal power plants under construction or in operation in the states of Arizona, Nevada, Utah, and New Mexico, much of whose output will be used in the more populous areas of the Southwest.

The coal contract with the Navajo and Hopi Indians, approved by Stewart Udall when he was Secretary of the Interior, guarantees a royalty of twenty-five cents a ton, and the mining operation will provide jobs for possibly three hundred Indians at better than their usual wages. The benefits are obvious, royalties and employment, but the injuries to the environment are in contention. Strip-mining has generally left the earth scarred and useless, unsightly and unproductive; but the Peabody Coal Company, the world's largest, claims that it will not only restore the land, but improve it. If it does, it will be a sharp departure from most strip-mining practices, but the area to be mined is a very small portion of the reservation and the contract requires that the land be left in a condition as good as it was found— which, economically, was not much in the first place. Beyond this, however, the region is considered by the Hopi Indians to be sacred.

The plant longest in operation of this group, that at Four Corners, New Mexico, has attracted the attention of many—including the Gemini astronauts, who in 1966 observed the Four Corners smoke plume. The relatively isolated location of the generating plants was expected to protect the power combine from criticism. Public criticism of the Four Corners plant has not been lacking, however, even though it is designed to remove 97 percent of the particulate matter from the stack discharge. For in spite of this, the power generation has introduced up to 250 tons of air pollution per day into the Four Corners atmosphere, more than produced by all of New York City. What was once desert clarity has been curtained in fly ash, carbon, and oxides of sulfur and nitrogen.

Whether or not the Peabody Coal Company restores the mesa to its original state, and whether or not the four-state power installations are able to decrease overall pollution of the atmosphere, a shift in the environmental cost of power production has occurred. In effect, the electricity-using communities are exporting their pollution to other sections of the country and paying for it with employment opportunities, coal royalties, property taxes, and other considerations. Whether the two regions—the cities of the Southwest and the relatively unpolluted countryside —both gain from such an arrangement depends upon the compensation paid for pollution damage and the capacity of the environment to absorb such damage. By most standards, however, Black Mesa and the Four Corners area appear to be losers.

Coal and Air Pollution

While losing ground to petroleum as an energy resource, coal is facing further challenge because of its pollution of the environment. Not only does coal combustion charge the atmosphere with particulate matter; it may also introduce sulfur dioxide into the air. Although some industry representatives dispute the hazards of dilute levels of sulfur dioxide in the air, the United States Public Health Service has accumulated persuasive evidence of the harmful effects of sulfur-dioxide pollution. In addition, sulfur dioxide affects more than the human respiratory system. In sufficient concentration, it mottles paint and destroys vegetation. In short, it imposes a burden (cost) upon the public, and communities have responded by legislating against the use of coal with a sulfur content above specified minimum levels.*

The restrictions against high-sulfur coal will have the greatest impact upon bituminous supplies, which provide about half the fuel for the steam generation of electricity. Bituminous coal varies widely in sulfur content—from 0.5 to 5 percent and above—and the coal industry has already been strained to meet the demand for low-sulfur fuel. The future supplies of low-sulfur bituminous coal will be forthcoming only through sulfur removal, a relatively undeveloped process in treating coal. A recent Bureau of Mines survey of mines east of the Mississippi

* Air pollution is considered in Chapter 11.

found that fewer than 10 percent produced coal with a sulfur content below 1 percent and that only 35 percent of the mines sampled produced coal that could be cleaned below 1 percent.

Natural Gas

The environmental crisis has made a seller's market for natural gas. It was not always so. In the early days of well drilling, natural gas was vented or flared as an unwanted by-product of petroleum production. Closely associated geologically with petroleum, sometimes taking the form of a gas-oil mixture, natural gas usually shares oil-production facilities and oil-reserves estimates. Gas is different from petroleum, however: Its extraction requires only that the deposit be tapped to bring it to the surface, and estimates of natural-gas reserves are less reliable than those for petroleum.

With natural gas entering economic life as an adjunct of oil production, the supply has been largely dependent upon what happened in the petroleum industry. Within the past few years, however, the pollution-free character of natural gas has attracted buyers to this fuel, especially large-city power producers.

Natural-Gas Pricing

Because until recently natural-gas production verged on over-abundance, and because the federally regulated gas price has been slow to respond to changed conditions, the industry has had little incentive to increase output—and possibly some incentive to delay expansion in anticipation of a later higher price. To the extent that petroleum is the dominant product of the petroleum-gas combination, increased natural-gas production will depend upon the decision to increase petroleum output. As gas becomes more important economically, however, investment in its discovery, and exploitation in its own right, will take place. But before this occurs, it may be necessary to free the natural-gas price from the control of the Federal Power Commission.

Assuming that the supply of natural gas is responsive to its price rather than simply a function of petroleum production, the effect of the FPC's price ceiling is to reduce natural-gas output below what it would be with a higher price. As shown in Figure 8.7, the effect of a price ceiling is to keep off the market output that would otherwise be offered at the higher, market-clearing price OB and at the same time to attract more purchases than can be satisfied at price OA, creating a shortage area, along CE on the graph. At OA, consumers want to purchase OE units of natural gas, but producers are willing to supply only OC units. (OD units would be supplied at the market-clearing price OB, and there would be no excess of demand over supply.) The demand-and-supply situation described in Figure 8.7 covers a period of time when it is possible for producers and consumers to respond to price changes with limited reorganization of consumption and output. The price ceiling of the FPC affects more than this short-run period, however. It prevents expansion of production facilities for natural gas, and the shortage of natural gas at the prevailing price frustrates consumers in their attempt to substitute gas for other types of fuel. A higher price would stimulate investment in gas production, increasing its future supply. With the gas price ceiling, however, the supply curve in effect stops at the price OA.

In addition to encouraging the development of domestic sources of natural gas, a higher price would stimulate the importation of gas, brought by pipeline and tanker. Mexico and Canada produce surplus gas, and tanker gas from North Africa is currently delivered in Europe.

Electricity

Electricity is coal, oil, gas, waterpower, or atomic energy converted to kilowatts. In the early 1970's, this energy conversion was not keeping up with demand. The blackouts in the eastern United States in the late 1960's were followed by uneasy brownouts to stretch the short power supply. This power shortage, or energy crisis, gave evidence of Murphy's Law: "What can go wrong, will go wrong." But it was *not* caused by an inadequate supply of the basic energy resources.

Figure 8.7. The Effect of a Price Ceiling for Natural Gas

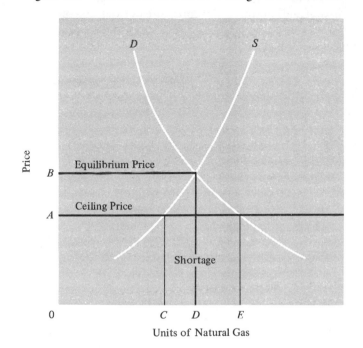

Units of Natural Gas

Electrical generation in the United States relies mainly on steam-driven turbines using coal, oil, or gas as fuel. Hydroelectric production, which depends upon the force of falling water to drive turbines, may be of considerable local and regional importance but accounts for only 16 percent of electrical output nationally. Nuclear-power production, once the bright hope of the future, is as yet an insignificant part of thermal generation, less than 2 percent, but is expected to increase progressively over the years.

The Anatomy of the Power Shortage

In the early 1970's, the power industry found itself caught in a shift away from coal as a fuel for thermal generation at the same time that planned nuclear plants encountered delays resulting from technical problems and public concern over the danger of radiation and thermal pollution. The optimistic expectations for nuclear-power production, and the pressure to reduce air pollution, made the electric utilities reluctant to sign long-term contracts with the coal industry. In turn, the natural-gas industry, which was unable to meet the increased demand for its relatively pollution-free fuel, was reluctant to expand production until the Federal Power Commission authorized a hike in the price of gas. In the meantime, the coal industry turned to the export market, especially Japan, for attractive prices and long-term contracts and did not expand mining operations because it feared further reductions in the domestic demand for coal. Earlier, the coal industry had cut back on investment in anticipation of declining sales and now it found itself unable to meet the higher foreign and domestic demand—a seller's market that was enhanced by shortages of railroad hopper cars and by decreased oil imports. But in the long run coal must rely upon indirect uses—such as liquefaction and gasification—to maintain its position in the market.

Power production lagged behind demand, which in the early 1970's increased at as much as five times the rate of population growth. Clearly, an unexplored opportunity to ease the power shortage through curtailment of demand was at hand, but neither the political nor the economic system seemed able to impose controls to promote this objective. Utilities still sold kilowatts at quantity discounts, advertised home heating by electricity, and generally encouraged greater consumption of a product increasingly in short supply. At the same time, the price of electricity, controlled predominantly by state regulatory commissions, was slow either to reflect the rising cost structure faced by the industry or to incorporate into the kilowatt rate a charge to compensate for the environmental abuse of expanding power production.

Long-Run Power Options

Conventional turbine electrical generation permits a modest range of flexibility in technology and energy sources, but nothing like the options in basic process that appear within reach in the future. A change in the basic technique of generating electricity cannot come too soon in the United States because, barring an unexpected decline in the growth rate of electricity use, the projected kilowatt consumption will greatly strain both the environment and the conventional energy sources, such as low-sulfur fossil fuels, within the next few decades.

Atomic Power

For a while it appeared that nuclear-power production would provide the solution to a lagging supply of energy without increasing environmental abuse; it generates neither noxious oxides nor fly ash and does not ravage the land in obtaining fuel or destroy fast-flowing rivers by damming. But atomic power has fallen short of its bright promise, partly because of technical difficulties in design and plant construction and partly because of growing opposition to such installations by concerned citizens. In any case, the early conventional power reactors * appear at best to offer temporary relief to the energy crisis, since the uranium-235 "burned" by these reactors is among the scarcest of our

* The first nuclear reactors in the United States were the so-called light-water reactors, which were cooled by water and developed heat by the fission of the U-235 isotopes. Unlike breeder reactors, which convert U-235 to U-238 and create a surplus of plutonium, the light-water reactors use less than 1 percent of the energy potential in a pound of uranium. The breeder is a more complicated and temperamental piece of equipment, however, and requires more sophisticated technology and greater capital investment. Although the engineering problems in breeder power production are formidable, they appear likely to yield to crash federal research-and-development programs. Whether problems of safety and commercial feasibility can be as easily disposed of depends largely upon Atomic Energy Commission standards and federal subsidies.

On the quite distant scientific horizon, possibly never to be reached, is the fusion reactor. Fusion develops heat not by splitting atoms but by combining light atoms such as hydrogen to form heavier ones. Fusion reactors are clean, involving no output of radioactive material that cannot be recycled, and can draw upon a virtually unlimited energy source, the hydrogen in water. For these reasons, some scientists have urged that research in this more nearly ideal source of power take precedence, but the less developed state of fusion-reactor technology has persuaded federal authorities to back the breeder reactor.

energy resources. Although Atomic Energy Commission estimates may be somewhat pessimistic, and projected reactor-con-
struction figures may be optimistic, present supplies of U-235
are expected to be exhausted by the early 1980's. (The development of high-temperature gas-cooled reactors that can use the
more abundant thorium as a fuel supplement may relieve the
pressure upon uranium supplies somewhat.)

But whether the reactor uses U-235, U-238, or thorium, the
electricity is still generated by the familiar steam turbine, tied
to an atomic energy source. And when this fuel is "burned" to
produce turbine steam, the heat loss is about 50 percent greater
than with conventional fossil fuels, causing massive thermal pollution where cooling waters are at all limited. (Dissipation of
heat by means of cooling towers is possible, but water cooling
is much cheaper. Moreover, dispersion of heat to the atmosphere is not without untoward side effects, such as heavy fogging
under some weather conditions.)

Although thermal pollution is the most apparent unwanted
by-product of nuclear-power production, it is by no means the
only possible environmental hazard. Radiation pollution is the
greater concern. There is no danger of a reactor explosion such
as occurs in the detonation of an atomic bomb, and if plant design, materials, and human controls all perform as expected, the
routine radiation emissions will probably have no significant health
impact. Even here there is disagreement, however, and some
scientists argue that we should not permit even minuscule radiation discharges into the atmosphere, since we are not certain of
their effect. But the more intense controversy surrounds the possibility of an accident—in management, operation, materials, or
from natural forces such as an earthquake—that would vent the
radioactive pile to the atmosphere, causing a wipe-out of nearby
population centers and an increase in the general level of atmospheric radiation. Such a discharge of radioactive materials
might occur if the cooling system malfunctioned and there was
a meltdown of the atomic pile, causing a breach in the cladding
of the reactor.

The early light-water reactors rely upon water as a coolant
and are equipped with back-up cooling systems, and with con-

trols to shut down the fission process. Breeder reactors, potentially more radioactively hazardous, generally employ liquid sodium as a coolant. Liquid sodium is much less tractable than water, burning when exposed to air and exploding in contact with water. The point at issue, however, is whether the nuclear-power-plant safeguards provide adequate protection against the possibility of accidental radiation emissions. The scientific community is at odds on this question, but obviously the chances of accidental radiation emission are not decreased by building more nuclear power plants.

Quite apart from the danger of environmental havoc from massive radiation emissions, the problem of disposing of radioactive wastes remains critical and unsolved. Solutions as desperate as rocketing wastes into outer space have been suggested by the chairman of the Atomic Energy Commission. Since some radioactive wastes remain lethal for hundreds of thousands of years, developing a foolproof program of neutralizing or disposing of such waste by-products of nuclear power production would seem to merit a first-order priority. Such has not been the case; the Atomic Energy Commission is still searching for a solution.

In spite of potential environmental hazards, the federal government in the early 1970's undertook a crash program to catch up with the English and Russians in fast-breeder nuclear-power technology. Two experimental demonstration plants were authorized and the United States energy policy has mainly emphasized the promotion of nuclear-power production—an objective that the Atomic Energy Commission has supported by various incentives and coercions since President Eisenhower's famous "atoms for peace" speech before the United Nations, late in 1953, in which he promised to share discoveries in the peaceful application of atomic energy. Actually, the United States already has one breeder reactor—the Enrico Fermi plant outside of Detroit, built by the Detroit Edison Company at a cost of 130 million dollars and operated at a full-power equivalent of twenty-one days over a period of eight years. The Fermi plant has suffered a rash of malfunctions: The graphite shielding was found to be inadequate, fuel-handling equipment didn't work, tubing in the generators sprang leaks, and a reactor metal plate fell into the liquid-sodium coolant. This displaced plate caused a disruption of the cooling process and led to a meltdown of a part of the fuel core. Whether the reactor will ever become operable is questionable, but its experience does not reinforce the contention that accident-free nuclear-power technology has arrived.

Magnetohydrodynamics (MHD)

Less awe-inspiring, but possibly as revolutionary as nuclear-power production, is electrical generation by magnetohydrodynamics. Such an imposing term seems to belong to science fiction, but in reality the generation of electricity by magnetohydrodynamics goes back to Michael Faraday in 1831 and the discovery that moving a conductor in a magnetic field induces a current in the fluid conductor. This generating process holds promise as a major pollution-free source of power. Although the basic principle of MHD has been known for over a century, only recently have other developments brought it to the threshold of commercial introduction.

The MHD generator has been built and operated experimentally in the United States, but its development has been limited to a few pilot models for peak-power output rather than base-load operation. Throughout its development, the MHD has received only modest support from the electric-utility industry and sporadic backing from the federal government, and even this limited research has been largely dormant since 1965. In the meantime, however, West Germany, Japan, and the Soviet Union have continued research, with Russia putting the world's first large-scale MHD generator into production in 1971.

There are other nonpolluting methods of generating energy, such as pumps to withdraw steam from the earth's subsurface or cells to collect the sun's rays, but the MHD generator is the only nearly pollution-free method that relies upon conventional fossil fuels. Not only is its generating process more efficient than that of the present steam turbine, but it produces about one-third less pollutant effluent, as a result of its high operating temperatures. But most important, removal of virtually all particulate matter, as well as nitrogen and sulfur pollutants, can be designed into the system necessary for the recovery of the potassium crystals used to increase conductivity in the generating process. Although this generating process operates at substantially higher temperatures than the standard steam turbine, no thermal pollution of water occurs because it is not necessary to concentrate steam for recycling. The heat produced can simply be dissipated into the air—or used for alternate purposes. Nor should the MHD's greater efficiency in fuel consumption be overlooked, especially since it makes possible the use of coal in an environmentally acceptable way. An Office of Science and Technology study has estimated that the introduction of MHD for new generating capacity between 1985 and 2000 could save 11 billion dollars in coal consumption at present prices without adding significantly to the atmosphere's pollution load.

The Marriage of MHD and Nuclear Power

As timely as the MHD generator appears in its ability to get more power with less pollution from conventional fuels, these advantages do not exhaust its full potential. The MHD process can be supplemented with an ordinary steam-turbine generator to withdraw heat from the exhaust gases, as is done in a full-scale Soviet MHD power plant, or the system can be adapted to more efficient nuclear-power production. The grafting of the familiar steam turbine onto the exhaust system of an MHD plant simply takes advantage of otherwise wasted heat, but nuclear conversion of the MHD process involves the design of a closed system that greatly reduces energy dissipation. The principle of the nuclear-fueled closed MHD system is different from that of the fossil-fueled MHD process, which involves combustion gases that pass through the apparatus. The closed-cycle MHD uses nuclear fuel to heat a high-velocity stream of liquid metal of helium gas which continuously circulates and creates a magnetic field of electricity. The nuclear closed MHD system is out of the experimental stage but has been applied only to small-scale military and space use. Further technological advances in high-temperature reactors or the use of gas for cooling are necessary to increase the scale of the closed system.

Future Electric-Power Growth

If power consumption doubles every eight years, as is sometimes forecast, environmental pressure will be intense: massive
thermal pollution of our rivers and lakes, increased air pollution,
larger areas of land blighted by transmission lines, added danger
of oil spills from greatly increased transport of oil, spreading
strip- and auger-mining, and an expansion of potentially dangerous nuclear-power production. The Federal Power Commission projects a considerably lower rate of increase in electric-
power demand than doubling every eight years, but even the
more modest sixfold increase shown in Figure 8.8 would strain
both our economy and the environment.

Is such a high growth in power use inevitable? The reasoned
answer is No. In the first place, a rapid growth rate eventually
declines; and in the second place, electricity consumption does
not follow a course independent of man's will.

The future growth curve will flatten because of changes in
home and industry consumption. The household demand for appliance electricity has reached a peak, and growing use by industry
will be moderated by the decreasing importance of manufacturing and heavy industry with the rise in service and commercial activities. From households, more appliance-electricity
demand will arise primarily as a result of the population increase
and the expansion of the appliance market to lower-income
groups. But the real stimulus to future household electricity
consumption lies in electric heating, vigorously promoted by
most electric utilities * and some heating-equipment manufacturers, such as the General Electric Company.

The shift to home electric heating would more than double
electricity consumption by households in most regions and
greatly increase the capacity requirements of an industry in
which capacity is already in short supply. Advertised as "clean,"
electric heating at first glance promises relief to the environment.
But it is clean only at the point of use, not where produced.

* New York's Consolidated Edison is a notable exception.

Figure 8.8. United States Electric-Power Demand,
1970–2000 *

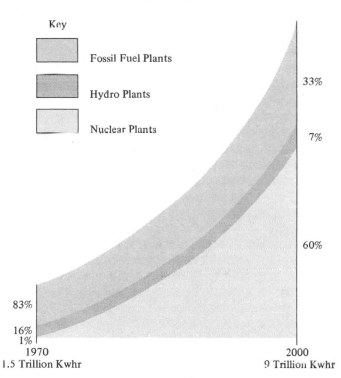

Key

Fossil Fuel Plants

Hydro Plants

Nuclear Plants

33%

7%

60%

83%

16%
1%
1970
1.5 Trillion Kwhr

2000
9 Trillion Kwhr

* Federal Power Commission. Reproduced in Department of the Interior, *United States Energy: A Summary Review* (Washington, D.C.: Government Printing Office, 1972), p. 13.

Whether conventional fossil fuels or nuclear power is used, the generation of electricity pollutes the air, the water, or both, quite aside from possible accidental radiation emissions. Moreover, electric heating is a wasteful way of using fossil fuels compared with heating directly with coal, gas, or fuel oil. As a result, resources are depleted at a more rapid rate to obtain a given heat output.

In many regions, heavy air-conditioning demand during the summer has caused a capacity buildup that has not been fully used in other seasons, causing utilities to search for a supplementing electricity market for the off-summer period. Electric space heating would of course provide the ideal supplement from the utilities' standpoint, but if extensively adopted, would shift the overcapacity to the summer. The short supply of the summer might simply be transferred to other seasons, where blackouts and brownouts would be much more physically distressing.

At some point, the stair-step increase in electricity consumption will be broken. Although it is not possible to change consumer habits and producer practices overnight, the expansionist policies of the electric utilities can be restrained with selective social controls. Utility prices are commission-regulated, and the rate schedules can be modified so that the pricing arrangements discourage large-scale electric use rather than encourage it: Higher rather than lower rates can be charged to large users, and there is no reason why this change should not apply to industry as well as to householders.

Utility prices do not now include the costs to society for environmental damages that are the side effects of power production—air pollution, thermal emissions, and ravaged lands from coal mining. If prevention and rehabilitation costs for these damages are included in the price of electricity, the higher rates will exercise an important dampening effect upon increased electricity consumption—especially for home heating. Finally, it may be necessary to limit the expansion of air conditioning and electric heating, to establish higher efficiency standards for lighting and for insulation in housing, and to restrict the use of electricity for some purposes, such as billboard illumination. In the absence of such social controls, a short-supply industry continues to promote sales that not only overload its capacity, but endanger the environment. The public interest will be served by saving the power industry from its expansionist policies.

References and Readings

Aaronson, Terri, "The Black Box," *Environment*, XIII (December 1971), pp. 10–18.

A review of the advantages and problems of fuel-cell generation of electricity, including a cost comparison with other forms of power production.

Abrahamson, Dean E., *Environmental Cost of Electric Power*. New York: Scientists' Institute for Public Information, 1970.
A brief but highly informative pamphlet on the social costs of power production, including nuclear-power generation.

Curtis, Richard, and Hogan, Elizabeth, *Perils of the Peaceful Atom*. New York: Ballantine Books, 1970.
A vigorous critique of the handling of nuclear-power development by Congress, the Atomic Energy Commission, and the power industry. The authors conclude that continued efforts to develop safe atomic power are not worth the risk and that complete abandonment of the nuclear-power program is the only sound policy.

Darmstadter, Joel, *et al.*, *Energy in the World Economy: A Statistical Review of Trends in Output, Trade, and Consumption Since 1925*. Baltimore: Johns Hopkins Press, 1971.
A massive Resources for the Future statistical compilation of world trends in energy use, including estimates of world reserves of energy resources.

Department of the Interior, *United States Energy: A Summary Review*. Washington, D.C.: Government Printing Office, 1972.
Estimates of energy supplies in relation to need compiled by federal agencies administering programs in various natural-resource areas.

Foreman, Harry, ed., *Nuclear Power and the Public*. Minneapolis: University of Minnesota Press, 1970.
This book is the edited transcript of a symposium held at the University of Minnesota on nuclear-power issues. The participants were drawn from a variety of professions and included critics as well as advocates of nuclear-power production. On the whole, both the prepared contributions and the discussions at the symposium are relevant and informative.

Landsberg Hans H., *Natural Resources for U.S. Growth—A Look Ahead to the Year 2000*. Baltimore: Johns Hopkins Press, 1964.
This book is a briefer version of an earlier study by Resources for the Future of the adequacy of natural resources for United States economic growth through the twentieth century. On the whole, resource scarcity is not expected to limit output through the period under review, although some resources may experience a moderate increase in price. The crisis in energy needs and the mounting environmental costs of continued economic growth, however, are largely unnoted in the study.

Landsberg, Hans H., and Schurr, S. H., *Energy in the United States: Sources, Uses, and Policy Issues.* New York: Random House, 1968.
A survey of the history and current trends of energy uses in the United States, including the generation and use of electricity.

MacAvoy, Paul, "The Regulation-Induced Shortage of Natural Gas," *Journal of Law and Economics,* XIV (April 1971), pp. 167–199.
An attempt to determine the effect of the Federal Power Commission's control of the price of natural gas upon its supply. MacAvoy's analysis is somewhat less decisive, however, than the article's title would lead one to expect.

Resources and Man. San Francisco: W. H. Freeman and Co. for the National Academy of Sciences, 1969.
A wide-ranging collection of articles presented by the National Academy of Sciences—National Research Council as "A Study and Recommendations by the Committee on Resources and Man of the Division of Earth Sciences." The articles include "'Interactions Between Man and His Resources," "United States and World Population," "Food from the Land," and "Energy Resources." The latter article, by M. K. Hubbert, is most relevant to this chapter.

Wolff, Anthony, "Showdown at Four Corners," *Saturday Review,* LV (June 3, 1972) pp. 29–41.
Four Corners is the area where power production utilizes strip-mined Black Mesa coal. This article is a critical but comprehensive examination of the economic, ethical, and environmental issues involved in this controversy.

Chapter Nine

Water Pollution, I: The Sources
and Magnitude of the Problem

*Throughout history man has been ravaged by plague and
epidemics visited on him by poor sanitation and polluted
water. In more modern times, the great typhoid epidemics
that swept London in the mid-19th Century underscored
the peril of water pollution and launched the first organized
steps to combat it. And until very recent times this stress
on preventing waterborne disease was the major thrust of
efforts to stem the decline of the environment.*

*Americans have acted, until recently, as though their rivers
and lakes had an infinite capacity to absorb wastes. Pollution
was considered the price of progress.—Environmental Quality* [1]

In the summer of 1969, two railroad bridges over the
Cuyahoga River, near Cleveland, were almost destroyed by fire.
This in itself was hardly news, but the fire broke out first in the
river and spread to the bridges. The source of the fire—the Cuyahoga River—is a turbid, chocolate-brown mass of diluted industrial wastes, carrying sometimes enough oily materials to be
inflammable, but never enough oxygen to support life—even the
leeches and sludge worms that are the last aquatic organisms to
survive in the lower reaches of heavily polluted water.

[1] First Annual Report of the Council on Environmental Quality (Washington, D.C.: Government Printing Office, 1970), p. 29.

The Cuyahoga River and a few others in the United States carry such a heavy burden of municipal and industrial wastes that they have lost their capacity to support aquatic life, and serve solely as avenues of waste transport. Before a river reaches this advanced state of degradation, however, it is usually able to recover its oxygen balance and life-sustaining capacity through the modification of the chemical nature of the waste products introduced into the watercourse. How much water pollution society will tolerate depends upon a variety of considerations, but probably the single most important factor is the purpose to be served by the river or lake. The Cuyahoga River and the Houston Ship Canal, for example, may be deemed suitable only to transport wastes. But the effects of these decisions extend also to the respective destinations of the waterways, Lake Erie and Galveston Bay.

If the level of pollution is kept well below that of the Cuyahoga, however, a watercourse may serve purposes in addition to waste disposal. Some uses require the absence of only certain kinds of pollution, such as minerals that corrode boilers. And some are less tolerant of pollution than others. For example, water which is to provide habitat for game fish (trout, salmon) requires a higher dissolved-oxygen content than does water for less exalted species (catfish and perch). Water serving as a trout stream is thus unavailable for waste disposal; one use becomes a cost or trade-off for other uses.

Although pollution of water and air occurs without man's intervention, from such natural causes as landslides and forest fires, natural environmental abuse is generally inconsequential except in areas of special devastation. Most pollution is the result of man's actions; the main sources are catalogued in Table 9.1.

Water Regeneration

Degradable Wastes

Human wastes, garbage, food-processing by-products, pulp- and paper-processing effluents, and other organic materials can be transformed by natural decomposition if a stream's regenerat-

Table 9.1.   Sources and Types of Water Pollutants

Source of Waste	Kind of Pollutant
Municipalities and residences	Human wastes, detergents, garbage, trash
Urban drainage	Suspended sediment, fertilizers, pesticides, road salt
Agriculture	
Crop production	Fertilizers, herbicides, pesticides, erosion sediment
Irrigation return flow	Mineral salts and erosion sediment
Industry	The widest possible range of pollutants, including biodegradable wastes in the paper and foods processing industries, heat discharge in a variety of activities, nondegradable wastes in the chemical and iron and steel industries, and radioactivity.
Mining	Acids, sediment, metal wastes, culm
Electric power production	Heat and nuclear wastes
Recreation and navigation	Human wastes, garbage, fuel wastes

ing capacity is not overburdened. The process by which such wastes are broken down into their constituent elements involves bacterial action, and may take place *aerobically* (in the presence of oxygen) or *anaerobically* (in the absence of molecular, or free, oxygen but with oxygen entering the process through various chemical combinations).

A stream can break down a light organic-waste load through aerobic bacterial action, but the process of decomposition causes a reduction in the water's dissolved oxygen. How injurious this process is to aquatic life depends upon how much depletion of dissolved oxygen takes place. If the stream's oxygen is greatly depressed, or if the oxygen requirements of the organisms present are high, stream regeneration takes place at the expense of aquatic life. In the process of regeneration, the selective destruction of aquatic life may significantly modify the character of the stream.

How much oxygen a stream can spare for aerobic decomposition depends upon its temperature and turbulence. Although oxygen absorption from the air is limited, a fast-moving stream restores its oxygen loss more quickly than a tranquil pool, and the amount of oxygen that water can retain varies inversely with temperature. A cold, white-water stream will carry more free oxygen than a warm, stagnant pool, and the former's capacity to degrade wastes—restore itself to an unpolluted state—is greater. This does not mean, however, that the appropriate waste-disposal policy is to select white-water streams. The stream with a high oxygen content is likely to have developed an aquatic population that is dependent upon the maintenance of this oxygen level, and even a modest reduction in the free oxygen is likely to wipe out much of the stream's life.

BOD, the Oxygen Sag, and Photosynthesis

Most streams in the United States can be likened to huge, open-ended tubes that periodically receive varying amounts of chemicals most of which have a profound effect upon aquatic life. Many of the polluting materials decompose and make available nutrient material that changes the character of the stream. The potency of the decomposing waste materials can be measured by the amount of oxygen that is used up in the process, generally expressed as "biochemical oxygen demand," or BOD. The designation BOD is sometimes used to cover a five-day cycle of waste decomposition.

The capacity of a stream to stabilize wastes depends upon a number of different factors: temperature, surface area, turbulence, and the presence or absence of toxic materials. The higher the water temperature, the more rapid is the bacterial action that decomposes the stream's wastes, and consequently, the greater is the demand for the stream's free oxygen. However, the saturation level of oxygen is lower in warm water, so a warm stream has less free oxygen available for decomposition than a cool stream. As a result, the dissolved oxygen content of a body of water may be reduced to zero during the summer, and waste loads that are decomposed aerobically during other seasons may decompose anaerobically during this period—especially when high temperature coincides with low stream flow. The degree of water turbulence and the amount of surface area affect a stream's exposure to air and therefore the rate of reabsorption of oxygen. Toxic wastes, even when neutral in oxygen demand, may destroy bacteria and oxygenating plants that have an essential role in stream regeneration.

Because of the various conditions that may prevail in a stream at different times and places, no single pattern is assured. Typically, however, in the process of decomposing wastes, a stream undergoes an oxygen depletion, or sag. If the water temperature is high and the stream's surface great, decomposition will be speeded and the oxygen sag will be steep and of relatively short duration; if decomposition is slow, drawing oxygen gradually, the sag curve will be flatter and longer.

An oxygen profile for the Ohio River, projected for 1980, is shown in Figure 9.1. Specific combinations of factors, including temperature, stream flow, and waste conditions, produce the particular sags illustrated. With different factor combinations, other sags would occur. The oxygen content of a stream during degradation and recovery from slight (*A*), heavy (*B*), and gross (*C*) pollution is shown in Figure 9.2. In some cases, oxygen depletion may be so great that a part of the stream may become anaerobic in the area of heavy waste disposal, as illustrated by the lower segment of Curve *C*. With a lighter pollution load, indicated by Curves *A* and *B*, the stream's oxygen is drawn down, but it remains aerobic. Knowledge of the nature of the oxygen loss in a stream is essential to determine the optimum pollution-abatement programs.

As waste products in a stream are degraded—broken down into constituent elements, such as phosphorus, carbon, and nitro-

Figure 9.1.   Dissolved-Oxygen Profile for the Ohio River,
Projected for 1980 *

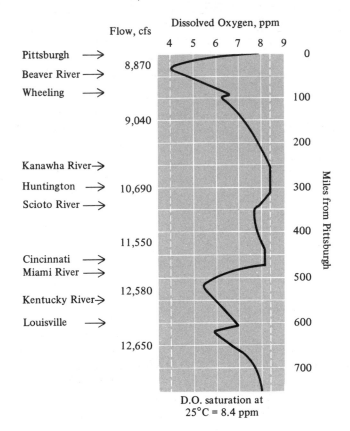

Assumptions: Medium economic growth, 70-percent waste load reduction, and temperature of 25°C.

* R. L. O'Connell, *et al.*, *Future Stream Flow Requirements for Organic Pollution Abatement, Ohio River Basin* (Cincinnati: Taft Sanitary Engineering Center, mimeographed, undated). Reproduced in A. V. Kneese and B. T. Bower, *Managing Water Quality: Economics, Technology, Institutions* (Baltimore: Johns Hopkins Press, 1968), p. 23. Published for Resources for the Future, Inc. by the Johns Hopkins Press.

Figure 9.2. Oxygen Sag Curves *

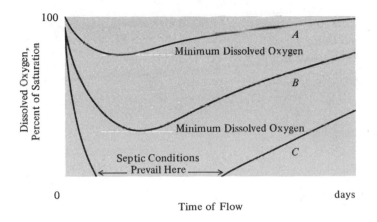

* Louis Klein, *River Pollution: Causes and Effects*, Vol. II (London: Butterworth & Co., 1962), p. 218.

gen—the released materials initially stimulate the growth of plant and animal organisms. Algal production is one of the more apparent results of the buildup of nutrients in the stream, and this further modifies the stream's chemistry. Through photosynthesis, the growing algae release oxygen into the stream; they also serve as food for other aquatic life, increasing its abundance. Photosynthesis is only a daytime process, and at night algae exert a drain on the free oxygen in the water; however, the net effect of algal growth is to raise the water's oxygen level. But growth cannot continue indefinitely. Eventually the abundance of algae may curtail light, a necessary ingredient of photosynthesis, causing rapid algal blooms to be followed by algal kills. In decomposition, the dead algae behave chemically as an organic waste, and exert a strong competitive pull upon the stream's free oxygen, decreasing that available for the support of stream life. The sudden drop in the supply of algae for food and as a producer of oxygen, if severe, can wipe out aquatic populations that were built up during the algal bloom.

Eutrophication

Along with algal growth, acceleration of plant growth generally is likely to take place in a water body when there is decomposition of waste materials. When a stream or pond is heavily fertilized by degradable wastes, the stimulation of plant growth will "age" it, and eventually cause its death by choking it with the plant growth. This evolutionary process—from lake to marsh to land—is termed "eutrophication," and takes place naturally when nutrient and sediment runoff from surrounding land causes a buildup of bog conditions, the growth of marsh grasses, and eventually the elimination of all water from the area. This natural process has been artificially accelerated by the increased production of organic wastes and the inadequate waste-treatment practices in the United States. Although treated wastes are lower in nutrient content than untreated wastes—thus exerting less aging impact—the fertilizer in all effluents except that from advanced treatment plants is sufficiently rich to cause unnatural growth.

The Eutrophication of Lake Erie—Pollution Showpiece. Lake Erie has been called many things in recent years—a 9,900-square-mile cesspool, a biological bomb, a dead lake. According to biologists, in the past half century the lake has aged fifteen thousand years from overenrichment. Some biologists believe it can be revived by stopping the flow of waste, but others contend that a major scouring of the lake bottom is the necessary first step toward revival. In certain regions of the lake, the bottom is covered by a 30-to-125-foot layer of polluted muck, heavily saturated with phosphates, nitrates, insecticides, and industrial chemicals. Already nearly 25 percent of Lake Erie's lower water level is frequently devoid of oxygen, and the aquatic populations have been drastically altered. Northern pike, blue pike, and sturgeon have been largely eliminated and only species tolerant of a lower-quality habitat, such as suckers and carp, have survived.

Lake Erie is not just aging; it is being choked to death by the domestic and industrial wastes from Cleveland, Detroit, and the other communities surrounding the lake. Cuyahoga River, whose bacterial count at times matches that of raw sewage, empties into Lake Erie, and the Detroit River unloads even more pollution into the lake. In the past, when the Detroit River was dredged, the bottom sludge from the river was disposed of simply by dumping it into Lake Erie, where it added to an already excessive deposit of waste materials.

In the early 1970's, Lake Erie served as the daily dumping ground from all sources for approximately 11 million pounds of chlorides, 137,000 pounds of phosphates, smaller amounts of nitrates, and undetermined quantities of cyanide, acids, oils, and various more exotic wastes. According to some estimates, simply to treat sufficiently the municipal wastes that flow into Lake Erie from the surrounding cities would require a municipal capital investment well in excess of a billion dollars and an investment by industry of more than a third of a billion dollars. And after that, there would still be the question of the bottom of the lake.

The Case of the Persistent Detergent.   Pollution of Lake Erie, although so dramatic that it attracted nationwide attention, is well removed from most of the population in the United States. Eutrophication from the use of household washing products brought stream pollution closer to home in most sections of the country. The household detergent has been responsible for more than a wash that is whiter-than-white. At first, some communities were plagued with water-supply problems when synthetic detergents built up in both ground and surface waters, and the early nonbiodegradable type of detergent created serious nuisance conditions at sewage-treatment plants. Later, when the chemical basis of detergents was changed to degradable ingredients, the breakdown of detergents was achieved at the expense of serious overenrichment of some of our major waterways. Finally, the modification of the detergents' chemical structure has raised a controversy over whether phosphorus or carbon is responsible for stimulating water-plant growth, further complicating the question of how phosphorus-based detergents should be changed to prevent eutrophication of our lakes and streams.

None of the above problems was anticipated when the first detergents were introduced in the United States in the middle 1940's and when they came into widespread use in the 1960's. Most of the first detergents were based largely upon a synthetic compound, alkyl benzene sulfonate (ABS), which had a high-sudsing quality and resisted biological degradation. The high-sudsing character gave the new washing material the resemblance of soap in household use, but unlike soap it continued to suds its way through sewage-treatment plants, surface and ground water supplies, and back into the home through the water faucet. Drinking water that strongly resembled someone else's wash water was bad enough, but the reminder that the water had traveled through treatment plants along with human waste was hardly comforting to the consumer. Even though no health hazard for humans could be established, a glass of water with a head of foam caused an uneasy reaction in most consumers.

ABS showed up in more than the home water supply. It turned streams into billowing paths of suds and falls into mountains of foam. It interfered with navigation on some lakes by obscuring landmarks, foamed its way out of settling tanks at treatment plants, where less than half of its potency could be withdrawn, and sometimes became airborne and drifted about the countryside, to the delight of children on nearby playgrounds and the distress of their germ-conscious parents. High-sudsing, non-biodegradable detergents had to go, and the industry turned to a degradable product based largely on phosphorus.

The new soft detergent was a great success—partly. True, it did not rise to the top of the water in mountains of foam, but neither did it sink to the bottom, an inert and innocuous substance. Instead, it injected, in effect, a massive dose of fertilizer into rivers and lakes and greatly accelerated the artificial aging of these bodies of water. In the early 1970's, numerous communities, some states, and Canada undertook to ban the sale of high-phosphorus detergents by legislation, and another search by the detergent industry was undertaken to discover a substitute for phosphorus. Initially, the most prominent candidate to replace about half of the offending phosphorus was a new synthetic, nitrilo-tri-acetic acid (NTA), which had been employed for a limited time in Sweden without causing overfertilization of waters or interference with treatment-plant processes. But a study by Samuel Epstein, a Boston toxicologist, checked the shift from phosphorus to NTA. Epstein found NTA potentially a health hazard, and it too fell from grace.

At this point, it would appear to be about time to reinvent soap. But the design of household equipment—automatic dishwashers and clothes washers—as well as of industrial appliances had locked in the use of low-suds detergents. Soap had not only fallen behind in the competition for a whiter wash; its use was likely to disable expensive household and industrial equipment. And if that wasn't enough, the manufacture of soap was less profitable. So the search for a harmless detergent ingredient stumbled on, rebounding from one environmental blunder to another.

Meanwhile, back at the laboratory a dispute was developing over which factor in waste water was actually responsible for stimulating plant growth. A new view challenged the generally accepted position that phosphorus is the main cause of excessive plant growth, and assigned responsibility to carbon. Those supporting the carbon-is-the-key school pointed out that massive algal blooms may occur when the phosphorus concentration in the water is low and that in any case phosphorus is almost always available in the stream or lake bed, so its presence does not explain the surges that take place in aquatic plant growth. Instead, carbon produced through the breakdown of carbon dioxide is considered to be the controlling growth factor. The phosphorus-is-the-key school responds that phosphorus is not found in high concentration during a growth surge because it is being used by the plant and that phosphorus in the stream bed is of no consequence since it is out of reach for algal growth.

The phosphorus-is-the-key school has more recently been challenged from yet another quarter—a pair of marine research workers studying coastal eutrophication. J. H. Ryther and W. M. Dunstan, of the Woods Hole Oceanographic Institution, contend that in coastal areas, eutrophication is primarily the result of excessive nitrogen fertilization, not of a high phosphorus content in the effluent. They contend that an excess of phosphorus is generally present in seawater, available for nutrient use, while the amount of nitrogen available is limited, and that although phosphorus may be the cause of algal growth in freshwater lakes, they believe nitrogen performs this key role in estuarine and marine algal growth. If they are correct, since approximately half of the nation's sewage effluent finds its way to coastal waters, a shift from phosphorus to nitrogen as a detergent base would hardly represent much of a gain unless the new detergent were carefully marketed on a regional basis.

The Waste-Carrying Capacity of a Stream

So long as the burden of waste decomposition does not significantly deplete the dissolved-oxygen content of water, self-purification will take place without degrading the stream's quality.* With abundant oxygen for decomposition—which is another way of saying, with limited waste in relation to water—assimilation of wastes will neither create offensive odors nor impair the stream's viability. The organisms responsible for preserving the quality of a stream by carrying out aerobic decomposition are the saprophytic bacteria; these are generally harmless to man but have an extraordinary ability to break down complex organic matter—including such apparently intractable materials as cellulose, lignin (paper-mill waste), rubber, paraffin, benzene, and petroleum. Indeed, the capacity of the saprophytes to oxidize petroleum is the basis of a plan to combat oil spills. A group of Florida State University scientists has suggested that such bacteria be cultured in much the same way as penicillin, freeze-dried for storage, and air-dropped upon oil slicks to degrade and emulsify the oil. This approach has obvious limitations, such as the time involved in oxidization and the difficulty of ensuring bacteria-oil contact in cases of turbulence, but the great advantage of the use of bacteria to neutralize oil spills is that harmful side effects are avoided. In early attempts to dissipate oil spills through the use of detergents, the destructive effect of the dispersant upon aquatic life was generally greater than that of the petroleum itself.

* Inorganic wastes, bacteria, and viruses that do not deplete the water's oxygen supply may of course impair water quality.

If the waste added to a stream reduces oxygen to less than five milligrams per liter, the stream's aquatic populations will be selectively modified. Five milligrams per liter is the minimum oxygen content that is necessary to sustain trout, and when the oxygen level drops below four milligrams per liter, other species of fish will be threatened and only those using the least oxygen —carp and suckers—will survive. Other aquatic organisms are also sensitive to the level of dissolved oxygen in the water, and so as the level falls, selective destruction of the stream's living populations takes place. The elimination of the smaller stream organisms may be largely undetected and hardly so arresting as the occasional fish kills that accumulate in odoriferous masses on the shores of lakes and streams. But the destruction of smaller organisms will be even more critical for the stream's capacity to sustain life.

Anaerobic Conditions. Eventually, the capture of the free oxygen by organic wastes may be so complete that the available oxygen is exhausted and decomposition takes place in a septic, anaerobic environment, producing noxious odors and destroying all but those few aquatic species that can survive in water largely devoid of free oxygen. This is the condition of some stretches of the Cuyahoga River and other rivers in the United States. But the loss of oxygen through the degrading of organic wastes may be only one result of pollution; nondegradable industrial wastes may build up in the stream, and toxic materials may inhibit or destroy the biotic process of waste oxidization. If bacteria, protozoa, and other organisms that contribute to the decomposition of organic wastes are wiped out by pollutants, it makes little difference what the stream's level of oxygen is.

The Broad Spectrum of Water Quality

A stream may have an oxygen content well above the five milligrams per liter required by trout, one of the more oxygen-demanding forms of aquatic life, and still not afford a suitable habitat for living organisms or be suitable for human consumption. Some of the traditional contaminants can be directly or indirectly measured by laboratory techniques; other pollutants, especially the newer synthetic chemicals, sometimes present exceedingly difficult problems of detection as well as elimination. For the most part, water-quality standards—the ranges of contaminants permitted for different water uses—have been framed in terms of the traditional factors, such as those outlined in Table

Table 9.2.   New York State Standards for Fresh Surface Waters *

Class and Use	Dissolved Oxygen mpl	Coliform Bacteria, per 100 ml	pH
AA. Source of unfiltered water supply and any other use.	5.0 minimum (trout) 4.0 minimum (nontrout)	Not to exceed 50	6.5 to 8.5
A. Source of filtered water supply and any other use.	Same as AA	Not to exceed 5,000 †	Same as AA
B. Swimming and any other use except water supply.	Same as AA	Not to exceed 2,400	Same as AA
C. Fishing and other uses except swimming and water supply.	Same as AA	Not applicable	Same as AA
D. Natural drainage, agriculture and industrial use.	3.0 minimum	Not applicable	6.0 to 9.5

* Condensed from New York Public Health Law, #1205, 5c, and Classifications and Standards, Parts 700–703. Reproduced in Division of Water Resources, Classifications and Standards Governing the Quality and Purity of Waters of New York State (Albany: New York State Department of Environmental Conservation, undated), pp. 504–507.

† A higher coliform count, 5,000, is permissible for the source of filtered water supply than for swimming and non-water-supply use because the Class A water undergoes chlorination and other forms of treatment before becoming available for human consumption, whereas Class B water is in contact with humans without further treatment.

9.2 for New York State. In addition to the measure of dissolved oxygen, the New York standard employs a coliform-bacteria count and a test for the extent of the water's acidity or alkalinity.

Acid and Alkaline Wastes

The New York standard for classifications from *AA* to *C* permits a pH range from 6.5, mildly acid, to 8.5, moderately alkaline.* Some inorganic acid wastes, such as those discharged by steel producers, may register as low as pH 1, while alkaline wastes may reach pH 12 and higher. Such extreme ranges of acidity–alkalinity will necessarily be reduced by stream dilution, but the stream's natural buffer mechanism may be adversely affected in cases of severe alteration of its normal pH, causing the destruction of water organisms. In addition to destroying aquatic life, acid wastes cause damage to metal and concrete structures, and high-alkaline cooling water causes scale in boilers, piping, and other industrial equipment.

The Coliform Test

Industrial-waste disposal is mainly responsible for the modification of a stream's pH, but coliform organisms in a water supply are considered presumptive evidence of contamination by human wastes. Themselves harmless, organisms of the coliform group grow mainly in the intestinal tract of warm-blooded animals, of which man is the most important, and do not survive outside this environment for long periods. Therefore, the presence of coliform organisms in water is a warning that water-borne disease may be transmitted by this water unless it undergoes further treatment.†

* The symbol pH is used to express the degree of acidity or alkalinity by values ranging from 0 to 14: 7 indicates neutrality, below 7 acidity, and above 7 alkalinity.

† In a study of coliform-bacteria survival in seawater, H. P. Savage and N. B. Hanes conclude that coliform growth may take place with sufficient nutrient outside the intestinal tract, and that bacterial density may actually increase. To the extent that the coliform bacterium is able to multiply in

The *Escherichia coli* is thus an indicator organism, and it performs an important function in the protection of health because of the ease with which its presence in a water supply can be detected and measured. The presence of *E. coli* can be found in two ways: by tests measuring indirect evidence, and by a count of the number of organisms. Evidence of *E. coli* can be indirectly inferred from gas generated when a water sample is incubated under controlled conditions, or more accurately determined by culturing the bacteria on an agar plate and counting the number of organisms per hundred milliliters of the culture medium.

The New York water bacterial standard permits minimum treatment of public supplies if the coliform count is sufficiently low, but modern treatment practices generally prescribe chlorination more or less automatically as protection against water-borne bacterial infections such as typhoid, paratyphoid, and salmonellosis. Protection against viral infections, produced by smaller, more persistent organisms, is not equally facilitated by chlorination—at least within the limits necessary to maintain a potable water supply.

Some viral diseases, such as infectious hepatitis, a cause of serious liver inflammation, may be transmitted to humans by shellfish grown in contaminated water and later consumed without adequate cooking. For this reason, polluted areas are generally posted against harvesting. Closing shellfish grounds because of pollution usually results in a severe economic loss to commercial fishermen, providing one of the more tangible measures of the costs of uncontrolled pollution. Because of the health hazard and the economic loss from the pollution of oyster beds, shrimp waters, and clamming grounds, the federal Environmental Protection Agency (EPA) has been granted special authority to intervene in cases where the shellfish industry is adversely affected by pollution.

Intervention takes the form of an enforcement conference between the EPA, representatives of state agencies, and the firms

---

open waters, its role as an indicator organism is impaired. See H. P. Savage and N. B. Hanes, "Toxicity of Seawater to Coliform Bacteria," *Journal of Water Pollution Control Federation*, XLIII (May 1971), pp. 854–861.

and municipalities considered responsible for the pollution problem. The massive pollution of Galveston Bay, Texas, by the wastes discharged by industrial firms into the Houston Ship Canal and by the untreated and semitreated domestic wastes added by municipalities has seriously impaired the aquatic life of this extended Gulf of Mexico estuary. Roughly 250 square miles of Galveston Bay have been closed to shellfishing because of the high *E. coli* count, causing an annual loss to the industry ranging from $359,000 to $1,045,000. An enforcement conference was called by the EPA in May, 1971, in an attempt to control wastes discharged into the Canal and Bay. Court action subsequently imposed restrictions on some firms discharging untreated wastes into the Ship Canal, but the magnitude of the pollution is so great that a truly heroic abatement program would be necessary to make much of an impression on the Canal.

The Troublesome Virus

In the treatment of both water for consumption and waste for disposal, viruses are more troublesome than bacteria, mainly because chlorine is more effective against bacteria than against viruses. Although viruses will not grow outside a host—such as an oyster or a human—they will remain alive for as long as six months under normal stream conditions. To prevent viruses in the first place from getting into streams, where they may continue to flourish in shellfish, massive chlorination of sewage effluent or filtration of treated wastes may be employed. Of the two techniques, the use of sand/soil filtration at the end of the waste-treatment process appears to be the more reliable way of preventing viruses from being introduced into our water sources. In sand/soil filtration, the virus is trapped by the affinity of the soil particles and held until it is no longer viable.

The Major Polluters

Less is known about many pollutants than is desirable for pollution-control planning. Of the various causes of water pollution, human wastes are probably most accurately measured in terms of biochemical oxygen demand (BOD), as are some industrial wastes, such as paper- and pulp- and food-processing wastes. On the whole, however, there is less information on industrial wastes, even though they are the most important single source of water pollution in the United States, and we have little more than preliminary estimates of agriculture's contribution to the burden of pollution in our streams.

Industrial Wastes

By traditional standards, the big polluters are not hard to identify. They are the producers of food products, paper, organic chemicals, petroleum, and iron and steel. But actually comparing the waste loads of different industries is more complicated. A measure of BOD can be derived for various industries, as shown in Table 9.3, but it may reflect only part of the pollution problem, and in some cases a minor part.

Table 9.3.   Estimated Volume of Industrial Wastes
Before Treatment, 1964 * [1]

Industry	Waste-Water Volume, billions of gallons	Process-Water Intake, billions of gallons	BOD_5, millions of pounds	Suspended Solids, millions of pounds
Food and Kindred Products	690	260	4,300	6,600
Meat Products	99	52	640	640
Dairy Products	58	13	400	230
Canned and Frozen Food	87	51	1,200	600
Sugar Refining	220	110	1,400	5,000
All Other	220	43	670	110
Textile-Mill Products	140	110	890	N. E.
Paper and Allied Products	1,900	1,300	5,900	3,000

Table 9.3—Continued

Industry	Waste-Water Volume, billions of gallons	Process-Water Intake, billions of gallons	BOD_5, millions of pounds	Suspended Solids, millions of pounds
Chemical and Allied Products	3,700	560	9,700	1,900
Petroleum and Coal	1,300	88	500	460
Rubber and Plastics	160	19	40	50
Primary Metals	4,300	1,000	480	4,700
Blast Furnaces and Steel Mills	3,600	870	160	4,300
All Other	740	130	320	430
Machinery	150	23	60	50
Electrical Machinery	91	28	70	20
Transportation Equipment	240	58	120	N. E.
All Other Manufacturing	450	190	390	930
All Manufacturing	13,100	3,700	22,000	18,000
For comparison:				
Sewered Population of U. S.	5,300 [2]		7,300 [3]	8,800 [4]

* Federal Water Pollution Control Administration, *The Cost of Clean Water*, Vol. II, *Industrial Requirements and Cost Estimates* (Washington, D.C.: Government Printing Office, 1968), p. 63; adapted from T. J. Powers, III, et al., *National Industrial Waste Assessment* (Cincinnati: Federal Water Pollution Control Administration, open file, 1967).

[1] *Columns may not add, because of rounding.*
[2] *120,000,000 persons × 120 gallons × 365 days*
[3] *120,000,000 persons × 1/6 pounds × 365 days*
[4] *120,000,000 persons × 0.2 pounds × 365 days*

Estimates of the relative importance of human and industrial wastes are expressed in the 1964 National Industrial Waste Assessment by three measures: the volume of waste water, the amount of BOD, and the amount of suspended solids. Each is a generalized indicator of environmental damage, but none is capable of measuring the full range of some pollutants, such as toxic industrial wastes. In all three categories, but most notably in the amount of BOD, industrial wastes exceed human wastes. But even so, the estimates in the National Industrial Waste Assessment understate industry's pollution role in the United States. Three important aspects of the industrial/human wastes comparison are not revealed by these measures: the more rapid rate increase of industrial waste, the greater abatement of human (municipal) waste, and the greater environmental destructiveness of industrial wastes. Only one conclusion is possible—industrial wastes are a substantially greater environmental burden than human wastes.

The Iron and Steel Industry. One of the big industrial polluters, the iron and steel industry, exerts little demand upon stream oxygen even though its discharge of waste water is unrivaled. But the steel industry waste waters carry ample non-BOD pollutants—acids, alkalies, and heat—from different stages of iron and steel production. Moreover, newer steel processes, unless specifically designed to limit water use, require more water per ton of steel production than the older techniques. Earlier iron and steel technology, for example, required less than 10,000 gallons of waste water per ingot ton daily, whereas advanced techniques use as much as 13,750 gallons. Obviously, as long as the supply of water is virtually costless and its disposal as waste is without penalty, there is little reason to curtail water use or to reduce the pollution discharge. With adequate incentive, however, plants can be designed to reduce waste discharges. For most products there is a range of production techniques from which the firm chooses on the basis of the relative costs of factor inputs. This flexibility in production techniques is well illustrated by the Kaiser Steel Corporation in water-scarce California, where the water use of the Fontana plant is less than 2 percent of the industry average.

The Pulp and Paper Industry. In contrast to the iron and steel industry, where new plant water use has increased over the years, the pulp and paper industry has shifted from the high-waste-producing sulfite process to the more self-contained sulfate (kraft) method of papermaking. The sulfate process has the double advantage of being less costly and causing less pollution as a result of the reuse of lignin, a major waste product of pulping, and the capture of more than 95 percent of the chemicals and wood substances used in the pulping stage of papermaking. The sulfite process cannot reuse these materials, particularly lignin, without incurring competitively prohibitive capital expenditures. The result is higher cost for sulfite paper and a pollution load from twenty to forty times that of the sulfate process.

Even though the kinds of paper produced by the sulfite and sulfate processes are different, virtually all of the United States papermaking facilities developed since 1940 have used the sulfate process. This has substantially reduced stream pollution below what it would have been if the added papermaking facilities had employed the sulfite process. Expressed otherwise, if the increased paper production in the United States since 1940 had used the sulfite instead of the sulfate process, the annual BOD waste load for the paper industry would now exceed 20 trillion pounds, only slightly less than the total BOD for all present industry.

The cost and pollution advantages of the sulfate papermaking process already have placed the sulfite firms at a competitive disadvantage. The older segment of the industry, much of which is concentrated in the Northeast, where pollution is already more serious than in most other sections of the country, will find it increasingly difficult to adjust economically to more stringent waste-disposal standards. Since competition from sulfate paper largely prevents passing higher sulfite costs on to the consumer, added pollution-abatement costs are likely to cause marginal firms to discontinue operation. Because the older, marginal firms are likely to be clustered in the same region, the economic dislocation will be more difficult to absorb.

Thermal Pollution. In the pulp and paper industry, pollution arises from the discharge of water used mainly in the preparation of pulp, the raw material from which paper is manufactured. Such waste water carries a heavy load of dissolved and undissolved solids, most of which exert a heavy demand upon stream oxygen. Another water use by industry, that of cooling or condensing, has little effect upon the quality of the water except by increasing the temperature of the stream into which it is discharged.

Until recently, the discharge of heated water into the nation's streams and lakes has been largely unregulated. But the growth of the power industry and the introduction of nuclear plants have combined to accentuate thermal pollution. The Atomic Energy Commission, which is responsible for establishing performance and safeguard standards for power generators, has not concerned itself with thermal pollution, however. The states retain the main responsibility for thermal regulation, with prodding by federal environmental agencies to raise standards.

The scientific community is in disagreement about the actual effect of increased heat upon various kinds of aquatic life. In late 1970, an enforcement conference called by the Federal Water Quality Administration in an attempt to win acceptance of more stringent control of heated waste waters developed into five days of largely unproductive disputes among scientific witnesses. Present evidence does not appear to justify ranking thermal pollution with other sources of pollution, however. Records of fish kills between 1960 and 1965 attribute only two of the 531 reported kills to thermal pollution. The estimate of fish lost in the two thermal kills was 620, as compared with almost 11.5 million for other forms of pollution.

The studies of the effects of temperature elevation upon aquatic life have established the upper limits of heat tolerance for a number of aquatic animals and some plants. As might be expected, the tolerance ranges vary; some plant and animal species are more adaptable than others. Most aquatic animals can adjust to a gradual temperature increase better than to an abrupt change, but among fish, the so-called game varieties—lake trout, salmon, brook trout—normally will not survive the higher temperatures. In general, an animal's metabolic rate increases directly with temperature, usually inducing more rapid growth, larger size, and shorter life. At other times, however, temperature increases may disrupt or impair the reproductive process—eggs may not mature or the hatch may take place too early in the season for survival.

Many industries rely heavily upon water as a cooling agent, but the undisputed thermal polluter in the United States is the electric-power industry. The electric-power industry has had such a high growth rate that a projection of its output increase to 1980 indicates a demand for cooling water that would use more than one-fifth of the freshwater runoff in the United States. This figure should not be misunderstood. It is not one-fifth of *all* fresh water, but one-fifth of the rainfall *runoff*. Eventually, process changes in power generation—such as the introduction of atomic fusion, magnetohydrodynamics, or the fuel cell—will reduce the power industry's demand for cooling water, but for the immediate future more cooling water will be required by this industry. Indeed, the shift from fossil fuels to atomic fuel for power generation involves more heat loss because of the less efficient energy conversion with atomic fission, thereby increasing the coolant requirement per kilowatt of nuclear power as compared with conventional thermal power.

The harmful effects of increased water temperature upon aquatic life have been summarized as follows:

death through the direct effects of heat;

disturbance of internal functions, such as respiration and growth;

death through indirect ecological effects, such as reduced oxygen, disruption of food supply, decreased resistance to toxic substances or disease;

interference with spawning or other critical activities in the life cycle;

competitive replacement by more tolerant species as a result of the above physiological effects;

reduction of a lake or stream's capacity to decompose organic wastes;

stimulation of plant growth or the development of undesirable forms, such as blue-green algae.*

* Adapted from John Cairns, "We're in Hot Water," *Science and the Citizen*, X (October 1968), pp. 187–97.

Although there is disagreement about how harmful thermal pollution is to aquatic life, there is agreement that the impact of increased temperature varies with different conditions. If the receiving body of water is large relative to the amount of heat discharged, the effect will be reduced through dilution, and may possibly be of minor consequence. In addition, the larger aquatic species are generally quite mobile, which means that the reaction of such species to higher temperatures may simply be movement out of the area. But species redistribution may cause food-supply and habitat problems, since unless the heat-polluted area is small, overcrowding and die-back of species may result. In any case, smaller organisms, such as aquatic insects, may be destroyed or the seasonality of their hatch disrupted, with a consequent modification of the food-chain relationship. On a larger scale, when the temperature gradient of a large portion of a lake is affected, the lake's stratification, or water layering, may be changed, diminishing the capacity of the lower levels to support aquatic life because warming of these layers reduces the free oxygen.

Of all the areas affected by thermal pollution, the estuary is perhaps the most vulnerable. It is shallow, usually at least moderately overenriched, and its productive existence depends upon an easily disrupted biotic relationship. Because of the abundant ocean water beyond the estuary, if may become a convenient causeway for the disposal of heat-charged water from nuclear plants. Under such circumstances, the spawning environment for a wide variety of species may be radically and destructively affected.

One of the frequently remarked consequences of increased water temperature is the acceleration of algal growth. Initially, this may be good—increasing oxygen and food for aquatic life —but if excessive algal growth takes place, it may be bad— cutting out light and checking photosynthesis, clogging the breathing mechanisms of aquatic animals, and upon death of the algae, drawing down the free oxygen in the water.

A group of University of Georgia research workers has been checking for such reactions in Par Pond for a number of years. This artificial pond near Aiken, South Carolina, has been subjected to massive discharges of heated waste water from a nearby nuclear installation, and the study has been financed by the Atomic Energy Commission. So far, no algal choking of the lake has taken place, but mammoth largemouth bass, turtles, alligators, and other aquatic animals have been produced. Although twenty-four species of fish have been successfully introduced into the pond, the largemouth bass has been the main object of research. This species has been found to mature earlier under the elevated temperatures—in two years instead of three—and to lay a larger-than-normal number of fertile eggs.

Whether the Par Pond research has lessened the controversy over thermal pollution is questionable. One conclusion from the study is obvious—heat has not increased algal growth to the point that it has inhibited aquatic life. But since Par Pond is an artificial body of water, uncontaminated by sewage or other sources of fertilizer, conditions are not strictly comparable to those generally found in our polluted environment. In many lakes and streams, sewage effluent, agricultural runoff, and other sources of enrichment provide nutrient for the algal growth that is stimulated by higher temperatures. No such interaction occurs in Par Pond.

Agricultural Wastes

Thermal and industrial-waste pollution have increased recently because of greater output and technological change. Agriculture reflects the same forces with identical consequences. There has always been some pollution from farming; erosion has displaced silt and soil minerals from cultivated lands, and at times runoff from grazing lands has carried animal wastes to nearby streams. But within recent times the occasional, moderate pollution by agriculture has changed to massive concentrations of animal-waste pollution from feedlot livestock production and overenrichment of watercourses adjacent to farms from fertilizer runoffs.

We now produce more food from less land with less labor. To do this, farming practices have changed—crop production involves larger amounts of capital equipment, improved biotic types, and extensive use of inorganic fertilizers and pesticides. Livestock production has also been drastically changed. At one time, the expanse of the open range was required to provide the pasture necessary for the nation's grazing animals. Now more and more United States livestock is raised in feedlots that are frequently closer to large cities than to the western ranges.

The same technique has been practiced for a longer time in poultry production, which for many years has increasingly employed factory-like structures where the animals are raised in confinement. (Even catfish production has recently been undertaken in submerged cages.) The new technique of animal production by confinement has been made possible in part through the routine feeding of antibiotics to animals raised in such concentrations, which otherwise incur greater risks of destructive epidemics.

New plant types, such as hybrid corn and miracle rice and wheat, require greatly increased amounts of inorganic fertilizer for optimum output. Not all of the fertilizer is consumed by the plant or absorbed by the soil, however. Varying amounts are carried in runoff waters to nearby streams, with a consequent increase in the phosphorus and nitrogen content of these waters. Over the years, the nutrient buildup in the streams and lakes near farming operations has increased enormously. In Illinois, for example, virtually all of the major rivers are overenriched from fertilizer runoff.

Feedlot Animal Factories. Feedlot production of livestock changes the ecology of farming in two ways: It deprives the soil of organic enrichment and humus from animal wastes, and it concentrates these wastes so that they create serious disposal problems. Just how much of a waste-disposal problem feedlot animal production is remains uncertain, but the burden of feedlot animal pollution upon our waters is substantially greater than that of the municipal/human waste load. Moreover, since this method of animal production is spreading, the problem of pollution will spread with it.

If all animal wastes were disposed of in the nation's streams, as fortunately they are not, the oxygen depletion would be equivalent to that caused by the wastes of somewhat more than 2 billion people. It is of course not likely that this upper limit of farm-animal pollution will be remotely approached in the near future, but already serious concentrations of pollution are occurring in some farm states and near some large metropolitan areas. In 1970, for example, South Dakota marketed over half a million beef cattle raised in feedlots. Half a million cattle produce a waste load equivalent to that of 2.5 million people and require essentially the same abatement facilities.

Feedlot waste disposal is not well controlled under existing legislation. State and local regulations have not been designed to cope with agricultural pollution, and where control has been exercised, it has consisted mainly of the enforcement of water-quality standards. Because of their number and political influence, agricultural enterprises have traditionally not been extensively regulated, and feedlot operations appear clearly to fall within this tradition. In the application of the recently revived 1899 Refuse Act, which requires a federal permit for waste disposal in navigable streams or their tributaries by polluters other than municipalities, feedlot operations have been excluded in cases where the lot size is below a thousand animal units, which is the equivalent of excluding from pollution control communities of five thousand population and below.

The Share in Pollution: People, Industry, Agriculture

In the imprecise statistics of pollution, the biochemical oxygen demands created by industrial, agricultural, and municipal/human wastes can be compared only in the broadest terms. At best, such estimates can establish a range of likelihood rather than a certainty of each source's contribution. Based on present imperfect knowledge, the range of the three major sources of pollution appears to be from a low for industry and agriculture of $\frac{3}{5}$ and $\frac{1}{5}$ respectively, compared with $\frac{1}{5}$ for municipal/human, to a high of $\frac{4}{7}$ for industry and $\frac{2}{7}$ for agriculture, compared with $\frac{1}{7}$ for municipal/human.

Such estimates are hazardous in more than one way. Not only are they based on data that are inadequate and of varying reliability, but they are national averages, which will necessarily be unrepresentative for some regions. Maine, for example, because of the high BOD output resulting from food processing and pulp and paper production, finds industry responsible for approximately 90 percent of the state's waste load. Other states, where industry is less important or where the industrial output creates less pollution, will fall below the national average.

One of the factors determining the magnitude of a state's water-pollution problem is simply the availability of water to pollute. A state with a limited water supply is not likely to attract industries using large amounts of water, whereas ample water means cheap water and usually less stringent control of waste disposal. As a result, industrial growth has frequently polluted most where water has been most abundant.

Even with better information, a meaningful evaluation of the pollution impact of people, industry, and agriculture is handicapped by the lack of a standard for comparison. Whatever the BOD contribution of industry and agriculture to the total pollution load in the United States, biochemical oxygen demand measures only part of the harmful wastes disposed of in our streams. Thermal discharges, pesticide runoff, toxic materials, and other by-products of changing industrial and agricultural technology have made the BOD test for pollution at least inadequate, if not obsolete. Not only are some of the new waste products, such as pesticide runoff, more virulent and more destructive of aquatic life than the older pollutants, but their effect is not limited to organisms within the polluted stream. It extends to higher forms of life—including man—throughout the environment. Measures of BOD and of suspended solids, and other traditional indicators of water pollution, may fix our attention on but one narrow flank of our threatened environment.

It would be wrong to give the impression that nothing less than complete knowledge of the environmental impact of water pollution must be available before a reasoned approach to the problem can be made. This is not the case. We do not have to know the precise dimensions of environmental damage, or be able to trace exactly the sources of pollution, in order to see that a large-scale abatement undertaking is called for. But inadequate information on how the various sources of pollution contribute to the overall problem makes difficult the choice among different approaches to environmental protection, such as federal subsidies to encourage municipal pollution abatement, effluent charges to impose the burden upon the polluter, and water-quality requirements to prevent stream deterioration beyond an established standard.

All of these approaches and more have been used in coping with water pollution in the United States, as will be shown in the next chapter, but deciding which to emphasize is a difficult exercise in social choice. The economics and ethics of pollution abatement impose important trade-offs, in the employment of resources, with other federal, state, and local uses—housing, education, and welfare, for example—and raise the difficult question of what we should choose to have less of in order to have more abatement of water pollution.

References and Readings

Brady, N. C., ed., *Agriculture and the Quality of Our Environment*. Washington, D.C.: American Association for the Advancement of Science, 1967.
> A collection of papers presented at an Advancement of Science meeting on the topic of the book. Papers are included on agriculture's role in water, air, and soil pollution and the extent of domestic and animal wastes in rural areas.

Clark, John R., "Thermal Pollution and Aquatic Life," *Scientific American*, CCXX (March 1969), pp. 19–27.
> One of the more comprehensive reviews of what is known about the effect of increased heat upon aquatic life, mainly fish.

Ehrenfeld, David W., *Biological Conservation*. New York: Holt, Rinehart and Winston, 1970.
> Mainly of interest because of some of the aspects of pollution considered in Chapter 2, "Factors That Threaten Natural Communities."

Eipper, A. W., Carlson, C. A., and Hamilton, L. S., "Impacts of Nuclear Power Plants on the Environment," *The Living Wilderness*, XXXIV (Autumn 1970) pp. 5–12.

An article by three members of the Cornell University faculty primarily devoted to the effects of thermal pollution from nuclear power production. The general nature of the problem is presented against a background of the Cayuga Lake nuclear power plant proposal. A highly informative article.

"The Great Phosphorus Controversy," *Environmental Science and Technology*, IV (September 1970), p. 725.

A brief account of the history and current status of the dispute in the scientific community over the role of phosphorus and carbon in eutrophication.

Klein, Louis, *River Pollution: Causes and Effects*, Vol. II. London: Butterworth & Co., 1962.

An important source of information on the biological aspects of water pollution, some of which are quite technical.

Kneese, A. V., and Bower, B. T., *Managing Water Quality: Economics, Technology, Institutions*. Baltimore: Johns Hopkins Press, 1968.

This work contains a brief but informative section on the biology of water pollution in the first part of the book. The latter part is relevant for the topic of the next chapter.

Water Pollution Control and Abatement, Parts 1A and 1B, *National Survey*. Hearings of the House Subcommittee of the Committee on Government Operations, 88th Congress, First Session. Washington, D.C.: Government Printing Office, 1964.

An extensive survey of the water-pollution problem and the present status of abatement practices. The hearings include both a national survey, cited above, and volumes on state and regional pollution problems.

Chapter Ten

Water Pollution, II :
The Options of Control

We are left . . . with only a single certainty. A large portion of all U. S. waters consistently demonstrate quality characteristics that violate established criteria. These violations occur in densely populated and sparsely populated areas, in humid and arid climates, in industrialized, in agricultural, and in forested regions, and apparently without reference to either the prevalence or the intensity of waste treatment. The lack of a pattern makes it impossible to judge whether conditions are improving or deteriorating; but the consistency of the pattern of pollution suggests that there may be inefficiencies in current approaches to pollution abatement.—The Cost of Clean Water [1]

The invisible hand, that remarkable device that Adam Smith finds operating in the market economy to direct resources in the simultaneous pursuit of private gain and the common good, appears to falter badly in guiding the use of some natural resources. The magnitude of water pollution in the United States, for example, as well as other cases of environmental degradation, is in large part due to the failure of the market economy to

[1] Report to Congress by the Water Quality Office of the Environmental Protection Agency (Washington, D.C.: Government Printing Office, 1971), Vol. II, p. 55.

impose the full environmental costs upon resource users. These costs, which take the form of polluted air and water, endangered wildlife species, and commercialized natural and scenic areas, are frequently shifted to third parties or to the public at large. This has happened because the private market has treated some resources, such as air, water, and wildlife, as essentially free goods, available for little or no charge as raw materials for production or as vehicles for waste disposal.

Because important environmental costs are not covered in the resource-use charges, the market economy's adjustment, in terms of both least firm cost and broader "public interest" objectives, falls short of the ideal. Since a polluting firm's prices do not fully reflect environmental costs, insufficient market distinction is made between production processes that create pollution and those that are without harmful effects upon the environment. If there were a price penalty for polluting, the costs of abatement would be imposed upon the production process and adjustments would be made in resource use.

If environmental costs are not included in the producing firm's production outlays, they emerge at a variety of other places: in increased treatment costs for municipal and industrial water supplies; in water recreation that is of lower quality and at the same time less available and more costly; in increased health hazards from polluted waters, and added expenditures for disease and associated rehabilitation; and in the aesthetic degradation that accompanies pollution. In determining the appropriate approach to pollution abatement, "internalizing" environmental costs within the firm is a secondary but important objective. Some approaches will achieve the dual objectives of abatement and internalization of costs better than others.

The Emergence of a Water-Pollution-Control Program

Because really obvious external costs of water pollution did not arise until recent decades, when population and technology overloaded the capacity of many of the nation's streams and lakes to absorb wastes, the early concern about water pollution was limited primarily to those cases in which it was a health hazard. Water-borne epidemics, such as typhoid outbreaks in the middle and late nineteenth century in North Boston, New York, and Plymouth, Pennsylvania, were the main reason for the early interest in controlling pollution, and the spread of chlorination of drinking-water supplies afforded most communities a less costly and more efficient means of protection than that of controlling pollution through waste treatment. Moreover, the pollution-abatement approach to water quality is more likely to be helpful to the downstream community than to the one building the treatment plant, and even with pollution abatement, moderate chlorination of the drinking-water supply is almost always recommended by health authorities.

Throughout the early half of the twentieth century, water pollution was viewed mainly as a local health issue; not until the mid-1950's did the federal government become active in promoting pollution abatement. The federal program, administered originally by the Public Health Service, consisted mainly of grants by the federal government to encourage the construction of municipal waste-treatment facilities. The construction-grants approach to pollution control is still the mainstay of the federal water-pollution-control program, but other regulatory features have been combined with it. Recently, the federal control of water pollution has been vested in the Environmental Protection Agency. This agency, established along with the Council on Environmental Quality in 1970, has been given responsibility for programs dealing with air and water pollution, solid-waste disposal, and other areas of environmental concern.

Although there are important cases of interstate water pollution, where wastes from one state pollute a river or stream flowing through another state, the fact remains that water pollution originates at a specific location and control must be imposed at this point. Following the traditional federal-state division of authority, the jurisdiction over water pollution by the federal government was originally restricted to interstate or navigable waters, narrowly interpreted,* and it does not extend beyond the three-mile limit in our ocean areas. These limitations, particularly the inability to exercise control beyond the three-mile limit, have restricted the role of the federal government in pollution abatement, preventing any effective check upon the many localities that dump their wastes at sea.

Because of the division of authority in the American system, the federal government has found it necessary to resort to stratagems of indirection to persuade states and localities to cooperate in pollution-abatement programs. The standard form of federal persuasion has been the matched grant—financial aid from the federal government to assist in the attainment of a specific objective, such as the construction by a locality of a waste-treatment plant or the establishment by a state of a system of water-quality standards.

The Federal Construction-Grants Program

Initiated in 1956 on a relatively small scale, the federal water-pollution-control construction-grants program reached a combined federal-state-local expenditure level of approximately 5 billion dollars annually in the early 1970's. Under this program, starting in 1973 the federal government contributed 75 percent, and the state or municipality paid the remaining 25 percent, for local sewage-treatment facilities. In addition to assistance for the construction of sewage-treatment plants and interceptor sewers, grants are available under the federal program for the training of sewage-treatment-plant operators, for research in waste-treatment techniques, and for the construction and opera-

---

* For some purposes, such as regulation by the Federal Power Commission, the Supreme Court has accepted an interpretation of "navigable waters" that is so broad—including any stream deep enough to float logs, for example—that virtually no limitation has been placed on federal control. (Citizens Utility Company v. FPC, 297 F 2d. 1; 34 PUR 3d 481 [1960].) In the case of federal water-control activities, however, states have been very jealous of their authority and protective of the cost advantages that industry within their borders enjoys as a result of lesser regulation. In recent years, however, federal jurisdiction has been extended to the tributaries of rivers flowing across state lines.

tion of demonstration waste-treatment plants, but these are of secondary importance compared with the outlays for municipal waste-treatment facilities.

The federal water-pollution-control program carries the clear imprint of the federal-state division of authority and the congressional policy intent. Since Congress cannot involve itself directly in the pollution-abatement decisions of states and localities, it has relied upon financial incentives to obtain compliance. For example, the contribution of the federal government to the construction of waste-treatment plants is contingent upon a minimum of secondary treatment under circumstances where the effluent from the plant is discharged into receiving waters protected by enforceable federal or state water-quality standards. By making grants contingent upon such qualifications, the federal government influences both the states' priorities of expenditures and the adoption of water-quality standards—increasing the states' share of water-pollution expenditures and stiffening the water-quality standards. By establishing qualifications for the receipt of a grant and then making the financial incentive attractive, the federal government virtually assures that the lower levels of government will take actions they otherwise might delay or neglect.

Congressional preferences have been apparent in another aspect of the grants program—the formula for apportioning funds to states and localities. During the early years of the program, the federal contribution was limited to $250,000 per project, which meant that the program did not make a significant impact upon the needs of the larger communities, for whom a $250,000 contribution was inconsequential. The ceiling on the federal contribution was raised over the years and eventually removed, in 1968, but by this time the effect of the limitation was clearly apparent in the lag in the construction of waste-treatment facilities for larger cities. Whatever was the cause of this early arrangement—the desire to spread funds instead of exhausting them in a few metropolitan areas, or simply a rural-town bias on the part of Congress—the effect was to allocate construction grants according to objectives unrelated to the severity of the pollution problem.

The 1972 Federal Water-Pollution-Control Act

In 1972, shortly before the November elections, Congress passed over President Nixon's veto one of the most comprehensive water-pollution-control measures adopted by the national government up to that time. The bill not only authorized a larger appropriation than previous bills—24 billion dollars over a three-year period—but increased the federal government's contribution to municipal treatment facilities to a maximum of 75 percent in comparison with the previous 55 percent, and initiated an approach to pollution control which was new for the federal government. Previously, the federal government had encouraged abatement by the carrot approach: grants to communities, and loans and amortization privileges to industry. Now, although still providing these incentives, the 1972 act required industry to use the "best practicable" technology to control water pollution by 1977 and the "best available" by 1981. Difficult as such regulations may be to define and administer, the fact of establishment of federal standards is a significant departure from the past approach to water pollution.

The Waste-Treatment Approach

The federal water-pollution-control program has directed its greatest effort toward municipal waste treatment. The larger and more complex problem of industrial water pollution has not been ignored, but nothing comparable to the considerable federal investment in municipal treatment plants has been available to industry. There are good reasons for this, only one of which is that already approximately 40 percent of the municipal systems' load consists of industrial wastes from firms that are connected to municipal sewers.

Virtually without exception, municipal pollution-abatement facilities are confined to primary and secondary waste treatment, based on mechanical and biological processes. Primary treatment, the first step in the treatment process—and sometimes the only step—consists of the mechanical removal of scums, solids, sticks, and various other debris, generally by settling. Even this limited form of treatment can reduce the biochemical oxygen demand (BOD) by as much as 30 percent. Unfortunately, the removal of sludge solids during primary and later treatment stages may simply redistribute rather than eliminate pollution, shifting it, for example, from the Philadelphia area to the New Jersey coast if sludge disposal takes place at sea. If the sludge is incinerated, pollution of the air is exchanged for pollution of the water. Attempts to "recycle" sludge as a fertilizer or soil conditioner have been less than successful. In most metropolitan areas, where there is large-scale production of sludge, the landfill approach accentuates an already critical shortage of nearby sites that can be used for waste disposal.

Secondary waste treatment accomplishes within the treatment plant the aerobic decomposition of wastes that otherwise would take place in receiving waters where there is sufficient free oxygen. Secondary treatment commonly employs either a trickling filter or activated sludge to achieve the decomposition of organic wastes. The trickling filter is simply a bed of rocks, tile, or similar rubble-like material, over which the waste water flows, increasing its exposure to oxygen in the air and providing a medium for the saprophytic bacteria that are largely responsible for the decomposition of organic wastes. The trickling-filter process requires a somewhat larger area for its operation and is less flexible than the activated-sludge process, as employed, for example, in the secondary stage of the South Lake Tahoe plant illustrated in Figure 10.1, but the end result is the same. In the activated-sludge process, instead of passing over a bed of rocks to increase its exposure to oxygen after leaving the primary settling tanks, the waste water is transferred to an aeration tank, where it is mixed with bacteria-saturated sludge and injected with air. If the process is operating properly and the bacteria are cooperative, a few hours is sufficient to reduce the BOD of most degradable organic wastes by as much as 90 percent.* If the waste

---

* A study by the Water Quality Office of the Environmental Protection Agency places the efficiency of the trickling-filter process in the United States at 81 percent mean BOD removal and that of the activated-sludge process at 87 percent mean BOD removal. (*Ibid.*, p. 13.)

Figure 10.1. South Lake Tahoe, California, Primary and
Secondary Treatment Facilities *

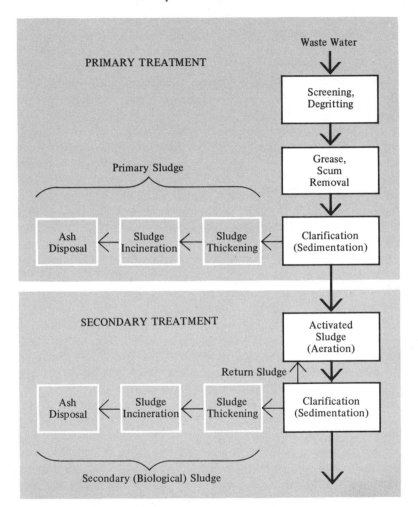

* Peter Forstenzer for *Fortune Magazine;* source for primary and secondary treatments: "Cleaning Our Environment—The Chemical-Basis for Action," American Chemical Society, 1969. Reproduced in *Fortune,* LXXXI
(February 1970), p. 104.

treatment terminates at this stage, chlorination of the effluent before it is discharged into a watercourse will remove most pathogenic bacteria.

After secondary treatment, the waste water exerts greatly reduced demands upon the oxygen supply of the receiving waters, but it may still carry a considerable burden of nondegradable materials which have effects ranging from subtle to lethal and which persist for a long period in the nation's streams without decomposition. Large amounts of phosphorus and nitrogen pass relatively unchanged through the biological treatment processes, and secondary treatment is generally incapable of breaking down salts, most dyes, acids, the hard insecticides and herbicides, and a considerable variety of the new synthetic chemical compounds. Advances in the chemistry of synthetics have kept well ahead of the development of techniques to prevent new compounds from polluting the environment. Indeed, present methods of waste treatment have undergone very little basic change in the past half century. Leon Weinberger, former assistant commissioner of the Federal Water Pollution Control Administration, made the following appraisal of the lag in waste-treatment techniques in testimony before Congress in 1966:

> Present waste treatment methods were devised generally, for the pollution problems that existed 40 or more years ago. Although there have been improvements in these methods, they are proving to be increasingly inadequate for the concentration and complexities of many of today's wastes and the requirements being posed by the increased loads on receiving streams. In addition, no satisfactory methods were ever devised for many industrial wastes and some of the impurities found in municipal wastes.[2]

In response to concern over the growing deterioration of the environment, the federal government in 1970 undertook to ensure secondary treatment facilities for every community needing

[2] *The Adequacy of Technology for Pollution Abatement.* Hearings of the House Subcommittee on Science, Research, and Development, 89th Congress, Second Session, Vol. I (Washington, D.C.: Government Printing Office, 1966), p. 139.

them and "also special additional treatment in areas of special need." At the time of the enunciation of this policy it was expected that the investment of the federal government would be somewhat greater than 2 billion dollars a year for five years—matched by a similar expenditure by state and local governments for a total of 20 billion dollars for the five-year period. Since 1970, the estimate has been revised upward for the required secondary-treatment investment, and if substantial advanced treatment is undertaken, investment costs will be many times those for primary and secondary facilities to process an equivalent amount of waste water.

The Costs of Transmission and Treatment

Before the wastes of home and industry can be neutralized by abatement, they must be collected and transported to the treatment plant. If a community does not have an integrated sewer system, the investment required to build such a system or correct the inadequacies of the existing system is likely to be much higher than the outlay for treatment facilities. And only limited financial assistance is likely to be available from higher levels of government to the local community for sewer construction. Assistance under the federal grants program is restricted to interceptor sewers and cannot be used for general modification of a sewer system. For the nation as a whole, the investment ratio of sewers to treatment facilities has been set at $1.75 for sewers to every $1.00 in treatment plants, and this ratio rises to $2.27/$1.00 in metropolitan areas. Although many sewer modifications are nonrecurring, they involve large investments and are a major financial hurdle for many communities.

Some smaller communities may find not only that the collection-and-treatment approach to pollution control involves large capital investment, but that the shift from ground disposal of wastes, as with the use of septic tanks, to stream disposal after treatment may actually accelerate environmental deterioration when the treatment-plant effluent enriches the receiving waters. By concentrating the discharge of nutrient-rich effluent, the collection-and-treatment approach to water pollution may actually accentuate nuisance growth of vegetation.

If the collection-treatment approach to water pollution is to check the fertilization of our lakes and rivers, biological treatment must be supplemented by more advanced physical-chemical techniques. Save for a few installations, such as the South Lake Tahoe, California, treatment complex, advanced treatment is still most likely to be encountered in the laboratory. Techniques of advanced treatment differ, but all are much more costly and complicated than the biological approach. The facility at the South Lake Tahoe plant, illustrated in Figure 10.2, is designed to combat two of the more troublesome by-products of modern society, phosphorus and nitrogen.

The Taft Sanitary Engineering Center, a federal pollution-control laboratory in Cincinnati, has devised a treatment process that performs much the same functions as that of the South Lake Tahoe plant, except for nitrogen removal. The Taft process is approximately five times as expensive as primary and secondary treatment combined, however, raising treatment costs to an estimated 58 cents per thousand gallons of waste water. This compares with an estimated cost average for primary treatment of 3 cents per thousand gallons and for secondary treatment of 7 cents per thousand gallons. Advanced treatment without nitrogen removal thus adds approximately 48 cents per thousand gallons to the cost. Any broad expansion of advanced-treatment facilities facing this order of expense will add substantially to the costs for sewer modification and expansion of treatment facilities throughout the United States. Indeed, the cost of advanced treatment is so great that alternatives to the treatment approach become increasingly attractive.

Storm Sewers and Sanitary Sewers

Even though a community has a well-developed sewer system, it may be the wrong kind for protection of the environment. Periodically, many treatment plants in the United States are flooded with storm waters that flush their wastes untreated

Figure 10.2.   South Lake Tahoe, California, Advanced-
Treatment Facility *

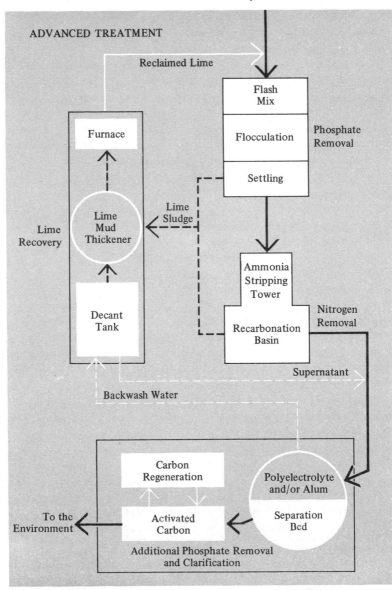

* Source: See Figure 10.1.

into receiving streams. This occurs because many communities, including large metropolitan centers in the East, have sewer systems that combine street drainage (storm water) with sanitary flow (domestic and industrial wastes). To prevent the treatment facilities from being overrun, causing raw sewage to be discharged into the receiving waters, either a separate sewer system must take care of the storm flow or storage facilities must be available to hold back storm waters and permit them to pass through the treatment system so gradually that they do not disrupt the biological treatment process. Although a separate system of sanitary and storm sewers is generally considered preferable to storage, it is substantially more expensive and does nothing to reduce storm-water pollution. And in some cases—as in New York City and other large eastern centers—the costs of separating sewers may be so great and the technical problems so difficult that storm-water storage is the only feasible arrangement.

On the national scale, the problem is little less than staggering. Recent inventories show as many as 1,300 communities in the United States with combined sewer systems, and the national cost of separating these systems would greatly exceed that of providing secondary treatment to the communities involved. A frequently quoted estimate of the American Public Works Association places the expenditure for separation at 48 billion dollars and the lower-cost alternative of constructing storage facilities at 15 billion dollars. Admittedly, such estimates are rough approximations, subject to a wide range of error, but there is no doubt that the cost of changing the existing sewer systems would be extraordinarily large. And since the federal water-pollution-control construction-grants program is limited to treatment plants and interceptor sewer development, the costs of sewer modification would fall almost exclusively with heavy and unequal force upon the communities.

In view of a recent study by the Water Quality Office, which indicates that storm-water runoff in some areas may be a significant source of stream pollution, the construction of storage facilities actually appears preferable to sewer separation. Impounding storm waters and treating them along with other waste water before discharge into streams may be the only feasible way of preventing runoff pollution from our cities.

If the estimated cost for sewer modification is added to that for extending secondary treatment to most communities in the United States, the approximate cost of attaining the 1970 policy objective can be shown as follows:

| | Cost, in billions of dollars | |
Investment	Low	High
Secondary Treatment	20	30
Sewer Modification		
Storage Facilities	15	
Separation		48
	35	78

The obvious question is, Can we buy clean streams and lakes for an investment of 35 to 78 billion dollars? By extending the federal grants program to provide all communities with secondary-treatment plants, will we eliminate water pollution? The 1970 federal policy goal strongly implies that the answer is Yes. Actually, the answer is clearly No.

Even if we separate our sewers and distribute secondary-treatment plants throughout the land, our lakes will not be free of algae and our streams will not run clear. In some cases, they may be even worse, overenriched by the concentration in the treatment effluent of nutrients that previously were reabsorbed by the soil through land disposal of wastes. The biological action of secondary treatment has little or no effect on certain industrial wastes and chemicals—salts, dyes, pesticides, mercury, phosphorous, and the like—and in addition simply changes the form of others, such as nitrogen, so that they remain in the treatment-plant effluent, only moderately reduced from their original loading when discharged. The form change of nitrogen —to nitrate—actually makes it more acceptable as a nutrient to a stream's organisms. As a result, the problem of the control of water pollution concerns more than the quantity of wastes generated by an increasing population and an expanding industry.

It also involves the nature of the wastes generated and the treatment processes employed in their abatement. Most of the recent increases in domestic and agricultural wastes—phosphorus-based detergents, phosphorus-and-nitrogen-laden farm fertilizer runoff, the same elements from human wastes—are only moderately checked by biological waste treatment. In spite of a significant increase in secondary-treatment-plant construction between 1964 and 1968, the federal Water Quality Office finds that during this period three out of every four pounds of the phosphorus increase were discharged into receiving waters. By any standard, this is not progress.

Alternatives to Waste Treatment

Few environmental issues involve so many private and public aspects and afford such a diversity of approaches as water-pollution abatement. This chapter has centered mainly upon the waste-treatment approach, the dominant present program, but has acknowledged the generally superior approach of process change induced by pollution charges. Waste treatment and process change do not exhaust the ways of coping with pollution, however. Aeration and low-flow augmentation provide additional options. Aeration, the injection of air into water to increase its free oxygen, has not been seriously considered as an abatement technique in the United States, but in the future it may constitute a lower cost abatement alternative to waste treatment and low-flow augmentation.

Low-flow augmentation is the controlled release of impounded water to dilute the level of pollution in streams, thereby raising the quality of the water. The release of water generally takes place during the low-rainfall period of the summer, and low-flow augmentation has been widely cited by the Army Corps of Engineers as a supplementary benefit justifying flood-control projects. This approach to pollution abatement has a special appeal to state and local governments because the costs of low-flow augmentation are wholly absorbed by the federal government.

There are also federal programs of financial support for the firm investing in abatement equipment, such as those of the Small Business Administration and the Economic Development Administration. The Small Business Administration makes and guarantees hardship loans to firms that are independently owned and operated, a small business being simply "not the dominant firm" in an industry. The Economic Development Administration provides assistance regardless of the size of the business if the firm is located in one of the "depressed" areas, which by definition cover approximately one-third of the United States. The EDA is specifically authorized to provide financial and technical assistance "if pollution abatement action should tend to limit modernization, expansion, or solvency"—a standard that is not overly restrictive.

Are We Winning the Battle Against Water Pollution?

As the quotation at the start of this chapter indicates, the question of whether the overall level of water pollution in the United States is getting better or worse is difficult to answer. In some problem areas, it is worse; in some regions, it is better. An equally important question is whether the construction-grants program is achieving the best results possible with this approach.

According to the United States General Accounting Office, the so-called watchdog agency of Congress that appraises such programs, construction grants have been allocated on the wrong basis. From fiscal 1957 to 1969, according to the GAO, the federal government made grants of about 1.2 billion dollars that generated treatment-plant construction of more than 9,400 units valued well in excess of 5 billion dollars because of the added contribution of state and local governments. In spite of this, however, the report finds that "the benefits have not been as great as they could have been because many waste treatment facilities have been constructed on waterways where major polluters— industrial or municipal—located nearby continued to discharge untreated or inadequately treated wastes into the waterways." [3]

The GAO's point is that as a result of a "first come, first served" principle in allocating funds, treatment-plant investments have not been placed where they will make the greatest impact upon pollution. Obviously, spreading small investments in treatment facilities over a stretch of river that is increasingly heavily polluted will only slow the mounting pollution, not keep any one portion clean. If, instead, abatement facilities were concentrated in areas where pollution could be checked or reversed, at least a limited improvement would occur. As the federal program has developed, municipal pollution has been the main focus of attention, while increasing amounts of untreated or inadequately treated industrial wastes have overwhelmed the efforts in the municipal area. Unless municipal waste treatment appreciably checks or reduces water pollution, the benefits from these facilities are minor. Obviously, municipal investments should be made where they will do the most good. The problem is to determine what is the "most good" and to have this decision accepted by the areas involved.

The Principle of Maximum Protection

Maximum protection or improvement of water quality requires that no pollution abatement be undertaken where it will have little effect, and that instead, concentrated investments be made where the impact will be greatest. So long as appropriations for investment are limited, the abatement program will be less effective than it could be in checking environmental deterioration if the allocation of funds for the construction of treatment plants is determined on a basis other than that of where the facility will bring the greatest improvement in water quality. For example, larger appropriations to low-income and populous states will not necessarily result in a concentration of plants where the improvement in water quality will be greatest.

[3] Comptroller General, *Examination into the Effectiveness of the Construction Grant Program for Abating, Controlling, and Preventing Water Pollution* (Washington, D.C.: General Accounting Office, 1969), p. 13.

The maximum-protection principle is simple enough, simpler than the usual basis for allocating federal grants, but its application on an individual treatment-plant basis involves analysis that is much more complex than the conventional approach relying on population and income. Achieving maximum protection involves more than simply finding what complex of investments will reduce BOD the most. It requires the determination of where a BOD reduction will bring the greatest improvement in water quality. Equivalent reductions of BOD in different areas—the Platte River in Iowa and the St. Croix River in Minnesota, for example—are almost certain *not* to yield equivalent benefits. What the benefits are depends also upon the use of the river—whether predominantly for recreation, irrigation, or waste disposal—the number of people served by these functions, the availability of similar water resources within the area, and the quality of the river in the first place.

The broader the area in which the treatment-plant investment is to be made, the more alternatives there are to consider in the process of selecting locations. To determine the optimum investment in municipal treatment plants on a national scale, a comprehensive benefit-cost type of analysis would be required, comparing the yield from an investment in one area with that of another. Given the magnitude of such an undertaking and the less-than-perfect results from benefit-cost analysis, such extended analysis appears unjustified. Instead, an economically valid abatement choice can be made on the basis of river basins, with the distribution of funds to river basins determined in terms of "maximum protection." Applying the maximum-protection principle on this broader basis would bring its application within comprehendible limits, reduce the number of investigations and comparisons required, and take advantage of some existing interstate arrangements, such as the Ohio River Valley Water Sanitary Commission (ORSANCO).

Although investment in municipal treatment facilities poses the same basic economic issue that arises with other public investment projects, there are significant differences in certain features of the water-pollution-control program. The main difference is that the stated objective of the construction-grants program is to extend secondary-treatment facilities to virtually all communities of any size, within a limited time. The investment decision, therefore, concerns not what communities to provide with treatment facilities and what communities to ignore, but what communities to equip with treatment plants now instead of next year or the year after. Under such a program, the benefit loss from the choice of a lower investment yield is limited to the time that elapses until the higher-yield plant is constructed, possibly as little as a year. Under the circumstances, the recommendation of the General Accounting Office that the timing of the construction of each plant be determined by a sophisticated form of operations research is clearly a case of analytic overkill.

Industrial Waste Control Options

Industrial wastes are more abundant, and many are more difficult to treat, than municipal wastes, but the range of options for coping with industrial pollution is also more extensive. For these and other reasons, the federal government has adopted different approaches to municipal and to industrial water pollution in the United States. This has not been the case with municipalities. The federal grants program has been justified mainly on the grounds that most local governments face difficulty in raising revenue and that waste treatment is the only feasible way to cope with municipal pollution. Industry presents an entirely different situation: No similar financial problem is encountered—abatement or prevention of pollution is a legitimate cost of economic output —and industry is not limited to the waste-treatment approach. It may employ other forms of reducing water pollution, such as modifying manufacturing processes, recycling waste materials, and changing the nature of its products. Under these circumstances, it is clearly undesirable to tie industry to waste treatment through government subsidy, since this would mean the closing of options, such as process change, that might be much more desirable approaches to industrial pollution.

Many industrial wastes—such as those from meat-packing, canning, and papermaking—are susceptible to biological treatment by conventional primary- and secondary-treatment plants. As a result, as much as 40 percent of the waste load of municipal treatment plants comes from industry. Industry's use of municipal treatment plants raises questions of ethics and economics.* The construction costs of municipal treatment facilities are shared by federal, state, and local governments. The federal-state contribution to municipal waste treatment does not come from any special set of taxes, and taxpayers contribute generally to these facilities whether they are direct beneficiaries of pollution abatement or not. Firms that do not use a municipal system for disposal of their industrial wastes, and those individuals who live in a community unequipped with treatment facilities, nonetheless share in the federal and state contributions to municipal treatment-plant construction, providing a subsidy to the firms using the community system.

By contrast, in financing the locality's share, which may be minor for the treatment facility but major for sewer modification and plant operation, there is usually a rough correspondence between the benefits and the charges for treatment. For meeting construction costs, the locality is likely to depend heavily on the sale of bonds, which are almost certain to be serviced and redeemed with revenue from the general property tax and sewage rental fees. The same revenue sources will be called upon to cover the costs of operating the waste-treatment plant, in which case the revenue paid is at least roughly related to the benefit from disposing of waste through the municipal system. The sewage rental fees, in particular, approximate the concept of a user charge or effluent fee. Depending upon their magnitude and how they are levied, waste charges may exert strong pressure to decrease pollution. Before such levies are likely to be effective, however, they must be both substantial and specific. If they are slight, mere token payments, they will become "licenses to pollute" and will be ineffectual. The solution to this situation is

---

* Whether to restrict industry's use of municipal treatment facilities is complicated by technical considerations. Economy of scale in treatment-plant size may be an irresistible economic inducement for the small and moderate-size community to accept industrial wastes in order to take advantage of the lower per-unit cost of larger-scale treatment plants.

simple, however—to raise the charge so that it provides an incentive to industry to reduce waste output.

The Effluent Charge and Its Variants

If we exclude the sewage rental fee, which generally takes the form of a flat fee or is related to the volume of waste discharge as reflected by water use, the use of effluent charges to decrease pollution has been quite limited. In part this has been because the conventional wisdom has endorsed the waste-treatment approach, but in addition serious questions have been raised about what to include in the pollutant index—BOD, dissolved solids, temperature, phenols, and so on—and how to monitor the discharge of the industrial firm.

In the few applications of the effluent charge in the United States, such as that initiated by Cincinnati in 1953, the assessment has involved simply a measure of BOD, and although this is clearly an incomplete pollutant index, the results have been impressive. After the introduction of a fee of 1.3 cents per pound of BOD, industrial loadings on the Cincinnati municipal treatment plant fell off by more than one-third, and they continued to decrease annually for the next decade. Other United States cities, such as Springfield, Missouri, and Otsego, Michigan, have also made effective use of the effluent-charge approach to curtail industry's use of their treatment facilities.

The Ruhr Experience. By far the most extensive use of effluent charges is that of the industrial cooperatives in Germany's Ruhr Valley, where water-management responsibility has been granted to these organizations by the state. Over the past fifty years, the cooperative associations have exercised control over water quality, land drainage, water supply, flood control, and waste disposal in the Ruhr Valley. To abate pollution of the Ruhr River, the associations have employed a system of effluent charges, with which treatment facilities are financed. Effluent charges are determined by one of two techniques, depending upon the Ruhr cooperative association involved, and the criteria are considerably more comprehensive than those employed in the few instances of such usage in the United States. One pollution index, although involving a number of phases, reduces essentially to the question of how much the industrial-waste discharge has to be diluted with fresh water in order for fish to survive. The other consists of a "population equivalent BOD" measure that accounts for both toxic wastes and biologically degradable material.

Even though the basis for determining effluent charges by the Ruhr cooperatives is considerably more advanced than that employed in the few United States applications, Allen Kneese, of Resources for the Future, an authority on the Ruhr case, considers the standards employed to be unsatisfactory. He points out that some substances, such as phenols, although neither particularly harmful to fish nor demanding of dissolved oxygen, may still be extreme contaminants in drinking water. In very small quantities, phenol—a by-product of the petrochemical industry —causes water to be unpalatable when chlorinated. The solution to the problem of inadequate effluent-charge criteria is to enlarge the factors covered, but this necessarily increases the complexity and the costs of administering the system. In spite of imperfections, however, the system of effluent charges adopted by the Ruhr cooperatives has induced extensive water-conservation measures by the firms in the Ruhr Valley. Moreover, the development of electronic equipment to monitor industrial wastes should make possible the expansion of the effluent-charge criteria without significantly increasing collection costs.

Pay to Pollute

A proposal that has few advocates among strict conservationists, but is advanced enthusiastically by those dedicated to the market allocation of resources, is the establishment of property rights in pollution. Although similar to effluent charges, the pay-to-pollute approach may differ in its ultimate objective. Both are designed to discourage pollution, but the pay-to-pollute approach implies permitting an "acceptable level" of pollution by those making the highest bids. An administrative agency, such as a state pollution-control board, is responsible for establishing permissible pollution levels and supervises the bidding for the right to pollute a particular watercourse.

The advocates of the pay-to-pollute approach contend that it will keep pollution within acceptable levels without distorting the market allocation of resources. The presumption behind this contention is that the highest bidder for the right to pollute a particular stretch of river is more productive than other polluters in the area. Other polluters, unable to buy pollution rights, will either have to change their production process to eliminate pollution, undertake waste treatment, or go out of business. Since the less productive firms are more likely to be unable to bid successfully for pollution rights, enforcement of strict pollution limits will have the greatest impact upon marginal and submarginal firms.

Social objectives as well as materialistic motives are considered to be within the recording capacity of the pay-to-pollute approach by its advocates. If conservationists decide that the pollution permitted by the control board for a reach of the Hudson River is too high, for example, they can enter the bidding and reduce pollution by buying rights and not using them. Finally, it is argued that by establishing a market in pollution rights, the efficiency of the market system can be brought to bear in the battle against pollution.

Superficially, the pay-to-pollute approach has much appeal: It strikes directly at the polluter, apparently with a minimum reliance upon bureaucracy to achieve this objective. Obviously, the establishment of property rights in pollution is an improvement over unlimited freedom to pollute. But as in the case of establishing water-quality standards, the key consideration is the enforcement of reduced pollution. The pay-to-pollute approach is an elaboration of the regulatory approach, as embodied in enforced water-quality standards, with reduced pollution allocated by competitive bid. And the enforcement of strict water-quality standards has repeatedly encountered state and local opposition because of the financial burden upon the polluters. Furthermore, the standards of the pay-to-pollute approach are not likely to be immune to pressure for moderation from firms and their employees, nor is such an approach likely to be successful without a large-scale administering bureaucracy.

The most serious drawback to establishing property rights in pollution is that the bidding process may not work. Although for some river stretches there are enough polluters so that spirited bidding may take place, this condition is absent on most rivers. Moreover, for those rivers that serve a concentration of polluting firms, it is not likely that the minimum standards of pollution will be established at very high levels. Where one or two large industrial firms pollute a river area, as in many single-industry communities, there will be too few bids to establish a competitive price for pollution rights—quite aside from the question of whether collusion in the bidding takes place with a small numbers of bidders.

Tax and Depreciation Subsidies

Accelerated depreciation or rapid write-off of machinery and equipment is sometimes permitted in the computation of a business firm's tax liability by states and the federal government. In 1971, for example, the federal Internal Revenue Service shortened the depreciation period by 20 percent in the hope of simulating economic activity. Investments by industry in pollution-abatement equipment are granted additional special accelerated depreciation privileges.

Durable machinery and equipment, such as blast furnaces and pollution-abatement devices, have varying life expectancies, and the payment for such assets is normally spread over the period of their useful life—ten, twenty, thirty, or more years. Different depreciation techniques may be followed, but the necessary condition for financial solvency is that the firm replenish the outlay made for the capital asset by the time the equipment is worn out or obsolete. If the equipment is paid for before it is used up—say in ten years when it will last twenty years—the first ten-year period will be one of high cost and low profit because of the increased depreciation charges, but the second ten-year period will be one of low cost and high profit because the depreciation charges will have been paid earlier.

Since in this situation costs are higher during the first ten years and profits lower, taxes based on net return to the firm are reduced during the period of accelerated depreciation. But this reduction is temporary unless the tax structure is changed, because in the second ten-year period, when the capital has been fully depreciated, profits will increase and taxes will be higher. Roughly, what is forgone in taxes in the period of accelerated depreciation will be made up later, when the equipment is fully depreciated but still usable.

Therefore, from the tax standpoint, rapid write-off is not much of an inducement to increase equipment purchases unless the business firm expects the tax rates to be more lenient in the period after the equipment has been fully depreciated. However, although the initial tax reduction from accelerated depreciation is a temporary, short-run gain for the firm, largely wiped out in the later period when taxes rise, compressing the payment for capital equipment into a shorter period of time does have an advantage: The cost of borrowing is substantially reduced. This reduction provides a stronger incentive to the firm to take advantage of accelerated depreciation. The cost of borrowing $100,000 for ten years is greater than the cost of borrowing this sum for five years. Savings in interest payments, rather than temporary tax reductions, make accelerated depreciation attractive to the business firm, especially during a period of high interest rates. Under provisions of the Tax Reform Act of 1969, the federal government permits firms to write off air- and water-pollution-abatement equipment in five years, irrespective of the useful life of the equipment, if it is added to plants that were in operation before January 1, 1969. In addition, six states also permit a five-year write-off of abatement equipment, and a few states exempt such equipment from sales and use taxes or allow credit against state corporation income-tax payments. But by far the most important tax concession involves the general property tax, which was not levied upon industrial-abatement equipment by twenty-four states in 1970, and the use of tax-exempt bonds to finance the purchase of abatement equipment. Industrial-revenue issues, a close relative of municipal bonds upon which many states have conferred the same tax-exempt status, are expected to be offered for sale in 1973 in an amount exceeding a billion dollars in face value. The saving in interest charges, which results from the bonds' tax-exempt status, varies with market factors, but the interest rate is not infrequently more than two percentage points below that of the non-tax-exempt bonds. This advantage extends to the bonds' maturity and represents a substantial saving in financing costs. Both water-pollution-abatement equipment and air-pollution-abatement equipment are eligible for industrial-revenue-bond financing.

The Direction of Water-Pollution Control

Although water-pollution abatement was one of the earliest areas of environmental concern because of water-borne disease, pollution of most of our lakes and streams is worse now than it was at the turn of the century. Treatment plants have not kept pace with either the volume of the waste load or the kinds of wastes that have been produced by our industrial system and increasing population. In part, this lag in the technology and capacity of treatment facilities has been a result of the efficiency of chlorination in protecting our water supplies: We could pollute our streams and still make them safe for use as water sources by chlorination. Only recently has the broader concern about environmental damage brought a new urgency to the abatement of water pollution.

But if water pollution is to be turned back in the United States, if the goal of "Clean Water by 1985"—announced by Congress with the passage of the Water Pollution Control Act in 1972— is to be achieved, waste-treatment facilities will have to go beyond biological treatment, industries will have to modify production processes, and more of the costs of abatement will have to be borne by industry. For the first time, the 1972 legislation on water pollution extends federal control to industry by establishing national abatement standards. If effectively administered, such standards will bring the "clean water" goal closer to realization.

References and Readings

The Adequacy of Technology for Pollution Abatement. Hearings of the House Subcommittee on Science, Research, and Development, 89th

Congress, Second Session, Vols. I and II. Washington, D.C.: Government Printing Office, 1966.

Testimony of government officials, industrial engineers, and others associated with the control of water pollution on the technical adequacy of present abatement techniques.

Comptroller General, *Examination into the Effectiveness of the Construction Grant Program for Abating, Controlling, and Preventing Water Pollution.* Washington, D.C.: General Accounting Office, 1969.

A report to Congress critical of the allocation procedure of the Federal Water Pollution Control Administration in making waste-treatment grants to municipalities. Useful factual information, but sometimes inadequate analysis.

The Cost of Clean Water. Washington, D.C.: Government Printing Office.

Annual reports of the federal agency responsible for the water-pollution-control program have been issued under this title since 1968, initially by the Federal Water Pollution Control Administration of the Department of the Interior and later by the Water Quality Office of the Environmental Protection Agency. The reports are important sources of information.

Dales, J. H., *Pollution, Property, and Prices.* Toronto: University of Toronto Press, 1968.

Primarily of interest because of the brief discussion in Chapter 6 of a "market in pollution rights."

Goodman, G. T., Edward, R. W., and Lambert, J. M., eds., *Ecology and the Industrial Society.* New York: John Wiley & Sons, 1965.

A collection of the papers in a symposium of the British Ecological Society. The papers dealing with the oxygen balance of streams, providing a survey of water-pollution problems, and discussing the ecology of sewage bacteria beds are especially relevant.

Imhoff, Karl, and Fair, G. M., *Sewage Treatment.* New York: John Wiley & Sons, 1940.

This is a classic in its field; it is old, but not out-of-date in its exposition of the basic primary- and secondary-treatment processes. The text is well illustrated and the explanations are clearly presented.

Kneese, A. V., and Bower, B. T., *Managing Water Quality: Economics, Technology, Institutions.* Baltimore: Johns Hopkins Press, 1968.

This is a superior treatment of the subject and is noteworthy in part for the chapter on the Ruhr, which describes a system of water-pollution control by penalty. Kneese has published essentially the same material on the Ruhr in a variety of other works, such as M. I. Goldman, ed., *Controlling Pollution*. Englewood Cliffs, N. J.: Prentice-Hall, 1967.

Pollution Control: Perspectives on the Government Role. New York: Tax Foundation, Inc. 1971.

A useful compilation of federal and state legislative approaches to air and water pollution.

Water Pollution Control and Abatement, Parts 1A and 1B, *National Survey*. Hearings of the House Subcommittee of the Committee on Government Operations, 88th Congress, First Session. Washington, D.C.: Government Printing Office, 1964.

Testimony of government officials and others on the nature and extent of the water-pollution problem in the United States. Parts of the Hearings other than 1A and 1B consist of a survey of the extent of water pollution in various parts of the United States.

Chapter Eleven

Air Pollution—Its Extent
and Control

As soon as I had gotten out of the heavy air of Rome, and from the stink of the smoky chimneys thereof, which being stirred, pour forth whatever pestilent vapor and soot they have enclosed in them, I felt an alteration of my disposition.
—Seneca, 61 A.D.

Take a deep breath, businessmen. Next thing you know, you might be paying to use the air.—The Wall Street Journal.[1]

The wisp of smoke that accompanied Prometheus' stolen gift of fire to man has grown to an enveloping canopy of pollution over many of the world's most modern cities.

Air pollution and its damage to man and his works are hardly of recent origin: The pall of soft-coal smoke over London, Pittsburgh, and St. Louis was heavier at the turn of the century than it is today, and the occupational risk of severe respiratory disability was early associated with chimney sweeps and others whose work brought prolonged exposure to the fumes of combustion and the emissions of industry. But while air pollution has long been a familiar blight on the land, the modern variety of con-

---

[1] Barry Newman, "Paying to Pollute," *The Wall Street Journal* (July 12, 1971), p. 24.

tamination is different; it is both more prevalent and more virulent. It combines emissions that are not only more varied than the smokes and dusts of the past, but when intermingled in the atmosphere produce more destructive combinations than when encountered as equal but separate elements.

Although most of the larger cities in the United States had passed smoke-control regulations by the first part of the twentieth century, these were generally ineffectual and did not significantly curtail the heavy industrial output of smoke during World War II and the immediate postwar years. During World War II, air pollution was at best a low-priority concern, and in the immediate postwar years the nation was preoccupied with the problems of the industrial changeover from war to peace, fearful of any action that might hamper the attainment of full employment. The change from coal-burning locomotives to diesel engines, and the increased use of natural gas for home heating, helped to keep air pollution from reaching even greater heights during the postwar period. Postwar prosperity gradually relaxed the concern over economic security, and attention eventually shifted to the deterioration of the atmosphere that accompanied rising industrial output and our affluent automobile culture. Public indignation led to stiffer air-pollution controls, and dramatic improvement in some industrial centers, such as Pittsburgh and St. Louis, took place through concerted citizen action. At the same time that some cities were improving their air by stricter industrial-smoke control and regulations on householders, however, an increasingly important source of air pollution went largely unnoticed—the automobile.

The automobile was late to be recognized as an air polluter. And when it finally was identified as the major cause of the Los Angeles smog by Arie Haagen-Smit, a California Institute of Technology chemist, the unique conditions of the Los Angeles air shed and climate were thought by many to be the main cause for the stagnation of the auto's wastes to the point of obscuring the sun and causing eyes to smart. But the experience of Los Angeles was to be repeated on a somewhat smaller scale in other major United States cities in the late 1960's.

The Thermal Inversion

Los Angeles County, where smog came of age in the United States, is an ideal environment for the maximum exposure to air pollutants. The area is a natural air trap and experiences thermal inversions on the average of three hundred days a year. A thermal inversion produces a cap of cool air that holds down the fumes and particles discharged from combustion which normally rise with the heated air and are dispersed above breathing level. Figure 11.1 shows how the atmosphere behaves at such times. At the same time that thermal inversions prevent emissions from escaping upward, the gentle prevailing westerly winds exert just

Figure 11.1.   Thermal Inversion *

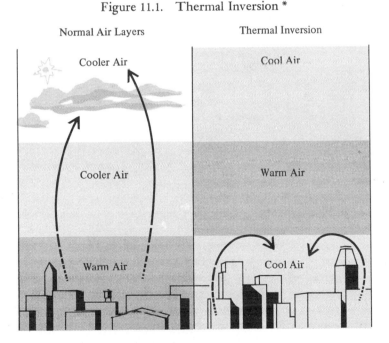

Normal Air Layers   Thermal Inversion

Cooler Air   Cool Air

Cooler Air   Warm Air

Warm Air   Cool Air

* David Bird, "Air Pollution Advisories Issued Along East Coast," *The New York Times* (November 19, 1971), p. 89.

enough pressure to pin the pollutants against a chain of hills to the east of Los Angeles, backing them up over the city and blocking their horizontal dissipation. The abundant California sunshine contributes to the eye-smarting smog by producing chemical changes in the pollutants. All the while, 7 million Angelenos go about their affairs submerged in accumulated airborne wastes—save when the winds shift and push the noxious vapors out to sea.

Entrapment of pollutants by thermal inversion, producing a degree of emission buildup directly related to the inversion's duration, has been associated with the more dramatic air-contamination disasters, such as those of Donora, Pennsylvania, in October, 1948, (20 deaths); London in December, 1952, (4,000 "excess" deaths); and the so-called "Thanksgiving Day" inversion in New York City in November, 1966, (200 "excess" deaths). These cases—all involving an abnormally high incidence of death and illness from respiratory impairment—have become accepted as classic examples of the effects of extreme air pollution, in these instances caused primarily by sulfur dioxide of industrial origin. The entrapped pollutants obviously differed from those of the Los Angeles smog in both variety and concentration, although monitoring has been incomplete at best.

While the experiences in Donora, London, and New York cannot be discounted, they should not be allowed to obscure the important but less dramatic day-to-day effects of lower levels of pollution that may in fact share responsibility for the deaths clustered at the time of heavy air pollution. Gradual impairment of respiratory capacity from continued exposure to pollutants may be more important in causing death than a temporary high pollution level. Moreover, other factors—advanced age, heart and respiratory disability, and various illnesses—may be the primary cause of death during periods of excess air pollution. In some cases, the abnormal number of fatalities recorded at these times results from a concentration of deaths that otherwise would be spread over a longer period of a few days or a few months.

The Varieties of Air Pollution

Not all thermal inversions trap the same kinds and combinations of emissions. The ingredients of Los Angeles smog are different from those of most other pollutant combinations, just as the frequency of the thermal inversions is different there. In Los Angeles, partly because of the pollution controls imposed before the automobile was identified as the main contributor to smog, air contamination from other sources is substantially less than in most other cities: Backyard incineration has been virtually prohibited, industrial emissions are rigidly controlled, and the use of coal for home heating has been banned. This leaves the auto as the primary malefactor, and the study of its effects on the California atmosphere has provided the rest of the country with advanced warning of the problems of automobile pollution. If we measure air-pollution emissions in the United States by weight, transportation—private cars, airlines, trucks, and railways—leads all other sources. Forty-two percent of the emissions are from transportation, and private automobiles are responsible for the greater share.

The main source of pollution from the automobile is combustion, which produces carbon monoxide, nitrogen oxides, hydrocarbons, and particulate discharge. Hydrocarbons are released to the atmosphere not only from incomplete combustion, but also when gasoline evaporates from the carburetor and fuel tank, and during fuel refining and transport—now largely controlled. The nitrogen oxides (NO_x) originate during the high-temperature/pressure phase of the engine cycle. These automotive waste products do not simply float around in the air, however, obscuring the sun until dispersed by a friendly breeze. Although the nitrogen oxides and the hydrocarbons are all spawned by the internal-combustion engine, their life cycle as pollutants is just begun when they leave the auto's tailpipe. When exposed to sunlight, these emissions create oxidants, and the result is smog. In addition to the more obvious pollutants, such as nitrogen dioxide and particulate matter, ozone—once considered a benign indicator of pure air—has more recently been identified as a harmful pollutant, especially of leafy vegetation. Ozone (O_3)—three atoms of oxygen in line—is most abundant in the upper atmosphere, where O_2 is subjected to energy in the form of ultraviolet light, but it is also produced at ground level from a variety of energy discharges. Although present in relatively small amounts, ozone plays an important role along with other pollutants in auto and industrial emissions. A breakdown of air-pollution emissions in the United States in terms of what they are and where they come from is shown in Figure 11.2.

The chemical composition of automotive fuel can of course be modified to decrease the output of certain kinds of pollutants, such as the highly reactive olefins.* Indeed, according to a study by the Bureau of Mines, by eliminating the so-called C_4 and C_5 olefins during the summer months, smog in some areas might be reduced by more than 25 percent. But olefins reach the atmosphere in two ways: from the discharge of incomplete combustion, tank evaporation, and the like; and from combustion in which various fuel elements are converted to olefins. Removal of the C_4 and C_5 olefins would not eliminate the production of ozone, but—depending upon the other chemical reactions in the air—it might help hold ozone to lower levels than would otherwise be the case. Some are skeptical, however, such as the chemist Donald E. Carr, who contends that "even if all the olefins could miraculously be removed from all the exhaust pipes, on a bright summer day in Los Angeles there would still be ozone in the afternoon." [2] Still more discouraging is the evidence that this ozone peak might be higher than the quick peaks caused by olefins.

Furthermore, the elimination of olefins from automotive fuel is unfortunately not without certain other environmental consequences. The olefins are not just smog producers; they are octane raisers, and their elimination on a large scale would require

---

* An olefin is a hydrocarbon that lacks the full quota of hydrogen atoms in its structure. These hydrocarbons are sometimes referred to as "unsaturated," and are more reactive than the "saturated" hydrocarbons, which contain a full complement of hydrogen atoms.

[2] Donald E. Carr, *The Breath of Life* (New York: W. W. Norton & Company, 1965), p. 95.

Figure 11.2.   Air-Pollution Emissions in the United States,
1968 *
(percentage by weight)

What They Are

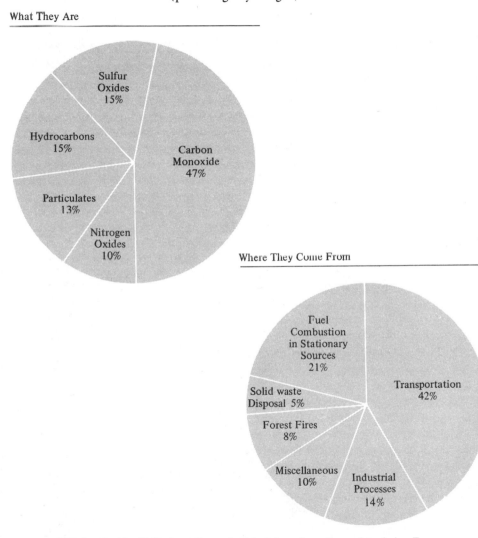

Where They Come From

* National Air Pollution Control Administration. Reproduced in *Environmental Quality: First Annual Report of the Council on Environmental Quality* (Washington, D.C.: Government Printing Office, 1970), p. 64.

either the addition of larger amounts of lead to gasoline or engine redesign to lower compression ratios. The use of larger amounts of lead in fuel is itself a source of particle contamination as well as being disruptive of catalytic exhaust-suppression systems. In addition, since lower-compression engines generally use more fuel at a given output rating, at some point the advantages of less pollution per gallon of gasoline consumed will be overcome by the larger fuel requirements.

Carbon Monoxide

The best-known and most deadly air pollutant, carbon monoxide, is a product of all types of incomplete combustion, but it is most frequently associated with the automobile because of the ground-level discharge of exhaust fumes and the heavy exhaust buildup during periods of traffic congestion. A thousand parts per million (ppm) of carbon monoxide in air are necessary to cause death in short order and—fortunately—no community in the United States reaches anything approaching this concentration of the deadly gas, even during the most heroic traffic jams. The highest measurement within the recent past in Los Angeles, the accepted bench mark for extensive auto pollution, was 72 ppm, and its pollution-alert levels for carbon monoxide—which involve decreased use of the automobile—have been established at 100 ppm, 200 ppm, and 300 ppm.

The research on the effects of carbon monoxide on health has been generally unhelpful. Not only has it not been possible to establish the levels at which carbon monoxide is harmful, but—outside of acceptance of the inescapable evidence that high concentrations cause death—opinions on its effects differ greatly. On the whole, there appears to be general agreement that carbon monoxide is not a cumulative poison, that it does not build up in the system, but is only temporarily locked with the hemoglobin of the blood, preventing it from carrying oxygen. Unlike some poisonous substances, such as lead and mercury, which when taken into the body tend to build up in vital organs, carbon monoxide is usually ventilated from the system in three to four hours by healthy individuals.

Beyond these points, however, agreement falls off rapidly, and some researchers find evidence of undesirable effects of carbon monoxide—impairment of judgment and coordination—at 50 ppm, while others insist that as much as 100 ppm involves no real danger. Experimental investigation in this area faces obvious limitations—notably the loss of the subject—when increasing concentrations of carbon monoxide are administered, but measurements of reactions to lower-level concentrations have been made in the laboratory, and by examining the reactions of those exposed to carbon monoxide, such as garage workers and tunnel police.*

Irrespective of what level of carbon monoxide is finally determined to be hazardous to health, two conclusions are inescapable: First, since it is hardly possible to consider carbon monoxide benign, even in small quantities, the prudent conclusion is, the less the better; and second, the air-quality standards for vehicle emission controls will reduce carbon monoxide, as well as nitrogen oxides and hydrocarbons, until about 1980; then, unless additional restrictions are imposed, auto pollution will again rise because the increase in the number of automobiles will have overtaken the abatement effect of emission controls.

* Examining the relationship between death rates and carbon monoxide concentration levels, two researchers of the California Public Health Department, A. C. Hexter and J. R. Goldsmith, found what they considered to be significant evidence of increased deaths when the carbon monoxide in Los Angeles averaged 20.2 ppm, the highest for the four-year study period (1962–65), as compared with the lowest average of 7.3 ppm. The average number of deaths on the days of highest carbon monoxide concentration exceeded that on the days of the lowest concentration by eleven.

Since the death rate is affected by factors other than the concentration of carbon monoxide, an excess of an average of eleven deaths on high-concentration days is more suggestive than conclusive. The link between cigarette smoking and cancer was eventually established from investigations that initially involved broad variables, but before the cigarette-cancer relationship could be considered demonstrated, more extensive evidence reinforced by laboratory work was required. A similar painstaking course can be expected in establishing the effects of sublethal concentrations of carbon monoxide.

The Taming of the Dragon

Only significant modifications in the operation of the private automobile will bring about improved air quality in most large cities.* Modifications in the automobile are expected to take place in three main areas: fuel composition, engine design, and the treatment of exhaust, for example by means of an afterburner or catalytic emission control. The engine may be redesigned to produce less pollution by using different kinds of fuel and achieving more nearly complete combustion. Fuels may be restructured, as a number of brands of gasoline recently have been, to eliminate such elements as lead, which is disruptive of the operation of catalytic exhaust-control devices and produces harmful particles.

Since automobiles are reasonably durable, changes in engine design and the selection of a specific kind of exhaust-abatement device will lock the auto and petroleum industries to a particular control approach for years to come. These measures will also raise the costs of transportation because of the necessary change in refinery techniques and equipment, additional costs for abatement equipment, and increased fuel consumption. The transition to a relatively pollution-free vehicle will take place in stages, resulting in a changing mixture of polluting autos, which will range from the pre-1968 models that have little besides crankcase emission-control devices to the new models incorporating the extensive engine redesign and exhaust controls that are expected to be initiated in 1976. During the early 1970's, however, pre-1968 cars that are not designed to use the lower-octane, lead-free gasoline have predominated, and some of these will remain on the roads for years to come. Therefore, leaded gasoline will

---

* William G. Agnew, head of General Motors' Emissions Research Department, contends that transportation is responsible "for less than 10 percent of the total U. S. air pollution problems." (Quoted in David Bird, "Car Makers and Ecologists Are in Conflict on Auto's Role in Air Pollution," *The New York Times*, May 23, 1971, p. 59.) Few outside the automobile industry are likely to agree with Mr. Agnew.

continue to be available to provide the higher-octane fuels these cars require.

Since leaded fuel, as little as a tankful, will impair the operation of a catalytic control device, the availability of such fuel—especially at a lower price—represents a continuing threat to the efficient operating of the newer control system. Raising the price of leaded gasoline so that it equals or exceeds that of the non-leaded fuel would eliminate the price incentive to use the leaded fuel, but since older cars are predominantly owned by the lower-income groups, an obvious equity consideration is involved. An alternative approach, such as subsidizing the production of nonleaded fuel from increased federal taxes upon the new autos, has merit. It would also involve somewhat more administrative costs and the uneasy reaction that is raised by subsidies to private firms, but since the need for the subsidy is limited to the transition period, the chances of it becoming entrenched are slight.

Redesign of the Pollution Machine

Adding exhaust controls, modifying automotive fuels, and readjusting the internal-combustion engine are the methods of minimizing automotive air pollution that are least disruptive of established products and practices. These responses will bring relief from auto pollution, but only as long as the reduced emission per vehicle is not overtaken by increasing numbers of vehicles, as shown in Figure 11.3.

Over the years, the American automobile has become an increasingly more powerful and massive machine. At times, it has been a means of ego expression as much as of transportation, and most of the improvements in engine design and operating efficiency have been neutralized by higher horsepower and greater weight. An obvious opportunity to reduce auto pollution is at hand, by legislating against private vehicles that exceed a specified per-mile standard of gasoline consumption.

In addition to providing relief from pollution, limitations on the size and power of private vehicles would reduce demands upon fuel resources and upon the materials used in auto manufacture.

Figure 11.3. The Trend of Auto Pollution *

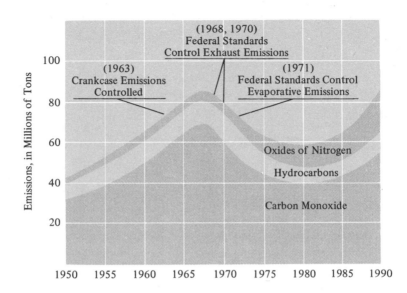

* Department of Health, Education, and Welfare.

Combined with increased emphasis upon public transportation, smaller cars would bring a substantial benefit from reduced traffic congestion. Indeed, if sufficient improvement and support were given to public transportation, much of the traffic congestion and the huge expenditures for road construction would be unnecessary. Reduction in pollution would be only one of the socially beneficial results of such a transportation revolution in the United States.

Not long after the automobile ceased to be a curiosity, the internal-combustion engine won out over the Stanley Steamer and the electric car—although the little old ladies in tennis shoes of that era clung to the electric car after the victory of the gas engine was apparent. Now there are those who suggest that a solution to the present auto-emission problem is the abandonment of the internal-combustion engine and a return to the ways of the past; others suggest the replacement of gasoline as a fuel for the present vehicle with natural gas, which burns without polluting.

The Electric Car

All of these suggestions have promise, but not much. The electric car has received the most attention because of the ready availability of the components required to build such a vehicle— batteries and an electric motor. And the quiet and virtually pollution-free operation of the electric car give it irresistible appeal during the stresses of the twentieth century. In addition to the disadvantage of less lively performance, however, the electric car is handicapped by its limited range between rechargings, and recharging is by no means so easily achieved as filling a gas tank. Moreover, the electric car is not so pollution-free as it appears at first glance. Its widespread use would simply trade the pollution discharge of the power utilities for that of the gasoline-powered automobile. Sulfur oxides and particulate matter would be increased, and carbon monoxide and nitrogen oxides would be decreased. Whether such a change would improve the quality of a community's air would depend upon the distribution of electric-utility facilities. Obviously, Black Mesa would lose by such a change and Los Angeles would gain. Other trade-offs would also arise as electrical generation in the United States shifted to nuclear fuel. Air pollution would be reduced and thermal water pollution increased. Again, whether this shift would bring environmental improvement cannot be assessed without examining the areas that would be affected. On the whole, however, the evidence against thermal water pollution appears to be less damaging than that against air pollution. Possibly the most persuasive argument for a shift to the electric car is that it would mean an enormous simplification of the control problem— regulation of a relatively small number of power plants instead of millions of individually owned autos and trucks. This advantage alone justifies serious consideration of the electric motor as a long-run replacement of the internal-combustion engine.

Different Fuel

Natural gas can be used as fuel in most automobiles with only slight engine modification, resulting in virtually pollution-free operation because of the nearly complete combustion of the natural gas. In performance characteristics, present vehicles using natural-gas fuel are inferior to those operating with conventional fuel, but as an even more compelling deterrent to widespread conversion to natural gas is simply the short supply of this fuel. Unless additional supplies of natural gas are developed or the supply is increased by coal gasification, its use as automotive fuel would be largely at the expense of space heating and power generation, causing an increase in coal and oil consumption in these areas. Whether the net effect of the fuel shift would be to reduce or simply to redistribute the overall pollution load is not immediately apparent, but certainly any net gain from such a rearrangement would be modest at best. A less frequent suggestion, the substitution of alcohol for gasoline, raises greater conversion problems than the use of natural gas as automotive fuel, and would require great investment; furthermore, alcohol is not a pollution-free fuel.

Other Alternatives

The electric car and different fuels are but two of many suggestions for superseding the present version of the internal-combustion engine. Some proposed replacements are quite exotic and untested, while others—such as the gas turbine, the diesel, and the Wankel—are developed engines that have already been employed as power plants. Of the three, the diesel and Wankel have aroused the greatest interest in terms of their potential for emissions control.

The Wankel is an internal-combustion engine using gasoline as fuel, but more adaptable to emission control than the conventional automobile power plant. The engine has significantly fewer moving parts than present engines—no valves, crankshaft, or pistons; it is already employed in a Japanese auto, and is being adapted for use by a number of European car manufacturers. General Motors has paid 50 billion dollars for the patent rights to produce the Wankel and is actively involved in research and development of this engine, which it plans to introduce in the Vega in 1975.

The diesel engine, which as all are completely aware, is at present the main power plant used by heavy trucks and buses, is adaptable to private passenger-vehicle use. Although creating a more unpleasant exhaust odor, the diesel engine operates at higher temperature and pressure than the gasoline engine, discharging less carbon monoxide and lead into the atmosphere, but substantially more nitrogen oxides. The diesel passenger car has advantages of economy in operation and maintenance, but it also has a hammering vibration and rackety sound that is not likely to appeal to those brought up on the smooth-accelerating Detroit product. Engineers suggest, however, that the vibration can be designed out of the diesel.

The Investment Establishment

No matter how pollution-free or adaptable to emission-control systems new power plants are, they face a very difficult hurdle —the massive investment in manufacturing and servicing that has been built up for the conventional internal-combustion engine. This investment is not confined to the machinery and tools of manufacture, but extends to engineering, repair, and maintenance talent as well. The more heavily capitalized an industry, and the more valuable and widely distributed its products, the greater the built-in economic resistance to radical product modification that will destroy this investment. In addition, if the industry is dominated by a small number of large firms, as is the auto industry, usually change must come from the established firms rather than innovating new firms. New firms have every incentive to design machinery and equipment to take advantage of new processes and new products; heavily capitalized established firms can do so only by writing off the value of existing facilities. As a result, change is more likely to be carefully rationed in an industry with the structure of the auto industry, with the greatest threat to the established firms coming from imports from abroad rather than innovators at home.

The approach to auto pollution in the United States does not contemplate either rapid or radical change. The conventional internal-combustion engine will be the auto's power plant for years to come, and its modification will take place gradually.* Whether this approach will be good enough will depend upon changes in other areas—public transportation, industrial pollution, and automotive fuels.

Industrial Air Pollution

On some days in the early 1940's it was hard to see across the street in Pittsburgh. By the end of the 1940's, however, the "smoky city" was no longer smoky, and at the present time this large industrial city is generally less afflicted with air pollution than Los Angeles, New York, or Denver. Partly this is the result of the automobile's greater contribution to air pollution in other cities, but it also demonstrates what can be done if clean air is considered important. Pittsburgh's achievement is largely a local reaction to industrial air pollution—the tons of fly ash, sulfur dioxide, and dust spewed from blast furnaces, steam locomotives, open-hearth furnaces, coke ovens, and other coal-burning equipment. Pittsburgh's air pollution was not colorless and odorless; it consisted of acrid fumes and heavy dark soot that soiled shirt collars when the day was only half over, sometimes required electric lights at noon, caused abnormal deterioration in the appearance of public and private buildings, and was a frequent irritant to nose, throat, and lung.

The banishment of smoke from Pittsburgh was not totally without discord. There were householders and industries that balked at the cost of changing from cheaper bituminous coal to smokeless anthracite, as well as at the requirement of mechanical

---

* Amendments to the Air Quality Act in December, 1970, authorized expenditure of 89.1 million dollars over a six-year period (1970–75) for research on a low-emission alternative to the internal-combustion engine. Results cannot be expected immediately.

firing in both homes and industry and of extensive smoke-controlling equipment in industry. Supported by a majority of the population and most of industry, however, the restoration of clean air in Pittsburgh was a notable community achievement and took place with a minimum of government intervention.

Because of the severe air pollution in Pittsburgh, controls were imposed there before other communities were aware that they might encounter similar problems in the future. In recent years, however, sporadic concentrations of smoke and particulate matter such as plagued Pittsburgh have occurred in many other industrial centers in the United States. Most of this pollution is from combustion. Noncombustion emissions from refining, from the preparation of volatile chemicals, and from the transportation and transfer of liquid fuels, contribute a relatively minor part of the total pollution load, about 15 percent by weight as compared to combustion's 85 percent. Most of the particulate matter in the atmosphere is produced by combustion, for which industry, including electrical generation, is mainly responsible. The automobile, which discharges lead salts and carbon, is a minor but increasing source of particulate pollution; its main pollutive effects are through chemical emissions.

Power Pollution

Although refineries, steel mills, and selected manufacturing processes may produce a somewhat greater variety of emissions, the single most important industrial source of air pollution in the United States is the generation of electric power. Along with the automobile, power generation, as shown in Figure 11.4, will be an increasing source of air pollution for some time to come. Increased pollution from electrical generation will occur even with the rapid development of nuclear-power production because coal-fired steam generators will continue to increase in use through the year 2000. Indeed, given present trends, by 2000 the demand for coal to generate electricity will be about four times that of the early 1970's, vastly accentuating a source of air pollution that is already causing critical problems in numer-

Figure 11.4.   Projected Electrical Generation by Source,
1965–2000 *
(Average Annual Generation)

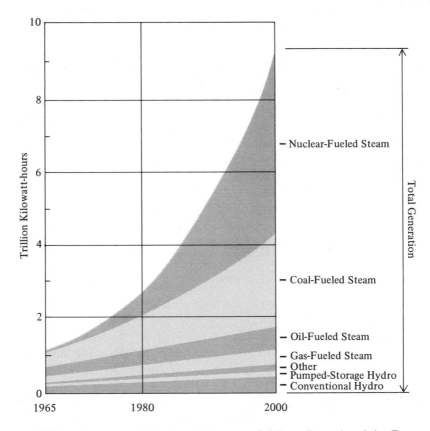

* Water Resources Council and Bureau of Mines. Reproduced in *Environmental Quality: First Annual Report of the Council on Environmental Quality* (Washington, D.C.: Government Printing Office, 1970), p. 81.

ous communities. The estimate of a fourfold increase in coal-generated electricity, consistent with the projections in Figure 11.4, is quite conservative in terms of the projected increase in demand for electricity, but is somewhat more liberal than the projections in Figure 8.8 (Page 191) in the share of the increased electrical output expected to be generated with coal as the energy source.

Power generation produces two kinds of air pollution: particulate matter and gases. The particulate matter consists mainly of fly ash, an unburnable mineral fraction, and soot, which is unburned carbon. Various gases are also discharged, of which sulfur dioxide (SO_2) and carbon monoxide (CO) are the most important pollutants. Some of the chemical emissions, such as carbon monoxide, can be reduced by increasing combustion efficiency through the introduction of more oxygen, while other pollutants, such as fly ash, can be trapped by various kinds of smokestack devices. The efficiency of some of these devices —such as the precipitators that entrap particulate matter by subjecting stack smoke to a charged electric field—is impressive, but they work best with high-sulfur coal. Unfortunately, they do not trap the sulfur along with the particulate matter, and this is released to the atmosphere to combine with oxygen in the air, forming sulfur dioxide, or under some circumstances, sulfuric acid. Other methods of removing particulate matter include wet scrubbing (which traps the particulate matter in water vapor), large vacuum-cleaner-like bags to collect the particles, and filters of various types.

Sulfur Dioxide Suppression. The removal of sulfur dioxide from stack gas, either that created when coal and oil are burned or that from solid-waste incineration, presents one of the greatest challenges in air-pollution control. Experimentation with sulfur dioxide suppression has followed a number of paths, but most frequently involves the use of limestone during combustion to trap the oxides chemically, or of a catalyst to convert the oxides to sulfuric acid. (In addition to sulfur dioxide, coal combustion also produces carbon monoxide and at times sulfur trioxide.) The emissions of high-sulfur coal can be cleaned of 85 percent or more of the sulfur dioxide by adding pulverized limestone to the coal when it is burned and wet scrubbing the stack gases. The chemical reaction between the limestone and the sulfur oxides produces large quantities of calcium sulfate and sulfite waste materials, however, and these create a considerable waste-disposal problem. Moreover, the limestone process does not work well in large-scale combustion chambers.

The suppression of sulfur dioxide by converting it to sulfuric acid requires a catalyst to produce sulfur trioxide, which becomes sulfuric acid when combined with the water vapor in the stack gas. The dilute sulfuric acid is then collected from the stack. It has some commercial value, but not enough to provide a strong economic incentive to use the catalytic process. Another approach, as yet confined to the laboratory, combines the removal of particulate matter with the suppression of sulfur oxides. In the conventional method of removing particulate matter, the effective use of the precipitators requires that electrostatic precipitation takes place before oxide suppression. In the simultaneous removal of particulate matter and sulfur dioxide, the stack gas is forced through a bed of closely packed granules that filter out the particulate matter at the same time that absorbent alkalized alumina captures the oxides. Suppression of sulfur dioxide faces difficult technical problems quite aside from the question of economic feasibility.

Low-Sulfur-Fuel Standards. In the absence of an economical method of suppressing sulfur oxides, some communities have imposed restrictions on the sulfur level permitted in fuels rather than on emissions. In 1969, New York City prescribed that both coal and oil not exceed 1 percent sulfur; two years earlier, Consolidated Edison, the beleaguered New York electric utility, had switched to 1-percent-sulfur coal and oil and natural gas, at an estimated increased fuel cost of 20 million dollars a year. The use of low-sulfur fuels has reduced sulfur dioxide by a significant 56 percent in New York City as compared with pre-1969 levels and the city plans further reduction, in later years, of the permissible sulfur content in fuels to 0.3 percent. Figure 11.5 shows the progress made by New York City in reducing sulfur dioxide emissions, and the projected effect of the more stringent 0.3-percent requirement. What the chart does not show is that even with the substantial overall improvement in reducing oxides, New York City still has SO_2 concentrations that are as bad as any in the nation, in particular in the Lower East Side, where because

Figure 11.5. The SO₂ Reduction in New York City
from the Use of Low-Sulfur Fuels *

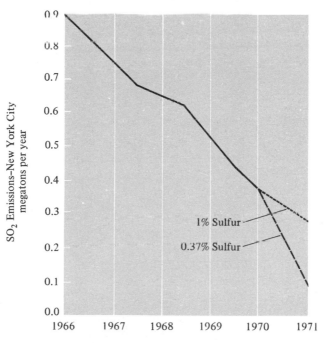

*From "Low-Sulfur Fuels for New York City" by Austin Heller and Edward Ferrand, in *Patient Earth* by John Harte and Robert H. Socolow. Copyright © 1971 by Holt, Rinehart and Winston, Inc. Reprinted by permission of Holt, Rinehart and Winston, Inc. P. 55.

of heavy incineration and atmospheric conditions, SO₂ at times reaches 0.13 parts per million.

Effective as the prohibition of high-sulfur fuels is in reducing sulfur oxides, it is a costly and limited approach. Low-sulfur fuels—coal, oil, and natural gas—are not only higher priced, but their supply is too limited to provide relief for all the communities that suffer from air pollution, even if the higher price is no deterrent. Natural gas, for example, is an almost pollution-free fuel, but the supply has not been able to keep up with demand in recent years because of lagging development of new deposits. Being commission-regulated, the price of natural gas has not responded to basic changes in demand, leading to supply shortages without compensating attempts to expand gas production. To stimulate natural gas output, which requires the discovery and exploitation of new deposits, a price more responsive to demand changes may be required. In addition, the conservation objective would be better served by an end to the fairly universal pricing practice of selling large quantities of gas at a discount to encourage greater use.

Fuel Desulfurization. The sulfur content of both coal and oil can be reduced by treatment. Fuel-oil desulfurization is considerably more successful under present technology than coal desulfurization and yields a marketable sulfur by-product, whereas cleaning sulfur from coal is much harder and doesn't yield a salable by-product. Sulfur is found in coal either because it was present in the plants that are coal's basic ingredient or because it leached from other sources during the period of coal formation. When the sulfur in coal comes from plant material, it is evenly distributed through a seam and virtually impossible physically to remove. When sulfur is deposited during the process of coal formation, however, it is concentrated as pyrites that may be removed by washing. Unfortunately, however, the Bureau of Mines reports that only 35 percent of coal samples taken from mines east of the Mississippi can be cleaned to a sulfur content below 1 percent with present desulfurization techniques. Although low-sulfur coal has long been a premium fuel considered essential for some industrial processes, such as coke production, air-pollution-control regulations have been responsible for the increased demand for it by large metropolitan areas and power plants. Since coal will remain a major source of fuel in the United States well beyond the end of the twentieth century, either advances in coal desulfurization or improvements in suppression of the oxides will be necessary to check air pollution from its use.

The Effects of the Sulfur Compounds. The effects on the environment of sulfur dioxide and trioxide are reasonably well agreed upon; the impact of other sulfur compounds is only imperfectly understood. Sulfur oxides have long been known to hasten the corrosion of iron and steel, to deteriorate stone and brick, and to destroy vegetation. These oxides have also been held responsible for the measurably greater respiratory distress that occurs in urban as compared with rural regions. Sulfur dioxide has been treated with special suspicion since the pollution disasters in Donora, Pennsylvania, in 1948 and in London in 1952, but the evidence of its danger to health has remained largely circumstantial.

Sulfur dioxide concentrations of 5 parts per million can be detected by most individuals, and prolonged exposure to this level is likely to bring on respiratory reaction, while exposure to 10 parts per million for an hour or less causes breathlessness and choking in most individuals. Whether SO_2 alone can be considered a respiratory killer at the levels found in the Donora and London smogs has not been established, however, and the evidence is strong that the toxic effects of sulfur compounds are enhanced by mixing with other pollutants. It is believed, for example, that sulfur trioxide and particulate matter form an especially lethal combination because the particles carry the SO_3 deeper into the lungs, where moisture produces a droplet of sulfuric acid, at best a harmful irritant and for the aged and those with respiratory disorders a likely contributory cause of death.

The generally lower incidence of respiratory distress in rural areas has been advanced as evidence of the harmful effects of polluted air, even though it has not been possible to establish precisely the health impact of particular pollutants. But other factors, such as working and living conditions, may contribute more importantly to the differences between rural and urban health histories. Another variable, cigarette smoking, appears to be a more important cause of respiratory disorders than environmental air pollution. Indeed the harmful effects from cigarette smoking reinforce the conclusion that pollution of the air is a health hazard since smoking is voluntary exposure to highly polluted air. Fortunately, no community experiences for any duration the concentration of air pollution that a smoker exposes himself to intermittently.

The fact that it is not possible to measure precisely what pollutant levels cause distress does not mean that air-pollution threatens
asphyxiation of a substantial part of the population before expenditures for its control are justified. It is sufficient that air pollution causes physical and aesthetic distress, is costly to the
community, and is within our economic and technical capacity
to moderate.

Federal-State Control of Air Pollution

The administration of air-pollution control in the United States
exhibits the same federal-state split personality that is found in the
approach to water-pollution control, with somewhat less well-
defined goals because of its more recent origin. Actually, the
first federal involvement in air-pollution control occurred in
1955, when Congress appropriated 5 million dollars for research,
data collection, and technical assistance for state and local air-
pollution-control programs. Substantial participation by the federal government in controlling air pollution did not take place
until 1968, when the first federal emission standards were applied
to automobiles. But the basic instrument for a comprehensive
federal program of air-pollution control had become available
a year before, with the passage of the Air Quality Act in November, 1967. By this legislation the federal government assumed a
major share of the responsibility for improving the quality of
air in the United States. On the whole, the approach encourages
the states to undertake air-pollution control, but provides for
federal intervention if a state fails to act. The 1970 report of the
Council on Environmental Quality outlines the main provisions
of the 1967 Air Quality Act as follows:

> The Secretary of the Department of Health, Education and
> Welfare must designate air quality control regions within a state
> or within an interstate region.
> The Secretary of HEW must promulgate air quality criteria
> which, based on scientific studies, describe the harmful effects of
> an air pollutant on health, vegetation, and materials. He must is-
> sue control technology documents showing availability, costs and

effectiveness of prevention and control techniques.

In the designated regions, the states must show willingness to establish air quality standards.

The states then set standards limiting the levels of the pollutant described in the criteria and control technology documents. *If the states fail to do this, the Secretary of HEW is empowered to set the standards.*

After the states have developed air quality standards, they must establish comprehensive plans for implementing them. These plans should set specific emission levels by source and a timetable for achieving compliance.[3]

Timetable of Emission Standards

Between June, 1968, and January, 1972, 247 federal air-quality-control regions with implementation plans were established. Three years later, in July, 1975, the ambient air quality—the overall quality of the surrounding atmosphere rather than that of the air near a point of pollution—must be "protective of human health." A secondary objective—ambient air quality "protective of human welfare"—involving more stringent control of emissions is planned to take effect in October, 1977. The background trends in air quality of selected areas is shown in Figure 11.6.

Controls are also planned to attain a 90-percent reduction in hydrocarbon and carbon monoxides in 1976 automobile models and a similar reduction in nitrogen oxide in 1977 models, but it is anticipated that additional restraints upon the use of autos will undoubtedly be required in some cities. Specifically, Chicago, Denver, Los Angeles, New York, Philadelphia, and Washington, D.C., are like to find it necessary to alter commuting patterns and increase the use of public transportation if the ambient air standards for these regions are to be met. Different regions face different polluant problems. Chicago, for example, has a troublesome extended concentration of carbon monoxide that not only will require strict enforcement of auto-emission controls, but will be likely to require restriction of private vehicle use as well. The

[3] *Environmental Quality: First Annual Report of the Council on Environmental Quality* (Washington, D.C.: Government Printing Office, 1970), p. 74; italics added.

Figure 11.6.   Trends in Ambient Levels of Selected
Pollutants *

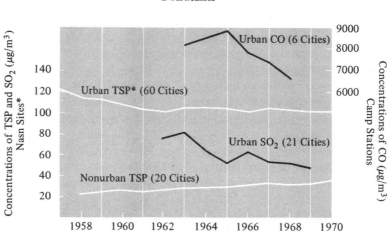

* The Mitre Corporation, MTR–6013; data from the Environmental Protection Agency. Reproduced in *Environmental Quality: Second Annual Report of the Council on Environmental Quality* (Washington, D.C.: Government Printing Office, 1971), p. 214.

† *TSP* stands for "total suspended particles"; *Nasn Sites* are sites of the National Air Sampling Network.

Northeast, on the other hand, may find controlling sulfur dioxide and particulate matter a somewhat greater problem.

In addition to the more familiar pollutants listed in Table 11.1, others will undoubtedly be added in establishing future air-quality standards, including nitrogen oxides, lead, fluorides, asbestos, and cadmium. Some of these materials are especially hazardous to health in the concentrations experienced in their normal use, as when asbestos is sprayed during construction work or is dispersed when a building in which it was used is demolished. For such pollutants, controlling the origination of the pollution rather than prescribing a low overall concentration in the air of the region is the appropriate approach.

Table 11.1.   National Air-Quality Standards: Protection of
Human Health *

Pollutant	*Level not to exceed*
Sulfur Dioxide	0.03 ppm [1]
	0.14 ppm [2]
Particulate Matter	75 grams per cubic meter of air [3]
	260 grams per cubic meter of air [2]
Carbon Monoxide	9 ppm [4]
	35 ppm [5]
Photochemical Oxidants	0.08 ppm [5]
Hydrocarbons	0.24 ppm [6]
Nitrogen Oxides	0.05 ppm [1]

* Reprinted from "National Air Quality Standards Finalized," *Environmental Science and Technology*, V (June, 1971), p. 503. Copyright 1971 by the American Chemical Society. Reprinted by permission of the copyright owner.

[1] Annual arithmetic mean.
[2] Maximum twenty-four-hour concentration not to be exceeded more than once a year.
[3] Annual geometric mean.
[4] Maximum eight-hour concentration not to be exceeded more than once a year.
[5] Maximum one-hour concentration not to be exceeded more than once a year.
[6] Maximum three-hour concentration (6–9 A.M.) not to be exceeded more than once a year.

Emission Controls Vs. Ambient Air Standards

Emission controls are the necessary bulwark of ambient air standards. Although the federal approach to air-pollution abatement has emphasized ambient air standards, clean air cannot be achieved by proclamation. Air pollution is the product of a number of different sources that may make quite unequal contributions to atmospheric degradation. If air quality is to be improved, the output of air pollutants must be checked at the origin rather than collected and neutralized later, as is done in water-pollution abatement. In our federal-state division of authority, determining what emission restrictions are necessary to meet air-quality standards is primarily a job for the states, since the output of pollutants takes place within state boundaries. But when the pollution affects a neighboring state, or a state fails to act, the federal government may intervene.

The administration of the Air Quality Act has expanded the role of the abatement conference, originally concerned mainly with promoting more vigorous state and local pollution-control efforts rather than imposing federal authority. Early abatement conferences were more bargaining sessions than enforcement proceedings, but in the Union Carbide case, the character of these conferences changed considerably.

The Union Carbide Case. Shortly after the air- and water-pollution programs were brought under the jurisdiction of the newly formed Environmental Protection Agency, a regulatory *cause célèbre* with the Union Carbide Corporation came to a head. For a number of years, a generally ineffectual battle had been carried on by the small West Virginia town of Vienna, across the Ohio River from the Union Carbide ferroalloy plant in Marietta, Ohio, to force Union Carbide to moderate its pollution of the Ohio River Valley air shed. Over the years, however, the corporation remained largely indifferent. Since the controversy was interstate in nature—air pollutants from the Ohio plant caused environmental deterioration in West Virginia—it fell within the traditional jurisdiction of the federal government. Moreover, Vienna's simple distaste for air pollution was not all that was involved: A Public Health Service study of the bistate area had found the Marietta plant to be mainly responsible for significant increases in respiratory diseases, such as asthma, emphysema, acute bronchitis, and pneumonia.

With such an apparently flawless case, in 1967 the National Air Pollution Control Administration (the predecessor of the Environmental Protection Agency) undertook an abatement conference in Vienna, West Virginia. At best, the conference can only be described as a failure. At worst, it stiffened Union Carbide's determination to resist requests to moderate its pollution. For the next two years the corporation declined to provide federal officials with complete data on emissions and refused entry to federal inspectors at the Marietta plant. The federal government at this point could have undertaken steps that eventually would have led to court action, but the process involved was time-consuming and legally tortuous. The federal case was difficult to make because Union Carbide could not be required to furnish emissions data or permit plant inspection. Unable to do much else, the National Air Pollution Control Administration called a second enforcement conference in October, 1969. Union Carbide officials didn't bother to attend.

But this second conference, using emission estimates and the incomplete data from Union Carbide, was able to piece together a set of recommendations. These recommendations, eventually adopted by the Secretary of Health, Education, and Welfare, called for the following: first, a 40-percent reduction in sulfur dioxide emissions within six months and a 70-percent reduction by April, 1972; second, submission of plans for stack-height modification by July, 1970; and third, a 50-percent reduction in soot and metal-processing emissions in excess of allowable standards by September, 1971. These recommendations, drawn up in 1969, became the basis for negotiations between the Environmental Protection Agency and Union Carbide in 1971.

Union Carbide's sulfur dioxide and fly-ash pollution came mainly from high-sulfur coal used to produce power. The cost of coal to generate the electricity used in alloy production is a major outlay for Union Carbide, about 4.5 million dollars annually, or roughly 20 percent of total costs. To achieve the 40-percent reduction in sulfur dioxide, Union Carbide had to resort initially to higher-cost low-sulfur coal in generating power, until it could install a system of SO_2 suppression employing limestone injection and the scrubbing of stack gas. Low-sulfur coal was calculated to add as much as 50 percent to the fuel costs of Union Carbide, and the firm initially expressed doubt whether the use of low-sulfur coal would bring a 40-percent reduction in sulfur dioxide emissions. In the early discussions with the EPA, the corporation contended that it would have to cut back production in order to meet the 40-percent goal, and as a result, would find it necessary to discharge over five hundred workers from the Marietta plant. The EPA did not relax its compliance schedule, however, and as time passed it appeared that Union Carbide had been unduly pessimistic about the extent of the layoffs that would be required to comply with the emission requirements. Finally, a change in the Union Carbide management brought a softening of its uncompromising policy.

It is not entirely clear what lesson should be drawn from the Union Carbide case, but certain conclusions are obvious: The National Air Pollution Control Administration did not have sufficient authority to enforce emission standards and the abatement conference is a cumbersome, time-consuming, and ineffectual way of attempting enforcement. But the eventual success of the Environmental Protection Agency's pressure on Union Carbide, even though long delayed, makes future regulatory action more likely to succeed.

Carrot or Stick

Once the noxious emissions that pollute the air leave the smokestack or tail pipe, there is no gathering of the pollutants for neutralization as in the case of the treatment of waste water. The focus of correction and control of air pollution falls more naturally upon the firm than it does in the case of water pollution. In the abatement of water pollution, industry has found it possible to shift part of the costs to the community through the use of municipal treatment facilities for the disposal of its wastes. A similar shift of the burden of air-pollution abatement is not possible, but essentially the same depreciation privileges and tax relief that are available for water-pollution abatement are extended by the federal government and the states to encourage firm investment in the suppression of air pollution. Accelerated depreciation similar to that available for water-pollution-control equipment is permitted by the federal government on a five-year basis for capital expenditures for air-pollution control. A few states provide similar depreciation arrangements, and some permit an even more liberal write-off period.

Tax relief to encourage investment in air-pollution equipment takes several forms, consisting mainly of tax credits for the purchase of pollution equipment in five states, of special property-tax reductions in twenty-one states, of exemption from sales and use taxes for abatement-equipment purchases in thirteen states, and of accelerated depreciation privileges in eight states. At best, the incentive effect of these inducements is moderate and they alone are not likely to encourage significant investment in equipment that is costly and does not add to the firm's revenue. To the extent that accelerated depreciation and tax relief do stimulate investment in abatement equipment, however, the "hardware" approach to reducing emissions is encouraged in place of the adoption of cleaner production processes.

The opposite use of taxes—as a stick rather than a carrot—to dissuade industry from degrading the quality of the air is even more limited in air-pollution suppression than it is in water-pollution control. But special taxes on lead in gasoline and on high-sulfur fuels have been endorsed by the Treasury Department and the Council on Environmental Quality and urged upon Congress by President Nixon. Congress has not enacted either tax, but it would be highly desirable to adopt the tax on leaded fuel before the introduction of the automobile catalytic emission-control system, in order to remove the price difference favorable to leaded gas.*

The tax upon high-sulfur fuels is more complex and more controversial than the proposed tax on leaded fuel. In order to decrease sulfur oxide pollution, it has been recommended that a tax upon the sulfur content of coal and fuel oil be levied at the mine or refinery and be increased over a period of five years from 1 cent to 10 cents per pound of sulfur. The resulting imposition of a price penalty upon high-sulfur fuel is expected to increase the output of natural gas, low-sulfur fuel oil, and low-sulfur coal, by encouraging the opening of new sources of supply and the desulfurization of existing supplies. Even without

* The price difference between leaded and lead-free gasoline has been at its greatest during the initial period, when refinery capacity for lead-free gasoline has been under construction. By 1975, the added price of lead-free gas at retail is expected to be limited to 0.2 to 0.9 cent per gallon, according to a study by the Environmental Protection Agency.

the sulfur tax, however, the increased demand for low-sulfur fuel has greatly increased western strip-mining, the main source of low-sulfur coal. As a result, the improvement in the air quality in the East is in part at the cost of extraordinary land devastation from strip-mining in the West—without any conscious determination of which is the greater blight, air pollution or land destruction.

The proposed sulfur tax also includes a system of rebates that is designed to encourage firms to suppress sulfur oxide emissions. In order to determine how much rebate is due the firm that reduces its discharge of sulfur into the atmosphere, two sets of data are required: the sulfur content of the firm's fuel supply and the sulfur discharged into the air when this fuel supply is used. The rebate due the firm depends upon how much of the sulfur in the fuel is kept from reaching the atmosphere. The tax-rebate system may not significantly decrease sulfur-oxide discharges, however, because the technology of sulfur control in combustion is still of very limited commercial application. The main effect will undoubtedly be due to the tax, not the rebate, and will result from the increase in the price of high-sulfur fuels, which will make the use of low-sulfur fuels relatively more attractive.

The prospect of enlarging the market for low-sulfur fuel by the sulfur tax has not gone unchallenged by the coal industry, which will find itself at a competitive disadvantage with the petroleum industry if this levy is imposed. Desulfurization of fuel oil is already commercially feasible whereas coal desulfurization still faces severe technological limitations. Because of this, the petroleum industry will gain an increasing share of the low-sulfur-fuel market as it builds up refining capacity in desulfurization.

The special character of the electric-utility industry and its dominant role in the purchase of fossil fuels—well over half of the total sold—is the major factor influencing the price of fossil fuels. Faced with increasing pressure to curtail sulfur-dioxide emissions, the electric utilities have turned to low-sulfur fuel—even though its use might be considered too costly in a competitive industry. The power industry isn't competitive, however; it is a regulated monopoly facing a rising market for its product, and it has experienced only moderate delays in passing on increased costs to the consumer through higher rates. Rebates for decreased sulfur emissions are not likely to exert much economic incentive on the electric industry to modify its practices, since the rebate, lowering costs, is essentially a trade-off for a rate increase. Public-relations objectives are likely to be a stronger reason than tax rebates for the suppression of sulfur emissions by the electric utilities.

The Costs of Air Pollution

At the third National Conference on Air Pollution, in Washington, D.C., in December, 1966, Allen Kneese, of Resources for the Future, charged that estimates of the costs of air pollution were indefensible guesses and should be abandoned. Indefensible or not, there is little prospect that such estimates will be abandoned. Indeed, they are likely to receive greater rather than less attention in the future. Since Kneese's dismissal of the estimates of air pollution in 1966, they have improved somewhat, but admittedly they are still inadequate. Basically, measurement of the costs of air pollution suffers from the inability to determine precisely the effects of different kinds and levels of pollutants upon such varied objects as vegetation, buildings, human health, property values, and air traffic. Unable to establish cause-and-effect relationships, the assessment of monetary damage from pollution rests upon an uncertain base. And in those cases where cause and effect can be determined, such as the destruction of vegetation by ozone, a further stumbling block is the absence of widespread monitoring devices to measure the presence of various kinds of air pollutants. The monitoring deficiency is less of a long-run problem than the lack of basic understanding of the effects of pollutants, however, since improved monitoring devices are being developed rapidly and additional measuring stations are being established.

Acknowledging that its evidence is "rudimentary," the second annual report of the Council on Environmental Quality contends that the benefits of decreasing air pollution clearly exceed the costs of its abatement. The Council concludes that the abatement of air pollution as planned through the present program to 1975 will reach an annual expenditure of 4.7 billion dollars, whereas the economic losses that this program will prevent will total at least 16 billion dollars annually in terms of 1968 prices. This is clearly a good investment—a benefit-cost ratio of more than 3 to 1. Moreover, since the benefits are measured in 1968 prices and the costs at those of a later date, the 3-to-1 ratio understates the benefit side of the equation.

The 16-billion-dollar annual benefit from abating air pollution is built up from the following:[4]

Costs Eliminated	*Billions of Dollars*
Medical care and work loss from air-pollution-related disabilities	6.0
Damage to materials and vegetation	4.9
Loss in property values from air pollution ..	5.2
	16.1

Although impressive, the 16-billion-dollar figure is clearly an understatement of the benefits from abating air pollution because it does not include extra-market factors that may be just as important as the measurable economic losses from air contamination. Save in the case of property valuation, the market does not reflect the aesthetic loss that occurs when corrosive air pollutants deface statuary and soil buildings or when a ponderosa-pine forest is defoliated. Nor do the medical-care costs and loss of income from illness represent anything but a fraction of the real costs that attend sickness and physical disability in the form of anxiety, discomfort, and a lowered capacity for the enjoyment of life. And finally, although impossible to convert to dollar terms, the elimination of the assault upon eyes and nose of the emissions of some industrial processes, such as papermaking and petrochemical manufacture, along with the auto-exhaust hydrocarbons, would be a most tangible benefit to those exposed to such

[4] *Environmental Quality: Second Annual Report of the Council on Environmental Quality* (Washington, D.C.: Government Printing Office, 1971), pp. 106–107.

malodorous discharges.* The failure of the market to quantify these disutilities makes them no less appropriate candidates for banishment.

References and Readings

Air Conservation Commission, *Air Conservation*. Washington, D.C., American Association for the Advancement of Science, Publication No. 80, 1965.
    A useful review of the major causes and effects of air pollution, with the exception of the disappointing chapter on "socio-economic factors."

Automobile Fuels and Air Pollution: Report of the Panel on Auto-

---

* Other estimates of the costs of environmental damage exceed those of the Council on Environmental Quality. Dr. Paul Kotin, former director of the National Institute of Environmental Health Sciences, is responsible for one of the most encompassing of all the estimates of the economic costs of impaired health from environmental deterioration. In 1970, before the Seventeenth General Assembly of the International Union of Biological Sciences in Washington, D.C., he placed the annual health cost from adverse environmental factors at 35 billion dollars. Dr. Kotin's assessment of health costs was not limited to the effects of air pollution, however, but included mental-health difficulties and physical diseases resulting from undesirable working conditions and the general stresses of modern life. He arrived at the 35-billion-dollar total as follows:

Costs	Billions of Dollars
Health services required because of adverse environmental factors (10 percent of total health costs)	7.0
Loss in wages and production during environmentally induced illness (1/3 of total illness costs)	25.0
Compensation and rehabilitation (1/3 of total compensation and rehabilitation costs)	3.4
	35.4

Such broad estimates are necessarily based on limited basic data and are subject to large margins of error. There can be no doubt, however, of the increasing importance of adverse environmental factors as a cause of health outlays.

motive Fuels and Air Pollution. Washington, D.C., Department of Commerce, 1971.
    A brief but authoritative examination of the fuel modifications and emission controls necessary to reduce auto air pollution. The report includes a series of specific recommendations for controls to decrease auto emissions.

Carr, Donald E., *The Breath of Life.* New York: W. W. Norton & Company, 1965.
    A short, sprightly book ranging widely from the chemistry of smog to the advocacy of the turbine as a replacement for the internal-combustion engine.

Cassell, Eric J., "The Health Effects of Air Pollution and Their Implications for Control," *Law and Contemporary Problems,* XXXIII (Spring 1968), pp. 197–216.
    A review of the knowledge of the effects of air pollution on health, in an issue of *Law and Contemporary Problems* devoted to the topic of air-pollution control.

Committee on Pollution of the National Academy of Sciences, *Waste Management and Control.* Washington, D.C., National Academy of Sciences, 1966.
    This is the so-called Spilhaus report, which covers a wide range of pollution problems, including air, water and solid wastes. The document is strangely organized and badly written in parts, but the treatment of air pollution is good.

The Cost of Clean Air. Reports of the Secretary of Health, Education and Welfare to Congress. Washington, D.C., Government Printing Office, 1969 and 1970.
    The first two annual reports of the National Air Pollution Control Administration, outlining the programs for air-pollution control and the anticipated costs of pollution abatement for selected industries.

The Economics of Clean Air: Report of the Administrator of the Environmental Protection Agency to Congress. Washington, D.C., Government Printing Office, 1971.
    The third annual report of the National Air Pollution Control Administration covers the nature and cost of controlling auto emissions as well as those of selected industries.

Hexter, A. C., and Goldsmith, J. R., "Carbon Monoxide: Association of Community Air Pollution with Mortality," *Science,* CLXXII (April 16, 1971), pp. 265–267.
    An account of a regression analysis of four years of data (1962–1965), including daily recordings of temperature, average carbon-

monoxide concentrations, and average total oxidants in Los Angeles in relation to the mortality rate. Statistical evidence is presented to show that carbon monoxide at levels occurring in Los Angeles is associated with increased mortality. No such relationship was found between total oxidants and mortality.

Proceedings of the first and third National Conferences on Air Pollution, Washington, D.C., December 10–12, 1962, and December 12–14, 1966. Public Health Service Publications No. 1022 and No. 1649. Washington, D.C., (Department of Health, Education, and Welfare, 1963 and 1967).

Like those of most conference proceedings, the papers in these volumes are devoted primarily to summarizing; they survey the present state of knowledge on air pollution, usually in a brief and general way, and reiterate the desirability of abating pollution.

Chapter Twelve

Solid Waste—Disposal and Resource Recovery

And Man created the plastic bag and the tin and aluminum can and the cellophane wrapper and the paper plate and the disposable bottle and this was good because Man could then take his automobile and buy his food all in one place and he could save that which was good to eat in his refrigerator, and throw away that which had no further use. And pretty soon the earth was covered with plastic bags and aluminum cans and paper plates and disposable bottles and there was nowhere left to sit down or to walk, and Man shook his head and cried, "Look at all this God-awful litter."—Art Buchwald (1970)

One growth rate that never seems to lag is the output of trash, and in this as in other more envied achievements, the United States is the undisputed world leader. In the 1920's, when Friday's fish came home in Thursday's newspaper and beer was carried in a bucket, the average amount of waste per household was slightly over 2½ pounds per day. But by 1970, mass distribution and factory packaging of products had caused a jump to over 5½ pounds per day, and by 1980 the household average is expected to rise to 8 pounds. And this is only household waste, the smaller portion of the economy's total output of unwanted materials.

The Proliferation of Solid Wastes

In 1969, the American economy produced over 4.3 billion tons of solid waste, the greatest part of which came from agriculture and mining. Industry—other than mining—contributed less than households, commercial establishments, and institutions, which were reported as a group by the federal Bureau of Solid Waste Management. Household, commercial, and institutional wastes, taken together, constitute less than 6 percent of the total, but they are nevertheless one of the most offensive sources of environmental damage. In tonnage terms, waste production in the United States is as follows:

Type of Waste	Millions of Tons
Household, Commercial, Institutional	250
Industrial	110
Mining	1,700
Agricultural	2,280
	4,340

Agriculture, the largest single source, until recently did not represent an environmental hazard at all proportionate to its output of waste. When cattle were raised on the range, a disposal problem was seldom presented by their waste, which gradually combined with the pasture land, but with the advent of feedlots, the concentration of large numbers of animals in confined areas close to cities has brought a concentration of wastes and pollution. At the same time, the burning of after-harvest refuse, which at one time passed virtually unnoticed, in some regions of the country has seriously added to air pollution.

The mining industry, in tonnage terms the other major waste producer, is frequently responsible for extensive solid-waste accumulation in particular places, but usually these areas are well removed from population centers. This does not mean that mining waste creates no problem, however, since the method of disposal—such as dumping into watercourses—may distribute it well beyond the mining site. The concentration of waste production at the mine, and the frequent uniformity of the waste, reduce collection problems and usually permit the use of less complicated systems of waste treatment. In part, these conditions also hold for industrial waste; it is concentrated at the point of production, and although usually less uniform than mining wastes, it is not so varied in composition as household wastes.

But industrial waste has other characteristics that make it a greater threat to the environment than its tonnage share of the economy's waste output indicates. Although mining waste is seldom innocuous, it usually consists of relatively inert materials, disposed of at some distance from population centers. Industrial waste, by contrast, usually originates in areas not so far removed from centers of population, and disposal generally occurs in nearby watercourses or municipal dumps. Unless pretreated, such waste may be toxic, impose heavy oxygen demands upon streams, or overburden municipal waste-disposal facilities. As industrial waste becomes more varied and complex, in consequence, for example, of the development of synthetic chemical products and by-products, the risk increases that materials will be introduced into the environment that will have harmful effects upon some life forms.

For most production wastes, whether mining, industrial, or agricultural, the greater opportunity of eliminating environmental damage lies in control at the source rather than in collection and disposal. When the wastes of industry, agriculture, and mining are permitted to accumulate, about the only approach that has been feasible in the past is the removal of these unwanted materials to a location in which they are relatively inoffensive. When the varied discards of our affluent economy have been scrambled by collection, the sorting necessary for reclamation and recycling may impose prohibitively high costs. Control at the mine or factory can involve a lower cost as well as a socially more desirable alternative to shifting the burden to the public through a materials-recovery program that reclaims wastes after they have been transported to the dump.

Until recently, however, little attention was given to materials recovery or waste control of any kind in the United States, other than the salvage operations encouraged by the market. The tra-

ditional approach to waste disposal has been simply dumping—
on land, at sea, into rivers and streams, or into the air through
burning—an environmentally damaging and obnoxious means of
discarding unwanted materials. Few communities have been
without that aesthetic and environmental horror, the open dump
—a poorly supervised cesspool of wastes, solid and otherwise, intermittently burning and generally vermin-ridden, which is at
once testimony to affluence and to parsimony. A slightly more
enlightened approach to waste disposal, sanitary landfill—so
called because a layer of earth is used to seal off the compacted
wastes—has been adopted by more progressive communities and
represents a first-step goal in the federal government's waste-
management program.

Increasingly, the solid wastes of home and factory have im-
periled the nation's streams and groundwater with leachate—
seepage from open dumps and other primitive forms of waste
disposal; large areas of the ocean have been contaminated to an
unexpected degree from dumping in "nobody's territory"; the
tidelands and estuaries have been overburdened by trash and
fill, impairing their natural functions; the air has been polluted by
improperly incinerated wastes; the terrain has been reduced to a
monotonous regularity and wildlife habitat has been destroyed
by waste landfill projects; and over the city and countryside an
uneven deposit of litter has affronted the eye and at times of-
fended the nose. There seems no escape from the problem—
even in Westchester.

The Unhappy Condition of Westchester's Dump

That symbol of upper-middle-class country-club living, Westchester County, New York, in 1972 was made painfully aware
that its solid-waste-disposal practices, like those of many other
communities, are increasingly costly, inadequate, and an environmental hazard. But in Westchester's case, the point was made with
the force of a federal-court decision charging the county with
pollution of the Hudson River because of its waste-disposal
practices. What Westchester officials refer to as a "sanitary landfill" operation, the court dismissed as a "garbage dump," and it

ordered that the soil cover over the refuse be increased 2½ times, which will add almost 2 million dollars to the annual cost of waste disposal. But this is the simplest of Westchester's problems. In spite of its suburban residential image, its jurisdiction includes industry and the waste that goes along with such activity. To prevent the pollution of the Hudson, the court ordered a drastic modification in the county's dumping practices: Westchester is to stop accepting liquid industrial waste until it is treated, to submit plans for a dike and treatment system to control leachate, and to determine how to protect the remaining marshland in the dumping area. The time allowed by the court to continue dumping any industrial waste is limited, and if the firms involved cannot find alternative dumping grounds or reduce their waste production, economic activity will be at least temporarily curtailed. Westchester's plight is typical of what is increasingly experienced, with variations, throughout the land.

The Federal Role

Of all the forms of pollution, solid waste—sometimes called the "third pollution"—has been the last to be recognized as a serious threat to the environment. Until solid-waste disposal was recognized as an important contributor to air and water pollution, the open dump was an accepted if not admired institution of most communities. It is still the predominant form of waste disposal in the United States, but with encouragement from the federal government, the states are very gradually establishing higher standards of waste disposal. Undoubtedly the most significant modification in solid-waste disposal, however, has resulted from the introduction in the summer of 1972 of a federal-state regulation restricting open burning at dumps. This regulation, designed to reduce air pollution, has forced many communities to upgrade waste-disposal practices and has encouraged compacting and sanitary landfill practices. The response to the directive has been uneven and incomplete, but for some communities it has been an important first step.

Until recently, few governmental functions have been more

strictly local than the regulation of solid-waste disposal. But in 1965, Congress passed the Solid Waste Disposal Act, creating the Bureau of Solid Waste Management, now a part of the Environmental Protection Agency, which was given responsibility for a variety of measures designed to improve waste-disposal practices and increase the recovery and use of waste materials. Research in solid-waste reclamation is encouraged through federal grants administered by the Bureau of Solid Waste Management and also by the Bureau of Mines, an old-line federal agency in the Department of the Interior whose responsibilities under the 1965 act have been expanded to cover research in mineral, metal, and fossil-fuel wastes. The federal involvement in the solid-waste problem has been directed mainly toward assisting localities to cope with the mounting output of refuse by undertaking activities beyond the scope of local governments: research in waste disposal and reclamation, training programs, and grants for demonstration projects.

The Costs of Collection

Although local governments are responsible for solid-waste collection and disposal, they are usually in a poor position to undertake any important modification of these practices. Highly resistant to innovation, the most extensive recent development in waste collection has been the replacement of the metal container by the plastic bag. This has decreased costs somewhat, but the change has hardly revolutionized waste collection. Costs of collection are still by far the greatest portion of waste-disposal expenses for the local community, averaging about 80 percent of total outlays for household collection. When litter pickup is involved, collection costs are even higher, averaging $88 a ton, which is four times as high as the average household collection cost.

Faced with high costs for waste-disposal services and strong competition from other government functions for budget allocations, most communities have not looked beyond waste collection to the disposal and reclamation problem. Moreover, the small and medium-sized communities find outlays for research in incineration and materials recovery financially unjustified—if actually considered—while the metropolitan regions are generally preoccupied with what are considered to be more critical problems. Except for the extremely high costs of waste collection in the large city, however, there are definite scale advantages in both the disposal of waste materials and resource recovery that favor the larger community. For example, since waste separation for materials salvage and pollution-free incineration requires large-scale equipment, the opportunities of the smaller community are limited because it cannot afford or fully utilize such equipment. In some cases, the solution to the scale inadequacies of the small locality is the formation of a regional solid-waste district that consolidates the refuse of a number of adjacent communities in order to take advantage of the use of larger processing equipment, different disposal techniques, or more suitable disposal sites.

Since the municipality is a creature of the state, the most effective way to achieve the establishment of regional waste-management districts is through state direction. The regional approach necessarily decreases the autonomy of the participating municipalities and reduces the authority of some public officials; hence, successful establishment of a solid-waste district is likely only if reinforced by state action.

How Much Does Solid-Waste Disposal Cost?

Familiarity with the unimposing local dump may give a distorted impression of the cost of solid-waste disposal in the American economy. Disregarding for the moment the social costs that are passed on to the public, the collection and disposal of municipal and industrial wastes involves an expenditure of over 5 billion dollars annually—and still leaves some communities in a semilittered condition. Five billion dollars is obviously a large amount of money, and it translates economically into heavy demands upon resources to move and dispose of society's wastes. In this age of nuclear aircraft carriers, highway programs, and defense cost overruns, billion-dollar sums have lost their attention-getting character. But there is no mistaking the magnitude of the problem: The expenditure for the handling of solid waste is greater than that for air-pollution and water-pollution abatement combined, and among overall public expenditures, ranks just below those for schools, roads, and national defense.

Even with such a huge outlay, however, the job of waste disposal in the United States has been only half done. As has been indicated, the greater portion of the expenditure for waste control has gone for collection, whereas the environmental impact of solid waste has come at the disposal end. In part, disposal problems have been ignored because collection has cost so much. And collection costs have continued to rise because except for minor specialization in trash vehicles,* this operation is still highly labor-intensive, and collectors' wages have sometimes increased more rapidly than the cost of living. Moreover, there is not much chance that labor-saving innovations in trash collection will soon take place, either in the design of trash-collection devices or the development of an alternative to household collection, such as pneumatic-tube trash transport. Within limits, less labor-intensive collection techniques can be designed into large-scale housing units and new communities, but a significant departure from the traditional system in established communities would at present require a prohibitively high capital expenditure.

Materials Reclamation

So far, most communities in the United States have considered their waste problem solved when they have moved their trash and garbage out from under foot to a more distant location. Sometimes disposal of waste by landfill has been put to community purposes, such as the creation of parks and airports, and certainly the most ambitious trash-garbage project of all is Mount

---

* A single-operator vehicle that picks up solid waste in uniform containers and deposits it in the truck without the operator leaving the truck cab is in use in some communities. This innovation reduces the labor requirements of trash collection and makes the work less unattractive.

Trashmore, a creation of the Chicago, Illinois, sanitary department. Mount Trashmore is a sanitary-landfill mountain being
made from Chicago wastes, and when completed will be used as
a ski and toboggan run. But in most places trash landfill is not in
heavy demand; instead, the problem is where to put it.

If it is not possible to continue to dispose of our increasingly
abundant waste by simply moving it from one place to another,
what can be done? A number of approaches are possible. The
waste can be compressed to space-saving size; it can be converted
into useful materials; or waste-creating items—such as bottles—
can be kept in service longer. The first approach, waste compression, can be achieved through the use of home "trash mashers,"
which increase the convenience of collecting and disposing of
household waste, but largely eliminate the opportunity for re-
covering resources, such as glass, aluminum, and paper, that are
in the compressed waste.* Finally, of course, industrial processes
can be modified to create less waste, and the packaging excesses
of American marketing can be restrained.

The reclamation of usable materials from solid wastes serves
two obvious purposes: the conservation of natural resources, such
as iron ore, bauxite, and trees, and the reduction in space needs
for disposal. The emphasis upon materials reclamation, largely
the result of federal research and demonstration grants under the
Resource Recovery Act of 1970, has produced a number of plans
of waste-recovery systems designed for communities of moderate
size. One of the more comprehensive resource-recovery arrangements, illustrated in Figure 12.1, has been designed under
the direction of the Aluminum Association, an organization of
aluminum producers and fabricators. The capital investment
is substantial, slightly less than 16 million dollars for a community ranging from 175,000 to 225,000 people, and the plant requires
ten acres of land. Depending upon the amount of material reclaimed—largely a function of the population served—and the
price of scrap, the recovery operation can be expected to yield
from $22,000 to $133,000 per year after covering expenses—not

---

* Separation of waste components after compaction may be achieved
where advanced techniques of shredding are used, but such practices are
very limited in application as yet.

Figure 12.1. The Aluminum Association's Plan for a Municipal Materials-Recovery Plant *

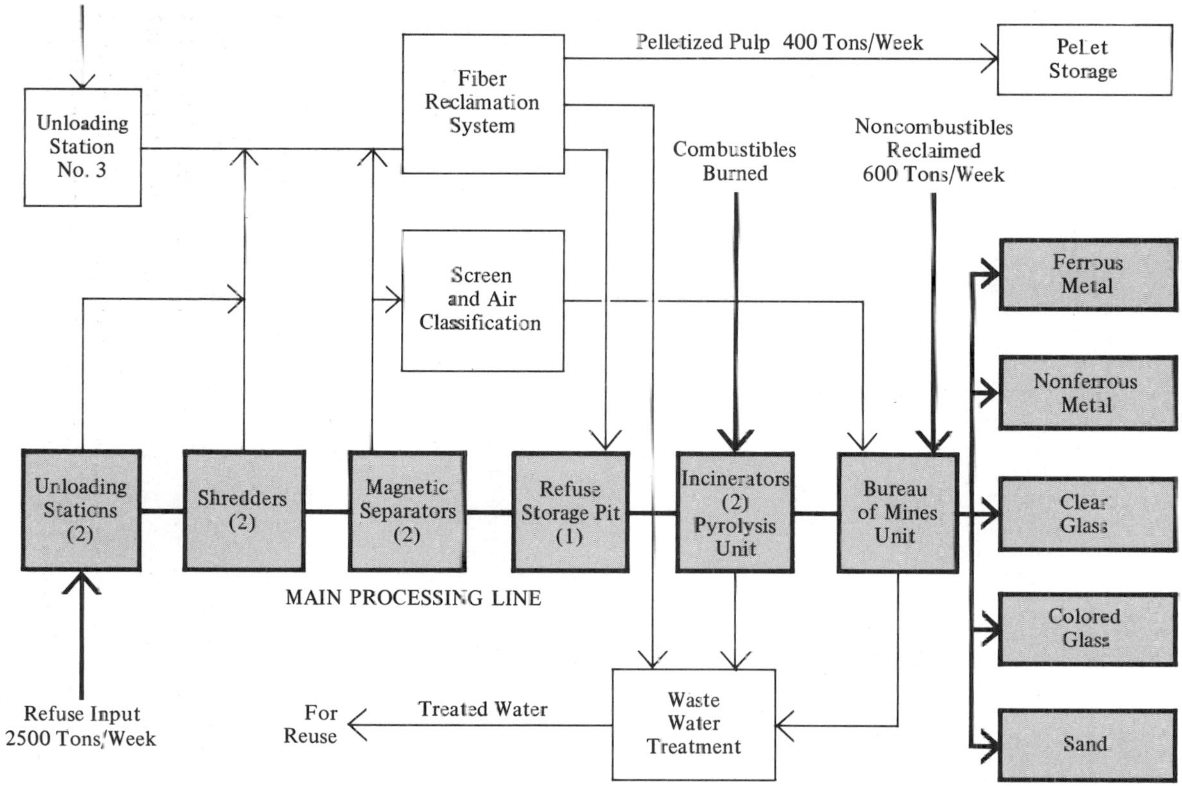

* "A Solid Waste Recovery System for All Municipalities." Reproduced from *Environmental Science and Technology*, V (February 1971), p. 109. Copyright 1971 by the American Chemical Society. Reproduced by permission of the copyright owner.

the kind of return on investment likely to set Wall Street on fire, but in an operation where losses are the general rule, managing to break even is an achievement. Whether this estimated profit will indeed materialize, however, depends upon the conduct of the scrap market and the actual cost experience of the plant. Materials reclaimed include aluminum, ferrous metal, metallic and nonmetallic glass, and sand.

The plant is basically flexible, permitting operation with only the main processing line with its two unloading stations, as indicated in Figure 12.1, or with the addition of Unloading Station No. 3, which adds a fiber-reclamation system and water-treatment facility. Combustible wastes are burned in non-air-polluting incinerators and a pyrolysis unit, a coke-oven-like affair that achieves combustion in the absence of oxygen and reduces materials to carbon. Electrostatic precipitators and tower scrubbers are standard equipment to prevent ambient air pollution and fabric filters control the plant atmosphere. The activated carbon produced in the pyrolysis unit can be employed in the advanced treatment of waste water, and the heat from incineration is converted to steam which is used to drive plant equipment, with the excess being sold.

Whether the Aluminum Association's recycling plant and similar systems are widely adopted depends largely upon the disposal costs facing the community.* The most important income source of the Association's plant, accounting for roughly half the plant's return, is the dump charge—$721,500 in a total income of $1,450,334. The other $728,834 is obtained from the sale of salvaged materials. These figures are speculative, however, like the cost estimates. Obviously, if a community's disposal costs are high, as are those of Washington, D. C., the highest in the

* The town of Franklin, Ohio, operates a small, 150-ton-a-day recycling plant that was built for $2,200,000, two-thirds of which was underwritten by the federal government. The plant employs the principle of a huge blender, crushing and pulping cans, wastepaper, glass, and other solid wastes. The salable wastes are separated from the conglomerate and sold and the others are burned. The sale of reclaimed materials does not cover the costs of the operation of the Franklin plant, but it is hoped that a larger and improved version of the waste blender will reduce costs of operation and come closer to this objective.

nation at seventeen dollars a ton, such a system may be an attractive investment. For the community at the lower end of the disposal-cost scale, however, this investment would have to be justified on grounds other than disposal cost. But since the talents of the technologists have just recently been directed to the development of such resource-recovery systems, these first attempts will doubtless be improved. A more important question is what price will be obtainable for salvaged materials, and whether it will decline as more salvage systems are put into use.

Almost everyone believes that recycling is a good thing; it is economically useful and individually satisfying. Countless bottles, bundles of paper, and cans have been culled from household waste and delivered without compensation to recycling centers. Unfortunately, however, recycling falls considerably short of its apparent promise. American industry doesn't run on salvaged materials to any considerable extent. In spite of the enthusiasm of environmentalists and the boasts of the container industry, volunteer materials reclamation in the United States is a tenuous and marginal operation. Without the help of volunteer workers and the subsidy price for used bottles and aluminum cans by some beverage and aluminum firms, materials recycling in the United States would be hardly noticeable.

This is not to say that the reuse of scrap materials is economically unsound. The American economy has a long history of the reuse of recovered materials, especially paper and ferrous metal. But a combination of circumstances, including changes in industrial materials requirements, the narrow resource guidelines of the market system, discriminatory freight rates, and tax disadvantages, has greatly reduced the market for salvaged materials.

Wastepaper

Wastepaper represents about half of the refuse of households and commercial establishments, and at one time was a steady source of income for most large office buildings. But the use of reclaimed materials in papermaking has declined since World War II, when waste provided about 35 percent of the raw material for paper and cardboard. It now constitutes an average of less than 20 percent of papermaking ingredients and this average may actually overstate the case. A more meaningful figure for recycled wastepaper would be closer to 10 percent because about half of the paper "waste" is salvaged at the time of production within the paper plant.

The decline in the use of wastepaper has been caused by a number of factors, some difficult to change and others that may be altered: higher costs of waste collection and processing; increased contamination of used paper by special coatings, inks, and plastics; improved wood-pulping techniques that make the use of virgin materials cheaper and yield better papermaking fibers (wastepaper fibers are shorter than virgin-pulp fibers and become shorter with reuse); and the integration of papermaking with pulpwood operations that include forest holdings, encouraging greater reliance upon industry-owned virgin materials.

Within limits, however, the proportion of used paper to virgin materials can be changed, and one of the determining considerations is consumer preference. Heretofore, most large-scale consumers, such as the federal government, cities, states, and large firms, either have been indifferent to the recycled content of their paper or, as in the case of the federal government, have actually specified 100-percent-virgin materials in their purchase orders. This has now changed. New York City recently placed its first order for "ecology" paper, stationery with 30 to 40 percent recycled content; commercial institutions concerned about their public image, such as the Bank of America and American Telephone and Telegraph, have specified used materials in their paper orders—100-percent-recycled paper being required for Bank of America checks; and notices that recycled materials have been employed for their manufacture are found with increasing frequency in books, including this one.

Part of this is a kind of harmless fraud—taking credit for recycling that isn't very different from past practices. But the widespread use of large amounts of recycled materials in papermaking will require more than the modest industry adjustments hitherto made to accommodate a small number of stationery and book-paper orders. Whether in full-scale use recycled materials will be able to compete with virgin materials, as the demand for recycled paper increases, depends in large part on the adaptability of the technology of papermaking. But with greater demand for recycled paper, especially if reinforced by tax incentives, the paper industry should be able to reverse the trend away from salvaged materials. On a small scale, 100-percent-recycled paper has already appeared in markets that were once the exclusive territory of paper made from virgin materials.

The Battle Over the Bottle

Possibly the most complex and controversial of all the issues to emerge from the environmental crisis involves the familiar glass container. The dispute centers on the use for beer and other beverages of the throwaway bottle, which together with tin and aluminum cans, has become a familiar sight along our roadsides and in our parks and playgrounds. Should the throwaway container be banned, taxed out of existence, endured and recycled, or attacked through greater litter prevention and control? It is possible that there is no single "best" solution to this problem. Various advantages and disadvantages are encountered in each approach.

The throwaway bottle has had a wide-ranging impact. It has increased greatly the output of the glass industry, raised the price of beverages to the consumer, and added significantly to trash and litter. The throwaway also decreases the labor and space requirements of the retailer, since he is not burdened with handling returned bottles, and at least in terms of the market's assessment, the consumer appears to favor the throwaway. The evidence is not strong on this point—opinion polls have recorded otherwise—and consumer behavior might shift if the very considerable social benefits of the use of returnable bottles were widely recognized. In the absence of this recognition, however, the returnable bottle appears to be a thing of the past, as is suggested by the trend lines in Figure 12.2. It was not always so.

Before the era of the throwaway, returnable bottles made the rounds between consumer and bottler about forty times before they were broken or discarded because of damage. Now, however, where returnables are available, the national average has

Figure 12.2.   Projected Trends in the Use of
Soft-Drink Containers *

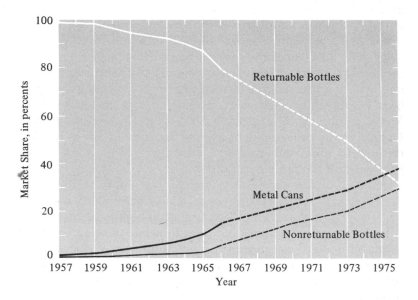

* William E. Franklin and Arsen Darnay, *The Role of Packaging in Solid Waste Management, 1966 to 1976* (Rockville, Maryland: Department of Health, Education, and Welfare, 1969). Prepared under contract by the Midwest Research Institute, p. 43.

dropped to fifteen rounds, and the figure is even lower in some areas of the nation, as in the urban Northeast, where the average is below four. Since the returnable costs more to produce—about ten or eleven cents as compared with four or five cents for the throwaway—the bottle must be used more than four or five times to pay for itself and to make possible the lower beverage price that is presumably necessary to encourage the purchase of beverages in returnable containers.

A deposit system has traditionally been employed to encourage the return of the bottles and maintain their velocity of circulation. But the two-cent deposit appears to have lost whatever persuasive force it may have had, and when the deposit was raised to five cents in a recent New York City test, virtually no change in the rate of bottle returns took place. The steady rise in the price level may have destroyed much of the incentive effect of the deposit system. How easily changed this reaction is will be better known when Vermont's and Oregon's requirements that a five-cent deposit be charged for all beverage containers take effect. These tests of the deposit approach, carried out over a wider area and reinforced by the emphasis upon litter control, may encourage more response than did the New York City test. Until evidence from such cases as Vermont and Oregon proves otherwise, however, it can only be concluded that the deposit approach does little to persuade the consumer to keep bottles from the trash or the roadside.

Container Recycling

If the throwaway bottle and the can are here to stay, secure in the support of the merchant and manufacturer and the indifference of the consumer to the bottle deposit, what about recycling as a second-best approach to the container waste problem?

Glass Recycling of bottles, although saving virgin raw materials, is not of much urgency for materials conservation, since the basic ingredient of glass is sand, one of the earth's most abundant materials. Glass does melt at a lower temperature than sand, and in this respect recycling bottles requires less energy than the manufacture of new glass, but the reuse of glass involves more than simply melting down old bottles. Control of the ingredients is extremely critical in glass production, and used materials necessarily contain unknown substances that may upset the furnace operation, leading to an inferior product or disruption of the production process. Another disadvantage of container recycling is that for it to succeed, at least as much individual effort must be expended, for less compensation, as is required for simple returning bottles to the grocer. Because the use of returnable bottles conserves more energy than recycling glass, some environmental groups oppose container recycling in general as an unsatisfactory substitute for the return and reuse of bottles.

The community gains from glass recycling through the reduction in litter. The question is how much of an impact the recycling of containers—glass and metal—has upon the waste-disposal problem, and whether the enthusiasm that has been demonstrated at the start of recycling programs will continue. If recycling succeeds where the use of the more environmentally protective returnable fails, it can only be because somehow recycling represents a more positive act of environmental protection to many than the prosaic job of returning bottles to the store.

So far, recycling has not succeeded where the returnable has failed. In 1971, a year that should rank high in recycling effort, glass from approximately 912 million bottles and jars was recovered in the United States; 912 million is a lot—except by comparison with total annual glass-container production in the United States, which is over 36 billion. Recycled glass containers thus represented slightly more than 2.5 percent of total output, hardly a consequential figure.

Ferrous Metal   The case of recycled metal containers is not much different. The so-called tin can is basically a steel can with an added coating made of tin or other materials and usually including copper. Because of the composite nature of the metal, either the copper or the steel can be reclaimed. If the copper is salvaged, the rest of the can is usually discarded; if the steel is reused, the whole can is compressed and fed with other metal scrap and raw materials into the steel furnace. In the past, when the open-hearth process was the predominant method of steel-making, the market for scrap metal was better than it is today. This process could accommodate a large scrap charge and was fairly tolerant of the kind of scrap used. Within limits, contamination of scrap by copper and other nonferrous materials did not disrupt the open-hearth process.

With the introduction of the basic oxygen process, however, the amount of scrap that can be used in steel-making has been decreased and much cleaner scrap—uncontaminated by nonferrous materials—is required. As a result, the market for ferrous metal scrap has weakened greatly, reducing the incentive to recycle tin cans and to salvage junked autos—to name two of the more familiar troublesome wastes of our society. Actually, tin-can scrap has never been an important source of the steel industry's raw-material supply, and interest in recycling has not altered this situation. Many cans have been cleaned, delabeled, smashed, and taken to recycling centers, but the effect on the industry's materials policy has been slight. As with glass containers, the number of tin cans collected and recycled is impressive, about 1.5 billion per year, but this represents only 2.3 percent of the annual output, and unlike glass containers, which constitute the major source of recovered material used in glass-making, recycled tin cans are an unimportant part of the supply of ferrous scrap.

Aluminum But if the recycled glass and steel containers have not made much of an impression on waste disposal or materials recovery, what about recycled aluminum cans? The Aluminum Association, the industry's trade group, reported a four-fold increase in recycled aluminum cans in 1971; these amounted to 770 million cans, or 3.7 percent of the annual aluminum-can output. The increase in aluminum salvage in 1971 was largely the result of publicity by the industry, encouraging recycling, and the payment of a bounty for aluminum cans by a number of beer firms and aluminum producers. The record of aluminum recycling is the best in the container industry, but even so, less than 4 percent of the cans produced in 1971 were salvaged.

Aluminum justifies a greater recycling effort than most other materials because of its longer litter life and the greater energy required to produce aluminum from bauxite. A postwar entrant in the packaging field, aluminum has gained widespread adoption in recent years as a beverage container, as a kitchen wrap, and in other household uses. It will contribute increasingly to solid waste in the future, as aluminum siding, roofing, and similar products are discarded. But already, along with plastics, aluminum has become one of the most offensive ingredients of

litter pollution. Tin cans rust and eventually degrade to incon-
spicuous brown debris, but aluminum retains its noncorrosive
luster long after most packaging materials have disintegrated.
Moreover, the distinctive feature of many aluminum beverage
containers, the pull tab, spreads litter that virtually defies collection and represents close to the ultimate in a socially indifferent
product design.

Because of the litter potential of aluminum containers and the
high energy requirements for aluminum production from virgin
materials, regulations limiting the use of aluminum may enhance
the social welfare more than private interests are impaired. An
obvious candidate for controls is the aluminum beverage container, which at best is of ephemeral benefit to the consumer,
but which creates greater social costs than other kinds of containers. A discriminatory tax on the aluminum container—
three, five, or ten cents, whatever necessary—could be imposed
to control its use. Such a levy would be a kind of internal protective tariff to limit the output of a particular item, but—unlike
the tariff in international trade—designed to increase public welfare
rather than private gain. A more cumbersome and administratively more costly approach would be to rebate the discriminatory tax if the aluminum cans were recycled, but this would
be generally less effective in eliminating the litter-pollution
potential.

Incorporating Disposal Costs in Product Prices

Can the market be made to serve the environment? The market
price of a washing machine or automobile does not include the
cost of its disposal. The consumer pays for this in a nonspe-
cific way through taxes and exposure to the various disutilities of
a high-waste society. But there is not much likelihood that the
individual's payment will coincide with the burden his purchases
place upon the disposal system, or that his payment will induce
efficient removal of the discarded product. Take the case of the
abandoned cars, for example, which have increasingly cluttered

metropolitan and rural America since the market for ferrous scrap fell into decline. In New York City, admittedly an area of worst offense, 72,961 cars were abandoned in 1970 as compared with 2,500 in 1960.

Some of the increase in abandoned cars is due to the larger number of cars in service in later years and to mounting car theft, but the abandoned vehicles have remained uncollected in large part because of the decline in the price of scrap metal, which has reduced the salvage value of many junk cars below the costs of towing and dismantling. Moreover, air-pollution regulations have prevented open burning to remove unwanted materials, such as upholstery, at the same time that the price for the salvaged materials has dropped. In view of this cost-price squeeze, it has been suggested that the purchase price of an automobile cover its disposal costs and that compensation be made to encourage proper disposal of the car at the end of its service. Attractive as this approach appears to be, in solving one problem it creates another. In the early 1970's, the vast majority of worn-out vehicles—up to 80 percent—were collected and processed through the regular scrap market. In order to ensure the satisfactory salvaging of the derelict 20 percent, a purchase-price fee would have to be paid on the 80 percent as well—clearly a case of overcharging the consumer. Largely for this reason, the Environmental Protection Agency decided against recommending this approach to the problem of the abandoned automobile.

If the scrap-metal market is permanently depressed, however, not only will more cars be abandoned as a result of the inadequate incentive for removal, but those in junkyards will accumulate, caught between low salvage prices and high costs of preparation for recycling. Some form of subsidy to cover certain kinds of costs, such as towing, will continue to be necessary unless the market for scrap revives considerably. But different disposal conditions are likely to make the inclusion of a fixed disposal cost in the purchase price of an article both discriminatory and administratively difficult. Rather than attempting to devise a system of charges that will take account of the very diverse conditions that arise in disposal situations, removal of the economic discrimination against the use of recovered materials may help reduce the burden of solid waste requiring disposal.

The Economic Disadvantages of Recovered Materials

Some salvaged materials are technically inferior to virgin materials, while others are superior, requiring fewer resources to process. But the market for recovered resources is curtailed in the United States by the economic incentives favoring virgin materials that have been built into our tax system. The depletion allowance and the capital-gains provisions of income taxation discriminate against recovered materials. Income derived from the ownership and sale of virgin materials is taxed at a lower rate than income from recycled materials. A further discrimination, higher freight rates, reduces the market range of salvaged materials. These are institutional factors subject to modification, but some—such as the tax depletion allowance—may be so vigorously supported by special interests that the prospect of significant change is limited.

The Depletion Allowance: Reward for Rapid Resource Use

The depletion allowance affords a lower federal corporation tax upon income earned from the sale of a wide range of exhaustible (depleting) resources. Since salvaged materials, although originally derived from the depleting virgin resources, are not regarded as depleting resources for tax purposes, this allowance encourages the development and use of virgin materials. The percentage of depletion permitted—a fixed deduction from annual gross income—varies with the mineral involved, but continues for the life of the corporation. In any one year, however, the depletion credit cannot exceed 50 percent of the net income for that year. Although originally designed primarily for the benefit of the petroleum industry, this special tax advantage has been extended to a large number of raw materials. A partial list of the minerals eligible for a depletion allowance, with the rate for each, is as follows:

Minerals	Deduction, in percents
Petroleum, Sulfur, Bauxite, Lead, Zinc, Tin, Mercury	22
Oil Shale, Copper, Iron Ore	15
Coal, Lignite, Salt	10
Sand, Gravel, Clay	5

Since the depletion allowance is available only the first time the raw material is used, not when it is recycled, salvaged materials are placed at a competitive disadvantage.

Capital-Gains Taxation: Lower Taxes on Property Returns

Capital gains occur when property, such as land, a share of stock, or a timber holding, has increased in value between the time that it is bought and the time that it is sold. If stock is bought at $50 a share and sold for $60, the capital gain is $10 per share.* How much this gain should be taxed, and whether it should be taxed at all, are matters of dispute, but under the present federal personal income tax and the corporate income tax, the capital gains-rate is generally lower than the regular tax rate. (Where the regular tax rate is lower than the capital-gains rate, the taxpayer can use the lower regular rate.)

In the taxation of corporate income, the capital-gains rate is 30 percent, in comparison with the highest regular corporate income-tax rate of 48 percent. Taxation of capital gains under the personal income tax attains a high of 35 percent, in comparison

* For tax purposes the computation of capital gains is considerably more complicated than this illustration suggests. To be eligible for lower tax treatment, gains must be "long-term"—from the sale of property held more than six months—and losses, the opposite of gains, can be used to offset gains over prescribed periods in addition to the tax year in which they occur. For the issue at hand, such considerations are not important.

with the highest regular income-tax rate of approximately 55 percent. Obviously, the higher the regular tax rate, the greater the economic benefit to those firms and individuals that can take advantage of the capital-gains treatment of taxable income. The issue here, however, is how this situation affects the recycling of salvaged materials in the American economy, and the answer is categorical—it discourages recycling. Like the depletion allowance, capital-gains taxation is generally restricted to income from the sale of virgin resources, not from that of salvaged materials. In the corporate income tax, for example, profits from timber operations and royalties from the sale of coal and iron ore are specifically defined as capital gains, whereas income from sale of such materials as scrap metal and wastepaper is denied capital-gains status on the ground that the waste materials are property held primarily for sale—a designation that would appear to apply equally well to coal, iron ore, and timber if it were not for the special treatment written into the tax law.

Finally, if the salvaged resource is able to compete with virgin materials in spite of the discriminatory tax treatment, its marketing range is likely to be limited by high freight rates. Transportation costs for low-value materials, whether virgin or used, are frequently decisive in determining whether a resource supply can compete in a given geographic area. If the used material, such as scrap metal, faces a higher freight rate than its virgin equivalent, in this instance iron ore, recycling is limited to the region in which transportation costs are not a significant factor. Since the freight rates on salvaged materials established by the Interstate Commerce Commission are as much as three times as high as comparable rates for virgin materials, the effective competition of salvaged materials is severely impaired.

Quite aside from the basic question of the equity of the preferential treatment for special interests through depletion allowances, capital-gains tax privileges, and discriminatory freight rates, such policies by discouraging recycling and aggravating the difficulties of disposing of wastes promote questionable private gain at the expense of the environment. While more than a reversal of these discriminatory arrangements will be required to bring recycling to the level where it contributes significantly to solving the problem of waste disposal, the present public policy favoring the use of virgin materials is peculiarly devoid of any benefit to the public.

References and Readings

Alexander, Tom, "The Packaging Problem Is a Can of Worms," *Fortune*, LXXXV (June 1972), p. 105.
> A survey of the contribution of packaging materials to the solid-waste problem, and of some of the approaches that have been suggested to alleviate the problem.

"Federal Redirections in Solid Wastes," *Environmental Science and Technology*, VI (April 1972), pp. 318–320.
> A brief article on the problems encountered in the federal solid-waste program and the future role of this program.

Franklin, William E., and Darnay, Arsen, *The Role of Nonpackaging Paper in Solid Waste Management, 1966 to 1976*. Washington, D.C.: Environmental Protection Agency, 1971. Prepared under contract by the Midwest Research Institute.
> The title indicates the area of study of this contract research project.

——— *The Role of Packaging in Solid Waste Management, 1966 to 1976*. Rockville, Maryland: Department of Health, Education, and Welfare, 1969. Prepared under contract by the Midwest Research Institute.
> A comprehensive examination of the expected trends in packaging, the disposal problems created by various kinds of packaging, and how these problems may be minimized.

Hannon, Bruce M., "Bottles, Cans, Energy," *Environment*, XIV (March 1972), pp. 11–21.
> The article examines the materials and energy requirements for the production of containers and concludes in favor of the returnable bottle. Recycling centers for throwaway containers are considered to be largely "public relations activities."

Hershaft, Alex, "Solid Waste Treatment Technology," *Environmental Science and Technology*, VI (May 1972), pp. 109–111.
> A review of recent developments in handling and disposing of solid wastes, including advances in materials reclamation.

314 ENVIRONMENTAL PROBLEM AREAS

Kenahan, Charles B., "Solid Waste: Resources Out of Place," *Environmental Science and Technology*, V (July 1971), pp. 594–600.

An article by the chief of the Solid Wastes Division of the Bureau of Mines on the reclamation techniques developed by this federal agency.

Small, William E., *Third Pollution: The National Problem of Solid Waste Disposal* (New York: Praeger, 1970).

A popular but comprehensive treatment of the solid-waste problem in the United States. The author is a former staff member of the Senate Committee on Public Works, which has been concerned with the solid-waste problem.

"A Solid Waste Recovery System for All Municipalities," *Environmental Science and Technology*, V (February 1971), pp. 108–111.

A description of the Aluminum Association's design for a waste-reclamation plant that is flexible in size and operation. Cost data on operation are included.

PART IV

Conclusion

Chapter Thirteen

Environmental Protection—
Tomorrow the World?

We have met the enemy and he is us!—Pogo

In the late spring of 1972, the United Nations Conference on the Human Environment was held in Stockholm to
work out ways to protect the world environment. Like most
United Nations undertakings, the attempts to reach agreements
in Stockholm were marked by sharp disputes and frequent ma-
neuvering in national self-interest, but in an important sense the
Conference was a success even before it took place.

Although the Soviet-bloc countries boycotted the Conference
in protest over the exclusion of East Germany, which is not a
member of the UN, 114 nations sent delegates to the twelve-
day session. The call to the Conference and the attendance by the
vast majority of the UN members was in itself evidence of increased concern over environmental deterioration, and what was
more important, recognition of the essentially commonplace origin of damage to the human habitat. Indeed, the bitter reaction
of many of the Third World countries—the poorer, developing
nations—to the growing concern for the environment in the
developed countries was really acceptance of the fact that damage
to the human habitat is largely the outgrowth of mankind's ordinary pursuit of material well-being. The Stockholm Conference

symbolized the acceptance of the view that twentieth-century industrial activity carries with it a serious threat to the environment and to mankind. In brief, the vulnerability of the resource base to deterioration from the by-products of commercial exploitation has become an accepted part of the conventional wisdom.

Only One Earth—Divided

The theme of the Stockholm Conference was "Only One Earth." But contention and acrimony were so widespread and persistent at the meetings that the passage of some measures was in doubt until the meeting's final hours. Officially, the Conference was limited to representatives chosen by the 114 attending nations, but an Environmental Forum was held at the same time as the official meetings, and produced a wide variety of vociferous commentary by members of the counterculture, Third World partisans, critics of the United States' Indochina policy, representatives from organizations such as the Sierra Club and Friends of the Earth, and various other interested individuals. Not only was the Forum used as a vehicle to attack the foreign policy of the United States for its contribution to "ecocide," as was the official conference even by a representative of the host nation, but the poorer nations took advantage of the Forum to press their opposition to recommendations originating in the developed world that population growth be brought under control and economic growth frozen.

The schism between the less developed nations and the wealthier advanced countries was not limited to the unofficial activities at Stockholm, however, but became one of the major areas of dispute at the official conference. The developing nations contended that the damage to the environment was not of their doing, that the industrial nations were primarily to blame, and that countries just now emerging from privation should not be expected to forgo the higher standard of living resulting from economic growth and industrial development in order to save what the wealthier nations have endangered.

China, only recently admitted to the United Nations, assumed the leadership of the Third World group at the Conference and generally opposed what was held to be interference with the internal affairs of the developing nations. In a major address before the Conference, Tang Ke, chairman of the Chinese delegation, stated:

> We support the developing countries in building their national economies on the principle of independence, exploiting their natural resources in accordance with their own needs, and gradually improving the well-being of their people. Each country has the right to determine its own environment standards and policies in the light of its own conditions, and no country whatsoever should undermine the interest of the developing countries under the pretext of protecting the environment.[1]

The developing nations were not content with asserting their right to go their own way in the world—accepting pollution as a concomitant of economic growth if necessary; they also confronted the wealthier nations with a bill of particulars designed to protect themselves from actions taken by the developed nations in cleaning up their own environments. Specifically, the less developed nations, which in many cases depend heavily upon sales of raw materials in the world market, sought assurance that their economic welfare would not suffer from restrictions placed against their exports for environmental reasons or from the competition of recycled materials in the industrial economies.

The less developed nations saw the growing concern for environmental protection in the industrial nations as a threat to their tenuous hold on the bottom of the development ladder. Greater protection of the environment in the advanced countries was expected to redound to their disadvantage in a number of ways, but especially by decreasing the poorer nations' sales in the world market. Lead, for example, harmful to humans as well as to the action of pollution-suppressing catalysts, was certain to encounter reduced sales as air-pollution standards in industrial nations stiffened. The market for sulfur could only be

[1] Quoted in Terri Aaronson, "World Priorities," *Environment*, XIV (July/August 1972), p. 4.

spoiled by the increased supply of that substance resulting from the desulfurization of fossil fuels and the availability of stack precipitator by-products. In like manner, recycled materials in general—iron, tin, aluminum, copper, and paper, to name a few—promised widespread encroachment upon the markets of the underdeveloped countries selling primarily virgin materials.

A decrease in sales in the world market was not the only prospect of environmental protection that disturbed the developing nations. They feared that the preoccupation of the aid-giving nations with environmental protection would shift funds hitherto devoted to foreign aid to domestic expenditures on environmental improvement. Foreign assistance by the developed nations was already falling below UN goals, and the gap between the developed and underdeveloped nations' level of living was widening. Economic welfare had increased least where there was greatest need; the poorer nations with the largest populations were among those lagging most. This increasing disparity raised a critical problem for the protection of the world environment, as pointed out at the Conference by Indira Gandhi, prime minister of India:

> On the one hand the rich look askance at our continuing poverty —on the other they warn us against their own methods. We do not wish to impoverish the environment any further and yet we cannot for a moment forget the grim poverty of large numbers of people. Are not poverty and need the greatest polluters? For instance, unless we are in a position to provide employment and purchasing power for the daily necessities of the tribal people and those who live in or around our jungles, we cannot prevent them from combing the forest for food and livelihood; from poaching and from despoiling the vegetation. When they themselves feel deprived, how can we urge the preservation of animals? How can we speak to those who live in villages and in slums about keeping the oceans, the rivers, and the air clean when their own lives are contaminated at the source? The environment cannot be improved in conditions of poverty.[2]

[2] Quoted in "What Happened at Stockholm," *Bulletin of the Atomic Scientists*, XXVIII (September 1972), p. 36.

The Additionality Provision

In an attempt to protect their already inadequate sources of livelihood, the underdeveloped nations at the Stockholm Con ference passed a resolution calling for compensation to be given them for trade damages resulting from environmental protection. Over the opposition of the developed nations, the resolution was passed by the Conference; it took the form of a recommendation to be considered by the United Nations General Assembly. The United States voted against the so-called "additionality" provision on the ground that a country's export earnings were affected by many things and it was inappropriate in principle to single out just one. The United States representatives also acknowledged that they believed the compensation requirement would discourage environmental improvement. The Conference delegates—whether from developed or underdeveloped countries—were mainly voting their own interests, a quite familiar UN procedure.

Unfortunately, the care and protection of the world environment may not be so easily split off from the problem of poverty as the developed nations appeared to hope at the Stockholm Conference. The wealthier nations can go their own way in shoring up their habitat, but the rest of the world covers more territory, and its population is both larger and growing faster. Increasingly, the impact upon the world environment will come from the developing areas, especially if the industrial nations correct their ways and the underdeveloped countries are not restrained in their abuse of the environment. Quite aside from the simple humanitarian motive of helping those in great need, the developed nations cannot remain isolated from what goes on in the rest of the world, a protected island in a sea of pollution. In the struggle for economic development, if Brazil's atmosphere becomes polluted because it has legislated lenient emission controls to attract industry, we cannot seal the air of Brazil off from the rest of the world, and all mankind is the poorer when the Serengeti Plains are stripped of their wildlife.

322   CONCLUSION

The Elusive Goal of Economic Development

But the developing nations need more than assistance. They
need to change some of their ways to make assistance work
toward greater growth and higher living standards. Although
Milton Friedman exaggerates when he finds most foreign aid
resulting in wasteful monuments to national pride, such as over-
seas airlines and steel mills seriously out of development phase
with the rest of the economy, the emerging nations must be
saved from ecological blunders, such as the Aswan Dam in
Egypt,* and they must be encouraged to bring about a better
distribution of their meager income among their own citizens.

Over the past decade, the underdeveloped countries have
lagged significantly behind the industrial nations in economic
growth. Two-thirds of the world's underdeveloped population
subsists on a per-capita GNP of less than $200 annually, with an
overall growth rate of less than 4 percent. Indeed, because of
rapidly increasing population in these countries, the actual per-
capita increase in income is reduced to approximately 1.5 percent annually. But even this does not tell the whole story. Not
only are the poor in these countries subsisting on incredibly
low incomes, but their share in their country's very meager increase in output is less than that of those who are better off. The
poorer nations are increasing output less than the richer nations,

* The Aswan Dam on the Nile River, built largely through Soviet aid,
cost the equivalent of 750 million dollars and the loss of many Egyptian
archaeological treasures. Although the project has the dual purpose of
generating electricity and extending agriculture through irrigation, ironically
the plains area previously fertilized by the Nile's annual overflow now requires the application of inorganic fertilizer, and the formerly productive
fishing area at the river's ocean mouth has been wiped out. Moreover, the
irrigation ditches have carried more than the water needed to increase the
output of grain, cotton, and fruit; snails have followed these watercourses,
spreading schistosomiasis, a blood disease caused by parasitic microorga-
nisms carried by the snails. Although the Aswan irrigation project has added
to Egyptian agricultural output, during the eleven-year period when the
dam was being built, the country's population grew from 26 to 34 million,
greatly diluting the project's effect upon living standards.

and the lower income groups in the poor nations are not sharing equally in the modest increases in GNP.

Over the past decade, one in which a special effort has been made to assist the developing nations increase output, India has raised its overall output, but those in the poorest 10 percent of its population have either not benefited at all from this increase or have actually grown poorer. This is not an isolated instance. Much the same pattern is found in other emerging nations, some of which are moderately advanced, such as Mexico and Brazil.[3] One of the ironies of the foreign-aid programs is that although the average living standards of the poorer nations may show improvement, income inequality may be worsened.

Important segments of the poorer nation's population, like the people of our Appalachia, do not share in the improved economic output generated by increased economic activity. Emerging nations with hybrid economies, part primitive and part modern, where much of the economic activity takes place outside of the market system, will show uneven effects of foreign aid upon different sectors of the economy. The capacity of developing nations to benefit from foreign assistance also differs. Some are able to absorb foreign aid well, with a stimulating impact carrying throughout the economy, while in others the original aid fails to generate much further effect. In the selection of development programs, those having the greater economic impact are of course preferred, but in nations with a large non-market sector, foreign aid is likely to fall short of raising output and income in this sector. Projects designed to raise output are almost certain to be introduced in the more advanced sector of the economy, thus adding to the income of those already better paid.

Take the case of the introduction of the miracle grains, which at first glance would appear to be equally beneficial to the rich and the poor farmer. In actual fact, the very poor farmer is likely to find the miracle grains either beyond his reach or not a

3 See Robert S. McNamara, *Address to the U.N. Conference on Trade and Development at Santiago, Chile, April 14, 1972.* (Washington, D.C.: International Bank for Reconstruction and Development, 1972).

great improvement over the common varieties, because to obtain the high yields possible with the miracle grains, greater inputs of fertilizer and irrigation and more intensive cultivation are required. These additional inputs, especially commercial fertilizers and irrigation systems, raise the capital costs of farming above the poor farmer's ability to pay. As a result, the wealthier farmer's output and income increase, but the poor farmer's stays the same or decreases, even though the nation's rises. Development programs cannot be expected to wipe out inequality. Indeed, they may be justified if the gains in increased output outweigh the disadvantages of increased inequality. For example, some increase in inequality, accompanied by an end to starvation with the use of miracle grains, would appear to be preferable to greater equality without their use and mass starvation.

Although an increase in inequality in a nation already suffering a subsistence standard of living is a cruel consequence of the attempt to raise national output, it may be a necessary cost of later improvement. For emerging nations, as for developed nations, per-capita economic growth requires increased productivity. Usually this involves employing more advanced production techniques, using more capital equipment, or both. More complex, highly productive undertakings generally impose highly selective human-resource requirements. The better-educated, more highly trained, and more mobile individuals are likely to be chosen—in short, those individuals in a developing country who already receive higher incomes. If, in addition, the productivity-increasing project requires a domestic contribution of capital, again the more affluent citizens of the country are the initial beneficiaries of the project.

The critical question is not whether most development projects increase inequality—they do. The real issue is what can be done to minimize this impact without unduly checking economic growth. A highly controversial value judgment is involved here, and some are willing to tolerate only a very little additional inequality in order to encourage economic growth. The controversy over what level of inequality is acceptable in development programs can be bypassed, however, by rephrasing the question to ask how a foreign-aid program can be modified to reduce the degree of the increase in inequality without seriously reducing the growth-enhancing effect of the aid.

The answer to this question in the case of United States aid programs is clear. In the past, United States foreign aid has been dominated by military assistance and to a lesser extent by large-scale capital projects, such as highways, reclamation dams, and power installations. Little can be said for the output-increasing effect of military assistance—unless it is that most such aid is counterproductive from the standpoint of the civilian sector of the economy. Big capital-using projects are also frequently less than ideal. Even when they add to the social-overhead capital of the developing nation, they are likely to inject large expenditures into a very restricted part of the economy. As a result, before such projects can raise the output of the developing nation, there is certain to be a sharp increase in income inequality. By contrast, aid programs that invest in human capital (generally by increasing training and education), and projects that raise the output of the mass of the workers (such as the introduction of improved agricultural techniques), are less likely to add to income inequality while encouraging economic growth.

The United Nations' Development Goal

Whatever the reaction to programs for economic development, the United Nations has accepted the responsibility of channeling aid from the wealthier nations into these programs. For the decade of the 1970's, the goal of this aid program has been set at 0.7 percent of the annual gross national product of each developed member nation, hardly an oppressive burden upon the wealthier nations. (Originally, this goal was set at 1 percent of GNP by the Pearson Committee of the UN, but it was later reduced.) Even this modest goal has not been attained in the early 1970's, and only France among the larger nations is expected to come close to meeting it. Contributions by the United States, which did not quite reach half the established figure in the early years of the decade, are projected to decline in the later 1970's. The failure to achieve this meager United

Nations goal is not good news for either the developing nations' standard of living or the world environment, especially in view of the rapid population growth that is in part responsible for the developing nations' plight.

The development issue occupied much of the Stockholm Conference's attention and was the subject of seven of the Conference's twenty-six principles, which attempt to set forth a code of international environmental conduct. Principles 8 through 14 bear directly upon the development issue, emphasizing the theme that the underdeveloped countries need assistance to raise their living standards and protect the environment. Perhaps the most forthright in calling upon the developed nations to aid the poorer nations is Principle 12:

> Resources should be made available to preserve and improve the environment, taking into account the circumstances and particular requirements of developing countries and any costs which may emanate from their incorporating environmental safeguards into their development planning and the need for making available to them, upon their request, additional international technical and financial assistance for this purpose.[4]

The feeling of the conference that the care and protection of the world environment is largely the financial responsibility of the wealthier nations could hardly be stated more bluntly.

The Structure of World Environmental Protection

Although the issue of economic development and aid to the emerging nations dominated the Stockholm Conference, arrangements to monitor world environmental changes were made, and a permanent organization to coordinate international eviron- mental affairs was established.

Earthwatch

The Conference approved a network of 110 monitoring stations to check on the climatic effects of pollution, under the

---

[4] "What Happened at Stockholm," *op. cit.*, p. 33.

direction of the United Nations World Meteorological Organization. Earthwatch will also monitor ocean pollution, radioactive wastes, food contamination, and plant and animal changes that may indicate environmental hazards. Not only will it be possible for the first time to obtain worldwide information on pollution of the environment, but ten benchmark stations in unpopulated areas will provide a frame of reference for evaluating the data from urban areas.

The Environmental Secretariat

The Stockholm Conference recommended the establishment of a permanent Environmental Secretariat to coordinate world environmental affairs. In addition to a small staff and an executive director, the Environmental Secretariat includes a Governing Council for Environmental Programs made up of fifty-four national representatives, which reports to the General Assembly through the existing United Nations Economic and Social Council.

A UN Environmental Fund

In his Environmental Message to Congress in February, 1972, President Nixon proposed the establishment of a voluntary world environmental fund. This proposal was adopted by the Stockholm Conference, and the fund, initially set at 100 million dollars over five years, will be used to establish Earthwatch and other projects of the Environmental Secretariat. The United States has agreed to contribute 40 million dollars, on a matching basis, toward the 100-million-dollar goal.

Special Environmental Concerns of the Conference

In addition to the considerable debate between the developed and the underdeveloped countries over environmental responsibility and the accomplishment of the job of determining the organization of the Secretariat, the Stockholm Conference was marked by action on a number of specific environmental concerns. A convention on ocean dumping was initiated to promote an international accord among nations to limit the disposal of waste in the ocean. The convention was convened by the United Kingdom under the authority of the United Nations.

To preserve unique natural and historical areas, the general conference of UNESCO at Paris in the fall of 1972 approved a World Heritage Trust Convention. The International Whaling Commission (IWC) was urged by the Stockholm Conference to adopt a ten-year moratorium on commercial whaling; at a London meeting of the IWC in late summer of 1972 this recommendation was rejected, but the establishment of whaling quotas and the near success of the Stockholm moratorium recommendation represented impressive progress. And Endangered Species Convention, also endorsed at the Stockholm meetings, was very successfully concluded in Washington, D. C., in February 1973.

From almost any standpoint, the work of the Stockholm Conference and its aftermath has been impressive. A comprehensive set of environmental principles has been adopted, a permanent organizational structure is established, and specific recommendations have been made in important environmental problem areas. The question that remains is whether the agreement obtained on matters of principle can be maintained when these principles are subjected to the pressures of national interests. The record of the parent organization, the United Nations, in resolving conflicts between member nations is far from impressive. Much of the success of the Stockholm Conference was due to the extraordinary efforts of its very talented organizer, Maurice Strong, and Strong will direct the Governing Council for Environmental Programs from offices of the UN in Nairobi, Kenya—a location that may be quite close to some of the world's difficult environmental problems. Moving from the consideration of principles to action for environmental protection, however, will require both talented guidance and more agreement than has generally characterized the affairs of the United Nations.

The World Environment in the Year 2000— Alive and Well?

Most long-range forecasts are likely to be forgotten by the time they come due, which may be just as well. Remembered or not, however, the recent concern over the environment has expressed itself in a multitude of forecasts—most of them heavy with gloom. Given the forces at work, it is hard to see how things can get much better, but some of the more pessimistic demonstrations, such as those advocating no-growth, conclude that we will be fortunate indeed to avoid disaster.

Where, in fact, is the world environment most vulnerable?

The greatest source of pollution comes from the developed nations, where industrial output is largest, but these nations are also more sensitive to the need for environmental protection and have the greater capacity to achieve it. The emerging nations are as yet responsible for little industrial pollution, but their potential here is great, and they present a truly awesome force for increasing world population. Moreover, given the Third World truculence toward environmental values, it is not likely that pollution abatement and population control will receive the highest priority in the struggle of these states to increase output. By 2000 or before, however, the impact of increasing numbers upon living standards in the emerging nations will provide strong persuasion for population limitation—especially if foreign aid is restricted to those nations with effective population-control programs.

The environmental problems that need technical solutions—such as air and water pollution and solid-waste disposal—show the greatest promise of yielding to increased research and increased expenditures. The resolution of problems involving human factors, such as population control, is much less predictable, and because it depends upon human decisions, will vary widely over time and place. By 2000, the pressures of population will cut across both city and country. Most vulnerable of all to the pressure from increased population and expanding industrial development will be the remaining open space and natural regions.

At the same time, concentration in the metropolitan areas will continue, not so much to intensify as to extend farther from the cities' centers, an inchoate spread of urban development.

With developmental and recreational pressures reaching into areas of previously remote solitude, the endangered-wildlife list can only increase. In some regions, such as the African nations, wholesale wildlife destruction as a consequence of agricultural development has already begun and can only accelerate. And agreements among the nations of the world may come too late to save from extinction such migrating wildlife as the whale.

The year 2000 will usher in an era with many more people, with the world still divided between rich and poor, with industrial output rising, but the natural environment more barren save for the abundance of man and his many works.

References and Readings

Brown, Lester R., *World Without Borders*. New York: Random House, 1972.
> Lester Brown is a former foreign-assistance administrator who is now a senior fellow with the Overseas Development Council. His book is a review of the causes for the increasing spread in income between the rich and poor nations, and a strong plea for the adoption of a new set of global priorities that include the elimination of poverty, the stabilization of world population, and the reduction of military expenditures.

Environmental Quality: Third Annual Report of the Council on Environmental Quality. Washington, D.C.: Government Printing Office, 1972.
> See especially Chapter 3, "International Aspects of Environmental Quality."

Matthews, William H., ed., *Man's Impact on the Global Environment: Assessment and Recommendations for Action* (Cambridge: The MIT Press, 1970).
> A comprehensive study of the global effects of pollution upon the climate and the ecology.

McNamara, Robert S., *Address to the U.N. Conference on Trade and Development, Santiago, Chile, April 14, 1972*. Washington, D.C.: International Bank for Reconstruction and Development, 1972.

A brief account of the prospects and problems associated with development assistance.

Ranis, Gustav, ed., *The United States and the Developing Economies*, rev. ed. New York: W. W. Norton & Company, 1973.

Three articles in particular are pertinent to the consideration of economic development and environmental protection: Milton Friedman, "Foreign Aid—Means and Objectives"; Charles Wolf, Jr., "Economic Aid Reconsidered"; and Max F. Millikan and Walt W. Rostow, "Criteria of Eligibility for Assistance." Friedman argues that foreign aid for development is of questionable worth and that if emerging nations really have a potential for development they can "do it themselves" under the market system; Wolf takes exception to this view; and Millikan and Rostow caution that certain preconditions must be present in the developing country for the foreign aid to be effective.

Ward, Barbara, and Dubos, René J., *Only One Earth*. New York: W .W. Norton & Company, 1972.

This is a skillful blending of the writings of two well-known authors—Barbara Ward, an economist, and René Dubos, a biologist. The book covers a wide range of environmental issues and economic development, and was commissioned by the United Nations Secretary-General as an unofficial report for the Conference on the Human Environment in Stockholm.

"What Happened at Stockholm," *Bulletin of the Atomic Scientists*, XXVIII (September 1972), pp. 16–54.

An unusually complete report of the Stockholm Conference, including transcripts of some of the more important addresses made there.

Index

Aaronson, Terri, 319
Accelerated depreciation, 248–250
Additionality provision, 321
Aerobic decomposition, 199, 231
Agnew, W. G., 262
Agricultural wastes, 219–221
Air pollution, 253–289
  Air Quality Act, 276
  carbon monoxide, 260–261
  catalytic exhaust control, 262–263
  cost, 285–287
  Donora, Penna., 7, 256, 275
  emissions in U. S., 259
  emission standards time-table, 277–278
  federal-state controls, 276–278
  hydrocarbons, 257–259
  London, 256, 275
  Los Angeles, 255–256, 257, 261, 265, 268, 277
  New York, 256, 268, 273, 277
  nitrogen oxides, 257
  Pittsburgh, 268–269
  power generation, 269–274

  sulfur dioxide suppression, 271–272
  sulfur effects, 275–276
  sulfur oxides, 265, 274–276
  thermal inversion, 255–256
  Union Carbide case, 280–282
  varieties of, 257–264
Air Quality Act, 276
Alaskan North Slope, 174
Alberta tar sands, 177
Algal bloom, 201–205, 218–219
Alkyl benzene sulfonate (ABS), 204
Aluminum Association, 298–299
Ambient air trends, 278
Anerobic decomposition, 199, 207
Aransas National Wildlife Refuge, 101
Aristotle, 40
Army Corps of Engineers, 109, 110, 117, 128, 158, 239
Asotin dam, 158–159
Aswan dam, 322
Atomic Energy Commission, 186, 187

Atomic power, 185–188
Auger-mining, 53

Bain, J. S., 126, 130
Benefit-cost analysis, 109–132
    alternate-source approach, 155
    interest rate, 119–124
    period of analysis, 125
    secondary benefits, 127–128
    taxes, 127
Biochemical oxygen demand
    (BOD), 198–199
Black Mesa, 178–180, 265
Bogue, D. J., 15, 34
Bonneville Power Adm., 153, 159
Borlaug, N. E., 57
Brower, David, 152
Buchwald, Art, 290
Bureau of Outdoor Recreation,
    151–152, 159
Bureau of Reclamation, 117, 125,
    128, 156, 159
Bureau of Solid Waste Manage-
    ment, 295

Cairns, John, 217
Calif. Central Valley Project,
    125–126
Calif. Edison Mohave, 179
Capital-gains tax, 311–312
Carlyle, Thomas, 41
Carr, D. E., 258, 288
Circular flow, 89, 90
Civilian Conservation Corps, 5
Coal, 178–181
    air pollution, 180
    sulfur content, 180–181
Coliform test, 209–211
Columbia River hydro projects,
    134–135, 137
Commoner, Barry, 8–9, 11, 81

Connally, John, 101
Consolidated Edison of N. Y., 190
Consumer sovereignty, 86–89
Council on Environmental Quali-
    ty, 227, 283, 285–286
Crawford, W. D., 165
Cross-Florida Barge Canal, 110–
    111
Cuyahoga River, 195–196

Darnay, A., 304
Degradable wastes, 196–198
Depletion allowance, 176, 310–311
Desulfurization, 274, 284
Dickens, Charles, 1
Discount rate, 124
Dominy, Floyd, 152
Doomsday, 41
Douglas, W. O., Justice, 140, 141
Dunstan, W. M., 205

Earthwatch, 326–327
Eban, Abba, 1
Economic Development Adm.,
    240
Economic growth, 61–80
    costs and causes, 63–64
    environmental protection, 79
    labor, 78–79
    large-scale production, 65, 66
    productivity, 73–74
    Structure of American indus-
        try, 67–69
    technology, 66–67
Ehrlich, Paul, 8–9, 37
Electric car, 265
Electricity, 182–192
    demand for, 191
    growth, 190
Endangered Species Convention,
    328

Energy, 165–194
  atomic power, 185–188, 189
  coal, 178–181
  demand and supply over time,
    167, 169
  electricity, 182–192
  fossil fuels, 171–182, 191
  magnetohydrodynamic, 188–
    189
  market shares, 172
  natural gas, 181–182
  offshore oil, 174
  petroleum, 171–178
  power shortage, 183–184
  price of, 171
  supply of, 168–170
Energy crisis, 165–194
English poor laws, 40
Enke, Stephen, 24, 36
Environmental impact studies, 160
Environmental Policy Act, 141–
    142, 159
Environmental Protection Agen-
    cy, 73, 210, 227, 281, 309
Epstein, Samuel, 205
Escherichia coli, 210
Eutrophication, 202–203
External diseconomies, 53

Faraday, Michael, 188
Federal Power Commission, 128,
    137ff, 228
Federal Water Quality Adm., 159
Feedlot animal factories, 220–221
Fermi reactor, 187
Fiscal dividend, 71–72
Fish and Wildlife Service, 128,
    129, 151, 159
Flood Control Act of 1936, 111
Forstenzer, Peter, 232
Four Corners power, 165, 178–180

Franklin, W. B., 304
Friends of the Earth, 318
Frontier philosophy, 4

Galbraith, J. K., 75, 107
Galveston Bay, 196, 211
Gandhi, Indira, 320
General Accounting Office, 240–
    243
General Electric Company, 190
Green revolution, 57–59
Greenhut, M. L., 121
Gross national product, 61–64,
    71–72, 75

Haagen-Smit, Arie, 254
Habitat issue, 7–8
Hanes, N. B., 209
Hansen, Alvin, 27, 75
Haveman, R. H., 120, 121, 131
Herman, Tom, 109
Hexter, A. C., and Goldsmith,
    J. R., 261, 288
Hickel, W. J., 98, 140
Hill, Gladwin, 165
Houston Ship Canal, 196, 211
Hubbert, M. K., 172, 174

International Whaling Comm.,
    328
International Whaling Conven-
    tion, 96
Interstate Commerce Comm., 312
Invisible hand, 86, 89

Jahns, R. H., 51

Ke Tang, 319
Kennedy, J. F., 109
Khrushchev, Nikita, 123
Kneese, Allen, 200, 224, 246, 251,
    285

Kotin, Paul, 287
Krutilla, John, 145, 152, 153, 156, 161

Laissez-faire, 40
Lake Erie, 196, 202–203
Land abuse, 2–4
Landsberg, H. H., 51–52, 59, 193, 194
Leachate, 294
Levy, W. C., 132, 142, 157, 161
Lewis and Clark, 132–133
Linden, H. R., 177
Low-flow augmentation, 239
Low-sulfur fuels, 272–274

Magnetohydrodynamic power, 188–189
Malthus, Thomas, 37, 38, 40–41, 56, 57, 60
Market standard, 115–116
Market system, 89–93
Materials Policy Commission, 6
Materials reclamation, 297–301, 305
Maya Empire, 3
Mayer, Jean, 19
McNamara, R. S., 323, 330
McPhee, John, 153
Meadows, D. H., 9, 41, 43
Middle Snake River, 132–162
    Appaloosa and Low Mountain Sheep plan, 143–145
    China Gardens dam, 148–149
    Environmental Policy Act, 141–142
    High Mountain Sheep and China Gardens plan, 146–149
    Low Mountain Sheep dam, 149–150
    Pleasant Valley dam, 149–150

power sites, 139
    value as semiwilderness, 154
    wilderness, 151–155
Mill, J. S., 38–39
Miracle grains, 57–59
Mishan, E. J., 75, 81, 107
MIT computer simulation study, 9, 41–48
Mount Trashmore, 298
Multi-purpose resources, 96

National Academy of Sciences, 15, 37
National Conference on Air Pollution, 285
National Environmental Policy Act, 141–142, 159
National Rivers System, 158
Natural gas, 181–182
Nature Conservancy, 102
Neman, Barry, 253
Nile River, 322
Nitrilo-tri-acetic acid (NTA), 204–205
Nixon, R. M., 61, 283
Nuclear power, 185–188, 189

Oakes, John, 61
O'Connell, R. L., 200
Office of Coal Research, 178
Office of Science and Technology, 189
Oil shales, 177–178
Opportunity cost, 112, 118–119
ORSANCO, 242
Oxygen profile, 200
Oxygen sag, 198–201

Pacific Northwest Power Company, 157, 159
Papandreou, Andreas, 91, 107

Par Pond project, 218–219
Peabody Coal Company, 178, 180
Pearson Committee, 325
Petroleum
    industry protection, 175
    oil shales, 177–178
    production, 175
    tar sands, 177
pH, 209
Photosynthesis, 201
Pinchot, Gifford, 4–5, 11
Population
    birth control in underdeveloped
        nations, 21–22
    Blueprint for Survival, 38
    Census Bureau projections, 30–
        31
    Commission on Population
        Growth and the American
        Future, 33
    composition and the standard of
        living, 25–27
    costs of a high birth rate, 32–33
    demographic forecasting, 29–30
    developed nations, 18–22
    economic efficiency, 29
    economic growth, 22–23
    ethnic issues, 20
    geometric growth rate, 40
    growth in U. S., 27–28
    illegitimacy, 27
    investment in decreasing, 23–25
    "law of large numbers," 34
    Mill, J. S., 38–39
    pill, 30
    resource depletion, 48–52
    underdeveloped nations, 17–19
    world, 17, 21
    zero population growth, 30, 32–
        33
Population growth

market effect, 49–50
Price functions, 93–95
Power shortage, 183–184
Powers, T. J., III, 213
Public investment, 118–119

Radiation pollution, 186–188
Recycling, 297–301, 305–312
    aluminum, 307–308
    ferrous metal, 306–307
    glass, 305–306
    transportation costs, 312
Reserve Mining Company, 54
Resource depletion, 48–52
Resource Recovery Act of 1970,
    298
Rockefeller Foundation, 57
Roosevelt, F. D., 6
Roosevelt, Theodore, 4, 11
Ryther, J. H., 205

Sanitary land fill, 293, 294
Santa Barbara Bay, 174
Saprophytic bacteria, 206, 231
Savage, H. P., 209
Schistosomiasis, 322
Scrap market, 308–310
Secular stagnation, 27
Seneca, 253
Side effects, 53
Sierra Club, 132, 318
Small Business Administration,
    240
Smith, Adam, 85–86
Social costs, 52, 53
Soil Conservation Service, 5
Solid waste
    agriculture, 291
    bottles, 303–306
    cost of collection, 295–297
    federal role, 294–295

household, 291–293
industrial, 291–293
mining, 291
Solid Waste Disposal Act, 295
South Lake Tahoe treatment
plant, 231, 232, 235, 236
Spillover cost, 53
Stalin, Joseph, 123
Stationary state, 8
Stockholm Conference, 317ff
Storm King Mountain case, 142
Strip-mining, 53, 179
Strong, Maurice, 328
Subsidies, 105–106
Sun Oil Company, 177
Surface mining, 53

Taconite, 53–55
Taft Sanitary Engineering Center,
235
Tar sands, 177
Tax on pollution, 105–106
Tax on sulfur, 283–284
Tax Reform Act of 1969, 249
Thermal pollution, 186, 215–218
Third world, 322ff
Threshold effect, 34
Thwaites, R. G., 133

Udall, Stewart, 140, 179
Union Carbide case, 280–282
U. N. Conference on Human En-
vironment, see Stockholm
Conference
United Nations
development goals, 325–326
Environmental Fund, 327
Environmental Secretariat, 327
University of Georgia, 218
U. S. Forest Service, 97

U. S. Geological Survey, 171, 172
U. S. Public Health Service, 180,
227, 280
Utility pricing, 192

Vanderhoof, John, 165
Van Loon, H. W., 15
Vienna, West Virginia, 280
Virgin materials, 311–312

Wallich, Henry, 61
Wankel, 266–267
Washington Public Power Supply
System, 157, 159
Wastepaper, 301–303
Water pollution
accelerated depreciation, 248–
250
acid wastes, 209
activated sludge, 231
agriculture, 219–221
algae, 201–205, 218–219
alkaline wastes, 209
alternatives to waste treatment,
239–240
Construction Grants Program,
228–229
detergents, 203–206
effluent charge, 245–248
industrial polluters, 211–223
iron and steel industry, 213, 214
1985 goal, 250
1972 federal act, 230
primary treatment, 230–231, 236
pulp and paper industry, 214–
215
Ruhr experience, 245–246
secondary treatment, 231, 236
sewer systems, 235–239
sources and types, 197

tax credit, 248–250
tertiary treatment, 235, 236
thermal, 186, 215–218
transmission costs, 234–235
trickling filter, 231
virus, 210, 211
waste treatment approach, 230–234, 236
water-borne epidemics, 227
Water Quality Adm., 216
Water Quality Office, 237, 239
Water quality standards, 207–209
Water regeneration, 196–201
Water Resources Council, 129
Water treatment
    costs of, 234–235
Weinberger, Leo, 233

Westchester County, N. Y., 293–294
Wetland resources, 99–102
Whale, 95–96
Whitman, W. T., 121
Whooping crane, 101–102
Wild and Scenic Rivers Act, 158
Wilford, J. N., 165
Woods Hole Oceanographic Institution, 205
World Heritage Trust Convention, 328
Wright, D. McC., 87, 88

Zero economic growth, 39, 69–71, 72, 74–77
Zero population growth, 39

DATE DUE			